"'From Shame to Grace' is no mere saying to me, it is a living statement and testament to my life in recovery. Without first healing myself, I would have had nothing to offer to my family and friends. Now I have grown to be available to my wife, my friends, my children, and their children. I have learned to let life happen and celebrate (most of the time) what may come, not despair what I was not able to control. After twenty-plus years in a marriage, through a whole lot of support and effort from the men I was introduced to in No More Secrets, my wife now has a husband matching of her worth and I have the wife I always wanted. I am a lucky man."

—Ben

"Jay and the No More Secrets program were the key to my successful recovery. I came to Jay because pornography and the adult industry were taking over my life, leading me to give up on my job and leading my wife to give up on our marriage. I was desperate. Through the course of working with Jay, I was able to stop my behavior, repair my marriage, and build a new life based on integrity and service. Jay and the NMS program were the strong medicine I needed to overcome my dire situation. I couldn't be more grateful."

—Gavin

"Jay has guided me to discovering my value and worth, and has helped me become the man I always wanted to be. I have re-created my marriage from a shambles and a farce into something sacred and precious. I am completely known, open, and free. An immense burden of secrecy and shame has disappeared from my life, and I have found dignity and grace. Jay has always guided me with love and compassion, which at times is the firm honesty that only a person who truly cares can provide, and has always acted in my best interest. No More Secrets is not for the faint of heart. Our contract with each other is to dig and explore, to expose our secrets in a safe environment so that we all can heal. This is hard and painful work at times, and it's also the most rewarding and meaningful work I've ever done. Jay is a fantastic guide, an invaluable mentor, and a loved friend."

—DB

"Jay Parker is brilliant when it comes to getting someone honest. Because of his understanding of addiction and the importance of getting honest before you can begin to heal. Jay creates the safe environment that many of us have never had. Jay saved my life."

—Stan

"I came into Jay's office over five years ago. I was anxious and fearful because my pornography use on my church office computer had been brought out into the open. I could have lost my job, my marriage, my children, and my reputation. I didn't know what to do, but a counsellor sent me to Jay Parker for help with my sex addiction. I was willing to do whatever I was told, so when Jay said I needed to attend SLAA meetings and become part of a men's group that would meet every week, I did it. I was part of that men's group for four years where I learned to be open and vulnerable, sharing my feelings, struggles and successes. Jay helped me to see how I could have a new life of sobriety and he helped me to renew my personal relationship with God.

God, my men's group, regular attendance and participation at SLAA 12-Step meetings, and Jay as my life coach gave me my life back. I kept my job, have reconciled with my wife, have a wonderful relationship with my children and grandchildren and I can look at myself in the mirror and like what I see. Thanks Jay"

—Luke

"After years and years 'In Recovery' and various therapies, I still didn't have protracted sobriety. Meeting with Jay and being in his program gave me real life-changing tools. My marriage, relations with my sons and my career were all at risk. I still have them all. Life is good now. Hard, but very good."

—Keith

"Simply put, Jay Parker has saved my life. His coaching and spiritual support have been absolutely the determining factor in my path from sex zombie to a productive, open and transparent member of society. He's been most patient with me and my struggles with getting honest and sexually sober. He's offered insights, tools and resources that I otherwise could not get anywhere else or certainly on my own. And when I have stumbled, he's always there to help pick me up and regain perspective. Jay makes sure I understand his experiences and those of others, so that I can leverage them to understand or re-learn that I truly am never alone in recovery—that I was and am not more sick than anyone else. Jay is generous with his time, forgiving and above all compassionate and empathetic. I've also hugely benefitted from Jay's direct communication and coaching approach. A recovering addict—especially one such as me, who is lifting out of the deepest depths of sex and love addiction—absolutely needs help with getting to their truth. While Jay can be and very often is soft and gentle in terms of demeanor, his messages time and again reflect the unvarnished truth."

—Dirk

"From the outside I was an attractive, middle aged woman raising two beautiful children. From the outside I was married to a man I adored who in return cherished me. From the outside I had people. People to socialize with. People to count on if I needed anything. People that knew and loved me. From the outside my life was beautiful. A fairy tale romance of opposites meeting, falling in love and building a life together. From the outside everything was fine.

On the inside, I lived in fear that if I didn't try to control everything, that everything would fall apart. On the inside, I lived in fear that if I wasn't pretty enough my husband would leave me. On the inside I lived in fear that asking anything from my marriage was too much and so I did so loudly and often, demanding my husband fix me by loving me enough. On the inside, I lived in fear that I couldn't any longer outrun the untouchable loneliness that was only lifted by the occasional illusion of connection. On the inside was an inferno of self-hatred, fiercely defended, with the belief that I could change the outcome of the train wreck of my life if only I worked harder.

And then the illusion fell apart along with my marriage, my family and my life. All the therapy, self-help books and introspection hadn't touched my warped ideas of love and so in January of 2010 I met with Jay. What I found in him was someone that understood things I was barely able to put into words, that could describe the warped characteristics of every relationship I had been in and someone who knew what it felt like to be desperate and out of options. Jay told me the first day he met me that there was a solution and then worked with me, until I could see that I too could heal, that I too could love myself and I too could feel worthy of respect and dignity. Jay Parker not only saved my life, but he connected me to a life I didn't believe was possible or that I was worthy of. Today I have a life worth living and am a woman I love to be."

—Vanna

"I was in my early fifties when I started in No More Secrets. I'd spent my life trying to be a good Christian man, husband and father. However, my secrets were killing me. I could not break my life-long attachment to pornography and masturbation. In No More Secrets, I learned about the root causes of this affliction. I was shown by example how to break the stranglehold these things had on my life. Today, as a result of the work I've done in No More Secrets, I am at peace with God AND myself. I am happy, joyous, and free. I have authentic relationships with men and women. And I look forward to each day and marvel at the opportunity before me to continue exploring this wonderful journey we call life."

—Nigel

"I would like to thank Jay Parker for his work with me and for his No More Secrets program and for his fantastic new book. I started working with Jay eight years ago as a hopelessly lost, depressed and addicted person going nowhere fast. I learned to live again as direct result of Jay's help. Jay became my guru and guide as I learned that I had value as a human being and had the opportunity to turn my life around and do something great with the time I have on this earth. I cannot put into words what the daily work with Jay Parker and the community of recovering addicts did for me! I try everyday to do for others what Jay did for me!"

—Harry

"When the consequences of my addictive behavior finally caught up with me--costing me my marriage, house, career, many friends, and my professional reputation--my father, Luke, knew exactly where to bring me for help. Almost three years later, all that loss pales in comparison to all the gifts that Jay Parker and my No More Secrets men's group have helped me find in sobriety. I've discovered a gracious and relentlessly loving God that I never believed existed, found my personal worth and integrity, and learned that misery is truly optional in recovery. Following my Dad's example, I did what Jay told me to do. Through working the Twelve Steps, attending SLAA meetings, working with other sex and love addicts, and becoming vulnerable and accountable to my blessedly large recovery community, I have traveled a road that is steadily restoring my life in every area--career, family, relationships, and emotional and spiritual health. While it is certainly true that sex and love addiction is handed down generation to generation, my own experience with NMS is proof that the solution can be generational too. My family was saved through NMS. We didn't give up before the miracle, right Jay?"

—Duke

"More than a decade ago, the Seattle 'S' community experienced a tremor. No More Secrets came to be. The endless cycle of addictive relapse began to be replaced by recovery from this devastating disease. One day at a time, one more recovering addict coming to my aid, and being surrounded by men who showed the way to God's grace, our wives and partners trust and my broken life, repaired. I'm not a member, nonetheless a recovering recipient. 'It takes a village to bring up a child,' so they say. It's taken an army of committed, recovering men to bring this addict the miracle of sobriety and sanity. I owe so much to the recovering men of NMS who gave me hope, helped me use the tools, showed the way and lifted me from the lonely abyss of predatory, sexual, self-immolation. I'm grateful and blessed."

—RW

"My attempts to get free from sex addiction failed. I tried to pray my way out of my brokenness, but that also failed. The first time I walked into Jay's office he told me that I was incongruent with my faith and that I was a predator—he was right. That night, I joined one of Jay's recovery groups and I haven't looked back. Today, I have personal integrity and real friendships based on honesty. I have released the secrets that were my shackles. I am not afraid to look at myself in the mirror. I am the man, the father and the friend that I was meant to be. In my opinion, the work Jay is doing through NMS, is divinely inspired. Jay has given me a life that I never thought was possible, and for that gift, I am and will be eternally grateful."

—DD

"For decades I acted out in so many ways, addiction numbed the deepest pains and darkest secrets. I could see myself extinguishing my life so quickly but not being able to stop the destructive behaviors. I was barely surviving and thinking of ending my life one too many times. I was living in the edge, risking the loss of family, relationships, job, everything. I couldn't see the end of it. I was out of hope when I crossed paths with Jay Parker and the No More Secrets Program. Out of desperation I surrendered to the guidance of the people that went through recovery before me. Jay asked me not to leave before the miracle of the program, I didn't, the hopeless pain went away and I got to save my life and my family. I'll be forever grateful for the journey. Now recovery is a lifestyle. It's all about thriving."

—Tonia

"I knew I was living a lie, but I didn't know any other way. I don't mean I told a lie or two, I mean my whole life was a sham. It looked great from the outside but inside I felt dead. Too much was never enough.

I was referred to Jay Parker by a dear friend. Jay was the first person who truly understood what was going on in my head and could tell me why I was out of control. He got me right away and, even better, had a simple and powerful solution. It's been hard, but life-changing work. Today my life is fulfilling, spiritual, connected and full of love. I have repaired my marriage, built a recovery community, achieved success at work, and most importantly I am now the great father my kids deserve."

—JAM

"My fear of intimacy left me and everyone else a mystery. Working with No More Secrets has allowed me to share all of who I am and to really know the men around me. I was alone and now I am a member of courageous and loving community. My family and I will be forever grateful to Jay."

—GH

"My life was out of control and I was dying inside. I was bankrupt as a going human concern. My sexual and romantic acting out behaviors were escalating at a dangerous and alarming pace. Jay Parker and No More Secrets saved my life by arresting this deadly cycle and launching me into a remarkable spiritual journey powered by Sex and Love Addicts Anonymous and Alcoholics Anonymous. I needed the rigorous accountability and nonstop emphasis on attacking the core of my disease—a male intimacy disorder—provided by NMS to rebuild, from the ground up, enduring relationships with other men and give the miracle of 12-Step recovery time to take root."

—Dean

"Jay Parker's No More Secrets program is like recovery cross-training. Plugging into NMS gives newcomers instant access to a wealth of experience, strength and hope from motivated men and women focused on a shared solution. The emphasis on transparency within the community results in an immediate level of support and accountability that could otherwise take months or years to build. Within my first week of joining, I learned about meetings close to home and work, got connected to a sponsor and had a list of men who had gone before me that I could call for advice and support. The number of opportunities presented to me quickly made it evident that my biggest barrier to recovery was my lack of ability to surrender, take risks and be vulnerable. Within the ranks of NMS men, I have had someone to help with any question or challenge I faced in my recovery journey—sobriety, spirituality, step-work, service, sponsoring— and to advise me on how to show up in relationship with honesty and integrity. Jay Parker's program jump-started me on the way to acceptance and serenity."

—Will

A Year of
No More Secrets

A Unique Recovery Model for
Sex and Love Addicts

JAY PARKER
PROFESSIONAL RECOVERY COACH AND
FOUNDER OF NO MORE SECRETS

ISBN-13: 978-1491207185
ISBN-10: 1491207183

For all those who are still sick and suffering,
there is hope.

CONTENTS

FOREWORD

The challenge of providing a culture of recovery for individuals troubled with addiction is a major concern and preoccupation of every conscientious residential therapist who treats individuals with addictive disorders. An addict's chance of relapse is frequently increased by an inadequate support system involving little accountability, minimal affiliation with a support group in an existing recovery community and a non-supportive home base following the trauma of the addictive behavior, intervention and treatment. I believe this is especially true for those who suffer from sexual addiction.

The language of treatment and the language of recovery are not the same language. This language barrier can be fatal for many addicts facing the tenuous path of rehabilitation and recovery particularly while navigating the stressful and anxiety laden journey into life after treatment without their addictive coping mechanisms. One might be able to relate to this if one thinks of an individual who is locked out of the house in their bathrobe on a blustery cold winter morning before the rest of the world has awakened. The experience is embarrassing, if not shame filled, awkward, and terribly uncomfortable with little hope for immediate relief from the situation.

If personal shame, loneliness, anxiety, and the loss of the original context of family and support are to be addressed as part of the continuity of care for the recovering addict, then acceptance, relational support, reassurance by example, and the healing of broken relationships is critical to successful recovery. The possibility of facilitating the above in light of my experience over several decades of treating addicts has often times been found wanting.

Jay Parker's *A Year of No More Secrets* presents a refreshing window into the world of recovery for sex addicts and their families and spouses few others are able to illustrate. The language of recovery is the language of faith, hope and love. Jay's work demonstrates in action the criteria the renowned researcher and writer George Valliant, author of *The Natural History of Alcoholism Revisited*, considers essential to the success of recovery and a healthy adaptation to life in general. In addition to the virtues of faith, hope and love, the positive emotions and altruism, the need for commitment and discipline and self-sacrifice in helping the still suffering other are major ingredients for Jay's formula of recovery.

I am privileged to have experienced the positive results of Jay's work in both being a therapist who has worked closely with him in the treatment and continuing care relationship and in being able to experience his community of recovery and see the positive results achieved with even the most broken of lives and relationships as a result of sexual addiction. A Year of No More Secrets is a worthy read for anyone involved in the treatment and recovery of sex addiction and provides hope for the possibilities of translating treatment into recovery for addicts and their families and building a culture of recovery.

Michael Morton, MA, LMFT
KeyStone Center Extended Care Unit
Philadelphia, Pennsylvania USA

PREFACE

The following pages contain an account of a year in the life of the No More Secrets program. This 12-Step based program helps men suffering from sex and love addiction find their way after blowing their lives up. Not all who start this journey make it. Those who do, develop tools to arrest their addictive patterns, address their Intimacy Disorder, put relationships back together and go on to live healthier, fuller lives.

To preserve confidentiality and protect anonymity, I have not used the actual names or personal attributes of any clients who are portrayed in this book as participants in No More Secrets (NMS).

At no time in my professional career have I ever been licensed to make any clinical diagnosis other than that of chemical dependency. As a recovery coach, any reference I make to a Diagnostics and Statistical Manual of Mental Disorders (DSM) code is made as an observer and not as a clinician.

Acknowledgements

Like the athlete on TV after the game winning play, I would like to start by thanking God, who has blessed me in all areas of my life and without His direction none of this would be possible. There is an old Yiddish proverb that, when translated, says "Man plans and God laughs." God keeps me humble and laughing, with my eyes pointed to the heavens while my feet are planted firmly on the ground.

Next on my list is my very kind, smart, funny, accepting, honest, and insightful wife Roz, whose "Normie lenses" on the world keep me anchored in reality. Roz supports me unflinchingly with my late nights, endless phone calls, countless meetings and a year round array of NMS events I am forever asking her to attend with me. She is my best friend and confidant. As I always say, I have the best wife in the history of wives and the best marriage in the history of marriages; that's not tongue in cheek, it's the truth.

Twenty-three years ago, former NBA all-star player and NBA coach John Lucas offered me a hand up and a way out at my time of need. During my time with John he taught me many things but mostly he modeled four things: "you're only as sick as your secrets," if you do recovery "you can get it all back," "all the instructions you need to do life is in the AA Big Book" and "you can't do it alone, community is a must." I can't thank him enough for saving my life. All he asked of me in return is that I pay it forward. John introduced me to the world of Bill Wilson who wrote the AA Big Book and started AA in 1935. Though he died in 1971, Bill's gift is still giving. I would also like to thank Dr. Patrick Carnes for taking the healing power of AA and making it transferable from alcoholism to sex and love addiction, helping millions afflicted with this debilitating addiction to recover.

In 1999 I met Dr. Hilarie Cash and since then my life has never been the same. Without her wisdom and encouragement, NMS would have never materialized. I can't say enough about her role in making this happen and for being my friend.

I'd like to thank Rokelle Lerner who is a highly renowned author and program director at Inner Path at Cottonwood Treatment Center in Tucson, AZ for her feedback and support though the years. I also want to give a special shout out to Michael Morton, who is the family therapist at KeyStone Center Extended Care Unit in Chester, PA, and to KeyStone's entire staff. In Michael I found a fellow traveler, and for me that is rare.

This book was gifted to me by eight recent NMS alumni who didn't want my book to die on the vine. Their tireless work has taken my words and made them real. The "gang of seven" (plus one) brought this book to life as editors, project managers, graphic artists, fact checkers, self-publishers, e-book experts and basic visionaries. I am forever grateful to these unnamed volunteers who made my dream a reality. I would also like to thank my webmaster [www.jayparker.org] and Mr. Phil McCoy who took time from being a filmmaker to direct and film me in my ninety second web promo. That experience was a true treat. I would also like to thank journalist, teacher and longtime friend Ms. Jana Thompson for her early edition editing work, insight and direction. Last but not least I'd like to thank Rich W, Clay F, and John J for keeping me sane on a daily basis. This book was my passion, yet with this passion comes a responsibility. I hope I did it justice.

I'm so appreciative of the assistance I've received creating this book. Any remaining errors, omissions, and generic faux-pas belong solely at my feet.

January

~

Honesty

JANUARY 1

ONCE UPON A TIME...

"Jay, if I've told you once, I've told you a thousand times: please, dear, color inside the lines." I can still hear Mrs. Cunningham's words ringing in my ears as if it were yesterday. If I had a dollar for every time she told me to color inside the lines I'd be a millionaire today, retired on a beach in Cancun, sucking on a rum and Coke—well, minus the rum. Looking back on it, I guess my Kindergarten teacher back at P.S. 176 in New York had me figured out. Maybe I had Oppositional Defiant Disorder, or maybe I had ADHD, or maybe, just maybe, I wore different lenses, ones that let me see things outside the box. Given a choice, I'd rather believe the latter.

I remember watching Evel Knievel do his crazy motorcycle jump over the Snake River. What I remember most was the disclaimer that appeared on the TV screen just before he took off. The announcer said it as I read it: Don't Try This At Home! Boy, I can relate. This would be a good time for my disclaimer: I'm not really sure my immersion program for sex and love addicts can be replicated. There are some real, fundamental lines that I color outside of when it comes to the coaching box, and I want to acknowledge this right from the start. My lenses often see beyond conventional strategies. I've learned to be okay with it. It fits me.

My program, "No More Secrets" (NMS), does not work for every addict. It is definitely not for the faint of heart. Along with being sex and love addicts, my clients all suffer from an Intimacy Disorder. The easiest way to define intimacy disorder would be in an exercise I give my clients. I write on a piece of paper, "in-to-me-see" then I ask them to read it back to me five times fast. As the connection starts to be made, they realize that they have spent a lifetime not allowing anyone to look inside of them. And most of all, that includes themselves. This can make NMS recovery messy. What I know about every form of addiction, whether substance or process (i.e., behavioral), is that addiction lays bare a simple truth: misery is optional, and recovery is done not at the speed of light but rather at the speed of pain.

My business is crisis-generated. Anyone who walks into my office is hurting enough to seek and gain recovery. Yet often, those individuals who present the greatest amount of pain and who express the most immediate appreciation turn out to be the ones quickest to forget their pain after the immediate crisis has passed.

Sex and love addiction is a disease that constantly tells sufferers that they don't have a disease. The conventional wisdom of Alcoholics Anonymous says that this illness is "cunning, baffling and powerful." I'll add the word patient. Addiction lies in wait long before raising its ugly head. The illness is metaphorically in the parking lot doing pushups, gaining strength to beat up its victims.

A lot of this is because the illness is culturally camouflaged. Our world and our media tells everyone that we can only be complete when we are either hypersexual or in a partnership, whether it's healthy or not. This concept is not new. Perhaps the greatest English romantic play ever written was *Romeo and Juliet*. Shakespeare wrote it more than 400 years ago. Take a step back and look at it through my lenses: the play takes place in true addict fashion. The central characters meet, fall in love, copulate and die within four days; Juliet was also fourteen, but I'm not going to go there. The rapidity of their romance was unhealthy.

Another classic is the childhood tale *Cinderella*. The story has nice intent with the evil stepsisters and the fairy godmother, but what about the prince? Once Cinderella transforms from a poor, tattered urchin into a beautiful, fair maiden, she dances with the prince for hours as they gaze into each other's eyes. Then, as the clock strikes midnight, Cinderella runs back to her old life. Now here's the kicker: the prince can only find Cinderella by her shoe! What about her face, eyes, hair, smile and voice? What exactly was he looking at for all those hours? Was he looking down her blouse? Little girls who embrace this story grow up looking for their Prince Charming, and when they think they have found him it turns out Prince Charming has problems with fidelity at worst or is just a jerk at best.

For over fifty years, young girls have grown up playing with Barbie dolls. A life-size Barbie would measure 39-18-36. Even though Barbie can have a profession like teacher or nurse, her best outfit after all these politically correct years is still the hot pants with the six-inch "I want to have sex" heels. In addition, all little girls who "do Barbie" learn that Barbie isn't complete without Ken! The truth is that Barbie is now considered tame and almost passé when going eyeball to eyeball with the newer "Bratz" dolls, which are highly sexualized and make me blush!

We live in an MTV world, for sure. That means that kids growing up in

Enid, Oklahoma get bombarded with the same media messages taken in by kids in New York or Los Angeles. A hot media question of the day was whether the MTV hit series "Skins" is child porn. Today's music with lyrics of "Ho" this and "Bitch" that conveys images intended to heighten sexual arousal while making the listener callous to the concept of monogamy. Such music portrays promiscuity as a rite of passage. Most of today's music comes with videos that are just short of porn. Former U.S. Supreme Court Justice Potter Stewart once commented that he couldn't define porn, "but I know it when I see it." It's been said that the porn industry in America made $10 billion in 2012. Truth is, we ain't seen nothing yet. For example, a company called Real Touch is developing an interactive sex toy called Teledildonics. I'll leave the particulars to the reader's imagination.

Sex industry staples like G-strings and strip club dancing poles have made their way into mainstream society disguised as thong underwear and exercise equipment. Teen girls wear shorts and sweatpants bearing phrases such as "Delicious" or "Eye-Candy" across their backsides. Where do the eyes of an adult male track when our "Eye-Candy" girls cross paths at the mall? Not to mention Abercrombie and Fitch's controversial padded push up bra/bikini designed for eight year-old girls. Where will it end?

Even the politically correct 1950 and 1960s had their share of music that carried messages not necessarily healthy for us. I remember all too well a hit song by The American Breed that says "bend me, shape me, any way you want me; as long as you love me, it's alright." How about that for a life lesson? When I recall the push-back the older generation gave to Elvis Presley or the Beatles, I have to laugh. Lyrics by the likes of Eminem, Public Enemy and Snoop Dogg make *I Want To Hold Your Hand* seem like *The Itsy Bitsy Spider*.

Recently I watched three highly regarded mainstream movies, and my lenses saw these loaded with the issues that I see in NMS every day. *Up in the Air* with George Clooney is a sad saga of a man who is a workaholic, love-avoidant, and a Type A personality with a severe attachment disorder. His female love interest is also a Type A personality; she leads a compartmentalized double life.

The second of the three movies was *It's Complicated*, a light romantic comedy with Meryl Streep and Alec Baldwin. Both their characters lack strong personal boundaries; his womanizing, in concert with a clear picture of the effects of divorce on children—in this case, all the children are adults—leads to an entertaining film loaded with sex and love addiction.

The last film was called *Two Lovers* with Gwyneth Paltrow and Joaquin Phoenix. This is an almost pathetic portrait of three traumatized late twenty to early thirty-something adults living with their parents who create a very messy love triangle. The woman who wants the man claims she will take care of him forever while the woman he pursues is more broken than he is.

The dichotomy is clear. Again, I see these dynamics every day, yet they are camouflaged in real life and in real time.

The world never knew beyond a shadow of a doubt about President Kennedy's dalliances with Marilyn Monroe. But with CNN and a twenty-four hour news cycle, President Clinton wasn't that lucky. His legacy will forever be linked to a semen stain on a blue dress of a twenty-two year-old White House Intern named Monica Lewinsky. He was impeached for lying about the affair. The expression "Doing a Lewinski" became part of the American sexual lexicon.

Famous and powerful men from Anthony Weiner to Tiger Woods have had to wear their indiscretions in the public arena. Woods's behavior was publicly labeled by the media as sexual addiction, which had rarely been done previously. Famous and powerful men seem to feel they are entitled to create their own set of rules. Regardless of fame and power, all sex addicts feel a sense of entitlement.

Finally in this rant, I get to the Internet, the greatest delivery system for antisocial behavior in the history of the world. Now don't get me wrong, I love my computer and I never want to go back to pencil and paper, but as with all technology there are downsides.

Think for a second about two of America's greatest visionary men, Henry Ford and Bill Gates. These men lived about a hundred years apart and each had a dream. Ford wanted to mass produce his Model T, make it inexpensive enough for every American to own and he did it. Gates wanted to put a computer on every desk and in every home, and he did it.

As forward-thinking as Ford was, he could not have envisioned in 1908 that in 2008 nearly 40,000 Americans would die in automobiles. He never envisioned seat belts, airbags, GPS systems, or DUIs (Driving Under the Influence). Despite all this, I do not want to go back to horse and buggy.

I make up that Gates never envisioned that porn would be the number one business online. He could not have seen that this technology would provide access and safe haven for pedophiles or sexual predators. I also believe that Gates never envisioned the availability of porn and the sex industry through websites, let alone the havoc wreaked on marriages. Ask any divorce attorney the biggest cause of divorce these days and you're likely to hear "The Internet." The Internet is accessible, affordable and anonymous. No "last call" or "blue laws" shut it down. This dope dealer is open for business 24/7/365 days a year and much of what is offered is free. This is scary to think about, especially if you are one of the minimum six to ten percent of the computer-using population who have become sex-addicted or are partnered with an active addict.

The wisdom of AA tells us that once you are pickled you can never be a cucumber again. "Just saying No" is no longer an effective course or option for those who have crossed the addiction line.

By the time a man walks into my office, the wheels have fallen off of his life. His spouse—or his boss or his child or the criminal justice system—has caught him in a behavior that gives his spouse the power to demand that he seek help. At that moment, the spouse has become both cop and parent. Nowhere in that unhealthy equation is there room for spouse, friend, lover, child, protector or employer. The addict's system is out of whack and all hell has broken loose.

This disease is more than an error in judgment. It's not a phase or a stage like acne that will be outgrown. It is chronic in history and obsessive-compulsive in nature, it cannot be stopped regardless of consequences, and it creates secrets. Sex addiction is real, as real as a heart attack, yet it does not enter lives uninvited. This disease has the same characteristics as any other disease. If left untreated it will get worse. It has the potential to be fatal.

As I begin the year and this endeavor, it is my intention to give readers a small window to this illness in all its manifestations. Through the years I have been urged by clients and peers to share NMS with the outside world. I believe NMS is a unique, innovative and effective recovery model. My goal is to communicate in the form of a year's worth of journal entries the powerful, important and sensitive work that we do here at NMS on a daily basis. I hope you enjoy the journey.

JANUARY 8

POST-HOLIDAY FALLOUT

This was a very hard week and I knew it was coming. I give all my clients a writing assignment based on a parable called "The Problem." This powerful piece is everyone's autobiography. One line in "The Problem" reads: "Our insides never matched what we saw on the outsides of others." The desire for home, hearth, holiday and a Hallmark card is overwhelming. The expectation of that perfect family with the trimmed Christmas tree, all the right gifts, old traditions relived, extended family all smiling, relationships rekindled, and the joy of reunion is never adequately met. For many in NMS, they really can't go home again.

The historic dysfunction in the families my folks come from makes this season what I call the sadness of a happy time. In a nutshell, proximity breeds contempt—not to mention resentment, anger, loss, grief and rage. Unmet expectations and emotional disappointment are inevitable. In every 12-Step fellowship, the time between Thanksgiving and New Year's presents the highest risk of relapse.

I closed my office Wednesday, December 23 and didn't go back in until January 4. Our final group meeting of the year was held December 16. That's a lot of time for our members to get undone, to isolate, and to have the addict raise its ugly head. I tell my clients all the time that while they're acting "as-if" they are normal and life is great, their addict is in training, doing pushups in the parking lot. This illness is cunning, baffling, powerful and patient. Even though we do a lot of prep work around the holidays, for a certain percentage of us the holidays end in relapse at worst and emotional upheaval at best. The first week back in the new year is about getting out the crazy glue and trying to bring order to the chaos. This is always one hell of a week, and this year was no exception.

I have been told that I have a great memory. I do not make chart notes or taped records of sessions. I do out-of-pocket consulting with a sliding scale. I have a personal mission that I will never let money be an issue. As a result of my approach, at any one time I am tracking more than fifty people's lives to a level that usually blows them away. I oftentimes can recall their lives better than they can, or I make reference to a fact given to me years ago that they had long forgotten. In that regard, I am blessed.

Another point of NMS is that I use examples of others, their successes and their failures, to teach, illustrate and, hopefully, illuminate. Most counselors go through hell and high water to ensure that one client never meets another client; they're all about confidentiality. This coaching program is built on the opposite theory. I want all my clients to know all my clients. I want to create a community where there are "No More Secrets." My philosophy is built on the wisdom of Alcoholics Anonymous: "You're only as sick as your secrets." The innate shame created by sexual compulsion and sexual betrayal is off the charts when compared with other types of shame-producing behavior. Would you rather tell your spouse she might need to take an STD test or call her to come bail you out of jail because of a DUI?

Beginning in the third week of December, I placed a client of mine, Dante, in an inpatient treatment center in Philadelphia called KeyStone Center Extended Care Unit (ECU). Throughout the course of my program, I have sent more than fifty men to this facility for a higher level of care. These are usually men incapable of stopping their behavior or who have a level of childhood trauma beyond the standard scope.

For me, a key component of what KeyStone does is their family piece. KeyStone provides a safe venue and outlines a format for the men to make full disclosures to their spouses concerning past behaviors. This facet of treatment is in line with our program. I am a firm believer that the only way for couples to heal from this deceit is if the woman has full knowledge of what her partner has done. For me, it's all about integrity and informed consent. Creating a relationship based on playing life's cards face up is paramount, and I believe that only with full disclosure can reconciliation be possible.

I believe the care patients receive at KeyStone can change their lives forever, even though any inpatient treatment facility is for discovery. 12-Step work, good coaching, outside psychotherapy when needed and strong support are necessary for a lifetime of recovery. Thirty days away does not equate to a lifetime of bliss. It's just a start.

Dante came to me in September on a referral by his psychiatrist. He had disclosed to her that he cannot stop looking at porn and that it is affecting his marriage. The therapist suggested he go home and confess to his wife, which he did. The results were less than stellar. All hell broke loose. After a further meeting with his therapist, she pushed him to see me. Grudgingly,

Dante came.

I see my clients in two-hour blocks. I do not believe in the traditional fifty-minute therapy session model. If at the forty-eight minute mark someone says something profound and two minutes later the counselor says, "Time's up, you've gotta go." That doesn't work for me. So I see only four clients a day, at 10am, noon, 2pm and 4pm. Sessions can get intense. I work in a different model than traditional counselors.

My first session with Dante was almost our last. I asked him questions about his sexual history that no one had ever asked him: times, amounts, frequency and specific behaviors. I asked for detail and he didn't like it. He presented as cocky, smart, macho and aloof. What he didn't know was that even though this was my first conversation with him, I had experienced this conversation a thousand times. When he had this conversation before with anyone else he could control the outcome. He couldn't do that with me. His cockiness, smarts, machismo and aloofness had protected him in the past. It didn't protect him now. It was not a level playing field, but I was the only one who knew that. He never stood a chance. When I asked him if he believed he could hide and continue his behavior forever, he said yes. Then I asked him to imagine what it might feel like in another ten years when his now three-year-old daughter finds Dad's porn on the computer or hears Mom crying when she finds out about an affair. That got his attention. I told him about going to inpatient treatment at KeyStone without putting any pressure on him, just planting a seed. I suggest KeyStone to about twenty-five percent of my first-time clients. I had a clear idea of who Dante was even without knowing the full extent of his abuse and trauma. Time was on my side. He jumped in fast. Within a week he was joining my newest group, going to SLAA meetings three to four times a week, seeing me on a regular basis, and talking to a sponsor.

The sponsor piece happened really fast, but that's because I fixed Dante up with one of my alumni. This alumnus has more than four years of sobriety. He had gone through a divorce followed by a protracted period of not dating. Within the past two years he also married a wonderful woman who knows his entire life story, including his participation in NMS. She got to make an informed decision about who she was partnering with. They are expecting their first child in July. Years ago, when this alumnus joined the program and his life was coming undone, he asked me what my goal for him was. I told him I wanted to dance at his wedding. A few years back, that came true. I blur the lines. I see people outside my office in different settings.

Back to Dante: During the previous three months he had struggled with sobriety and healthy boundaries with his current and past partners. As I do with all the men I coach, I pushed him to try to get his partner to call Hilarie, my colleague. Hilarie is a classically trained cognitive behavioral therapist who, at the time I met her, was president of the Seattle Counselors Association. Through the years, she has been open to learning about addiction treatment and has become the point person for the women connected to my men. With the NMS concept as the premise for my program, I have honest and open dialogues concerning the people I see. It seems to work. If I hit a snag with one of my guys or if he has hit a plateau, I suggested to him to see Hilarie for counseling, to try her specialty, which is voice dialogue, a type of embodied cognitive behavioral therapy. Her technique seems to work well with addicted men. If Hilarie feels a female client of hers is primarily presenting addiction issues, she suggests a recovery coach such as me. We both assist couples with their reconciliation work. It flows very easily. For the NMS model, it seems to work.

Within two weeks, Dante's partner Tonia was sitting in Hilarie's office. That, in and of itself, was a welcome event. Nineteen percent of the partners of the men I work with want no part of this process. They are clear and vocal. In their minds, their male partners are the designated "Sick Ones." These women are resistant to doing any work. I believe that stance can be a determining factor in the long-term efficacy of recovery and in the success of the partnership itself. Those women are more than happy for their men to go and get well, but they do not want to be part of the process. I liken it to dropping your clothes at the dry cleaners at 6am and coming back at 6pm to pick them up all fluffed and folded. When Tonia jumped in, I was pleased and so was Dante.

Very quickly Tonia was going to her own Sex and Love Addicts Anonymous (SLAA) meetings. She joined one of Hilarie's women's groups, found one of Hilarie's recovering females to act as a sponsor, and saw Hilarie on a regular basis. Soon Tonia started to do her own work. She started to find her voice and she began to face her own relationship addiction issues. Dante ended up not liking Tonia's new-found voice all that much, yet he could understand on some level that her healing was necessary.

One of the first places I start is to get the men to see that since pre-pubescence they have had a love affair with their penises. Once porn was introduced and connected to ejaculation, the die was cast. Most of the men I work with cannot go seventy-two hours without an orgasm before they first come to see me. I had one client who was so addicted to his own dopamine that he was averaging six orgasms a day. He would look at porn on the computer while having phone sex using chat lines, and all that would happen before noon while he was at work.

I put Dante on a thirty-day, unilateral sexual fast. No sex, even with his partner. He was willing to face the challenge and thought it would be a piece of cake. Tonia responded the way most females respond. At first they are relieved. But as the days go on they begin to not like it. The sad fact is that they have always known that sex was their partner's most important need. Without being able to use their sexuality as currency, their fear of abandonment, coupled with losing their number one bargaining chip to controlling his behavior, often puts them in an emotional tailspin.

Tonia began to see clearly her own pattern of sex and love addiction. Maybe it was the fact that Dante was married with two small children when they met ten years ago and that she was the "other woman." Or maybe it was that now that they were partnered, Tonia now worried Dante had a job opening for a new mistress. She didn't like the feeling. Either way, her eyes were opening and, from the women's end of this program, she was starting to hear a consistent message: Don't have sex with him again until he makes full disclosure of his behavior.

On the seventeenth day of their fast, he said to her quite casually that he was counting the days, only thirteen to go. She informed him of her new awareness and her unilateral new boundary. He was not a happy camper with her new-found recovery. All of a sudden, with his sexual supply cut off for an undetermined period of time, he started thinking that maybe her participation in a recovery program wasn't the best idea. Whoops. But he knew he couldn't stop the process now even if he tried. Be careful what you wish for, you might get it.

Through the next six weeks, their relationship at home deteriorated more and more. The ugliness on both sides: arguing, yelling and shaming, escalated almost nightly, at times taking place in front of their three year-old. The need for Dante to go to KeyStone became increasingly evident.

As a result of the openness of NMS, Dante had personally known more than ten men who had gone there. One of them, Sam, had been back only a week and urged Dante to go. Mustering all the courage he could find and dipping into his 401(k), Dante finally got there. The daily chaos in his home was over for now.

For the first ten days at KeyStone, all clients are subject to a phone blackout. That equates to no contact with the outside world. The silence is important and difficult for both parties. On the eleventh day, I am usually the first person to call. I ask the same question: Did I send you to the right place? With each of the fifty-plus men I've sent there, the answer has always been "yes."

January 4 was the start of Dante's third week at KeyStone. On the Thursday of that week, Tonia was scheduled to go there for two days to hear his disclosure. Our entire community was braced for the fallout. The closeness within the NMS family means that when something big happens to any of our members or couples, there is a huge ripple effect.

Our motto has always been: "we either go together or we don't go at all." For people with Intimacy Disorders, this is the perfect antidote: a supportive community coupled with a high degree of accountability. Now, during our first week back after the New Year's, we were waiting with baited breath.

Sam is a forty-five year-old man in a long-term marriage with three kids. He is devoutly religious. He is highly connected to his church, a Sunday school teacher, and a pillar of his religious community. Sam also has a secret life.

His wife is a petite Asian woman who, as a college exchange student, was wooed, groomed and courted into marriage. She gave up her family, her country and her culture for this man. Their relationship has been dictatorial in nature; that's one of the reasons he chose her. She has been clueless about all but about ten percent of his behavior. Silent and compliant, she has played the part of the good, dutiful wife to the max. Her mantra has been the same as that of so many of the partners connected to NMS men: "What do I have to do to not know?" If they knew of and acknowledged the behavior, they would be forced to do something about it. Denial is a bitch.

Sam came to see me more than a year ago. His wife had found his porn and had started to push back. But even more compelling was that Sam's behavior was out of control. He presented as suffering panic attacks. He was starting to think something might be amiss.

I knew from the first time we met that he was a KeyStone candidate. There is an easy way to break down who needs to immediately go to inpatient treatment. The basic elements are whether the behaviors are going to get someone dead, arrested, fired or divorced. It's a clear and simple barometer. In Sam's case, all four could have happened, but none had. That's amazing considering the variety of his behaviors for more than thirty years.

After being in NMS for more than a year, Sam went into inpatient treatment. Three of my KeyStone alumni took him to dinner and gave him the hard sell. The delay was tactical since he had a new job, financial concerns, and tremendous fear about disclosing his behavior to his wife. For the previous six months, he had been on a sexual fast. His wife had begun counseling with Hilarie, was participating in a women's group, and was beginning to find her voice—very much to Sam's chagrin. He was used to his wife being both passive and submissive. She had found strength and kicked him out of the bedroom some months before.

During his third week at KeyStone, Sam's wife flew out to hear the truth about her husband. Even though she thought she was prepared, she had not come close to imagining the full extent of his sexual acting-out. She was devastated. After the first day she was so distraught, she wanted to abort the process and come home. I had to talk her into staying for the second part. He reported that she shouted words in rage he had never heard his polite, reserved, religious wife ever utter.

11

Since his return from KeyStone, Sam has been out of his home and living with an NMS recovery buddy who had been to KeyStone a year earlier. Sam needs the safe harbor. This is the first real consequence he has suffered for his behavior, and he hates it. His wife set up a clear "no-contact" boundary—the equivalent of two boxers going to neutral corners, knowing full well if they re-engage center ring, someone will get knocked out. All communication between the couple goes through a neutral third party, commonly known as a go-between. Sam has access to his children at prescribed times and has been forced to find another church to attend. He has given up his position as a church leader and is trying not to fall apart.

The NMS community has done a great job of propping him up. During Sam's group this week he announced that he is going to have a meeting with a leader of his church to learn his religious penance and to find out how his future will look. He has tremendous fear, sadness and loss about where this might lead, yet he understands that the only way out of this is honesty. I told him to remember that he is not a bad man trying to get good but a sick man trying to get well. It's a hard concept to embrace when the world judges you a scoundrel.

Sam left word today that he was headed to see his church leader and wanted me to keep him in my prayers. I also just found out that Dante will be moving in with Sam and his NMS friend when he comes home later this week. The drama and trauma of NMS continues and it's only the first week of the year.

JANUARY 15

THE STORY OF STAN AND MARIANNE

Today started out great. My colleague Hilarie and I were invited to give a presentation about our practice at the Seattle Counselors Association's (SCA) monthly breakfast speaker's meeting. It had been ten years since our last speaking opportunity at the SCA. Any time I have a chance to speak to professionals about this topic, I welcome it. We fielded many questions during the ninety-minute presentation. My goal was clear. I wanted to give these clinicians different lenses and new information. Some were open to it, and some were not.

I talked about a current news story here in Seattle. A forty year-old woman was reported missing, and her live-in boyfriend was being sought as a person of interest. Within days he was arrested and charged with her murder despite her remains not having been found. In a story in last Sunday's Seattle Times, several of her friends were quoted as saying that she had fallen for this guy fast and hard, and that she had believed he was the best thing to happen in her life and the best thing that ever would happen in her life. She had been aware of his conviction on an aggravated sexual assault charge in 1994. At the end of the lengthy story, a couple who had befriended her was quoted as having told her she probably should learn how to be happy alone before partnering with a man. On Tuesday, searchers found her charred remains. Her death was probably ruled a homicide. My lenses saw it as sex and love addiction.

I challenged the SCA counselors to determine what diagnosis they would have made had she walked into their offices. The obvious diagnosis would have been Battered Women Syndrome connected to the potential for domestic violence. Hindsight is twenty-twenty. Speaking to the counselors was rewarding and uplifting, then it was back to my real work world.

Things have quieted down somewhat after New Year's, but life in NMS is anything but boring. This disease guarantees a certain level of angst. It comes with the territory.

I wish I could say that when we created this program more than ten years ago we had a clear vision of what it would look like. But that's not the case. This program has evolved over time prompted by a ton of trial and error. I like to tell my NMS folks that this is just one huge experiment and the only thing missing are the guys in the white lab coats with the clipboards. Somehow along the way we have settled into a working formula for combating this illness without sitting down and crafting a mission statement. I do, however, have a construct in my head. It centers on building a supportive and helping community.

I cut my teeth in this field at John Lucas' NBA treatment center in Houston in the early 1990s. John was the head coach for the San Antonio Spurs, Philadelphia 76ers, and the Cleveland Cavaliers in the National Basketball Association. Before his coaching career, John was an All-Star point guard well on his way to a Hall of Fame career. He also played professional tennis and holds the distinction of being the only person to play both sports professionally. Then came addiction. In 1986, John was released by the Houston Rockets for cocaine use and entered a rehabilitation program. John had twice been waived by the league for cocaine use. But he saved his career by seeking treatment. He subsequently created the first treatment program for athletes in the history of professional sports. My involvement with his program started in 1991.

His program started with basketball players but eventually he was helping anyone from the sports world who sought treatment. John took in pro baseball, football, and tennis players. He even took a professional weightlifter addicted to steroids. The distinctive piece of his program was that after the traditional thirty-day inpatient stay, his athletes transitioned into a house that John had bought. It housed eight to twelve athletes, had a live-in house manager, and created a sober living community like no other. His motto was part of his own story: "If you stay sober, you can get it all back."

Their mornings consisted of early prayer and meditation, exercise, and a therapy group bracketed by community breakfasts and lunches. In the afternoons, they attended addiction lectures and education. Worked into their week was a one-on-one therapy session with a case manager. Late afternoons were all about basketball. They held workouts in the gym, where they could regain the skills that got them into the league and landed the now-gone huge contracts. Working on sobriety first and basketball second was a consistent message of John's program.

At the end of each day, they would wrap up with a community "here-and-now" group. This was where all the gripes of the day would be cleared and aired. Sometimes things got a little rocky. Those groups put a lot of big egos and testosterone into a very small place.

What I witnessed were the positive, redemptive values of a recovery community. The gift of freedom and safety the program afforded each man as he sorted out his life both on and off the court was priceless. John had created a safe haven from the hailstorm of addiction. John's efforts were a noble experiment, and it worked. The program ended in 1992 when he became head coach of the San Antonio Spurs. But the model continues. Today, every major professional sport has a program similar to it. John's program was truly cutting edge. That was my model. Many of those former NBA players who went through his program realized John's motto. They did get it all back.

After group on my first Wednesday back, I turned on my phone to find a text from Beth who is a member of one of our women's groups. It read: "Stan is drunk, how do I support Marianne?" I was floored. Stan had more than twenty months of sobriety from sex and alcohol, and was strong in his desire to stay sober. His marriage to Marianne hinged on it. His drinking has always been a conduit to his relationship with the sex industry. The thought of him drinking scared me. My first priority was to reply to her text, so I responded quickly. "Tell Marianne to stay still."

Through the past twenty months, Stan and Marianne had been on quite a merry-go-round ride. It started when he showed up at my office looking like a deer caught in the headlights of his own life. Only a few days before, he had been on a business trip in Southeast Asia when he woke up from an alcoholic blackout in a closet. He was in a house of prostitution. He was petrified. The worst part was he didn't remember if he had had sex with anyone. His history says he had. He panicked but managed to exit the premises.

He caught a plane home and looked online for help concerning his sexual acting-out. He found the Sex and Love Addicts Anonymous website. As fate, or God, would have it, he saw they were having their annual men's retreat. In a state of quiet desperation, he decided to go.

He was there only a short time when he got freaked out by the frankness of the discussions about sexual acting-out. He tried to make a beeline for the parking lot. He was intercepted by one of my guys, who calmed Stan down by sharing what it had been like for him before, what had happened to him, and what he was like now. In recovery parlance, that's called "twelve-stepping" someone. I guess it worked because on the very next Monday, Stan was sitting in my office. That was two years before, almost to the day.

I was clear from our first conversation that Stan needed to go to inpatient treatment at KeyStone. He did not push back very hard. The other noteworthy facts were that he was in a long-term marriage, had three adult children, and his wife was aware of maybe two percent of his acting-out behavior. I knew from the start this was going to be difficult.

The treatment was ultimately successful even though Stan's disclosure was brutal. Marianne joined the women's group right away and started to educate herself about the disease of addiction. Even though she was armed with support and information, the disclosure brought Marianne to her knees. She felt she had been thrown under a bus. She wanted Stan gone from the home so she could be free to decide where to go from here.

It took eighteen months and a ton of individual and couples work to save this relationship. Marianne went to a weeklong retreat led by Rokelle Lerner called InnerPath. It is housed at Cottonwood, an addiction recovery center in Tucson, Arizona. Marianne also went to another addiction center called The Meadows outside of Phoenix on two separate occasions for her own work, while Stan stayed sober, sane and safe. After an eighteen-month absence from the family home he had been back home a little more than three months when I received the text from Beth. This was a definite setback and could have been a "Deal-Breaker" for Marianne, but in the end, NMS worked.

After I texted Beth, I saw that Marianne had called me. I quickly called her back. To my amazement, she was calm and clear. She went on to tell me that she had been on the phone with Stan, who was on the East Coast and she knew he had been drinking. She heard the entire conversation as he was pulled over by a state trooper because he had called her as soon as the cruiser's lights had gone on. To her amazement, Stan didn't lie once. For some reason, the trooper let him go. Six beers and four shots of vodka and the trooper had let him go. Later I told Stan that we'll know in a year whether that was a good thing or a bad thing. The future will ferret out the reality of his "good luck."

Marianne was immediately concerned for his safety and told him to stay still. Then she called her group member and recovery sister Teresa for support. Teresa told her husband Kevin, who is in Stan's group, and Kevin called Kelly, another group member, all of them KeyStone men. Between the two men, they stayed on the phone with Stan through the night, talking to him as he drove to his hotel, keeping him safe from three-thousand miles away. In the middle of it all, one of the women called Beth, who texted me.

I write about the details to illustrate the closeness of their group and the community as a whole. At 7am I was on the phone with Stan. He was in a shame spiral and still hung-over. He said Marianne "would be better off without him," and I agreed while differentiating between a sober Stan and a toxic Stan. I asked him to make me a commitment to stay sober today and come on home. He came in Monday morning and we processed the entire genesis of the alcohol relapse. He was honest and open. He was also committed to dusting off his ass and getting back on the recovery horse.

Marianne was able to own her sadness and fear while staying connected to her support system. She supported her husband, but in no way did she give him a get-out-of-jail-free card. She was clear that the best part of this event was that it did not end with him acting-out sexually. She was clear long before the relapse, and she remains clear now that any kind of infidelity is her forever "Deal-Breaker."

They came in as a couple yesterday and, truth be told, I didn't have to do much repair work. In the past week, they had processed the events surrounding the relapse and were in a pretty good place. On Saturday night they went to a SLAA meeting together. Stan took a "One Day at a Time" beginner's coin while his group mate and recovery brother Kelly celebrated two years of sobriety. The power of the NMS community was clear. The model worked. This little vignette ended happily. But this story is ongoing, forever one day at a time.

Also this week, Dante came home from KeyStone. He came directly to my office, and then he attended his group. Dante presented as a bit shell-shocked. That's normal given that he was in a treatment center for thirty days. Dante definitely showed more humility and willingness to take suggestions from others. It's a good start. Most people come out of KeyStone with what I call a "bounce." It's kind of like dropping a basketball from a third-story window. The first bounce is big and each one thereafter gets a little smaller, until the ball finally comes to rest. The challenge for Dante will be to sustain the momentum towards recovery that he gained in treatment. Time will tell. He is currently living with two other NMS brothers in recovery, so he is safe for now.

Dante will try on what being a part-time dad of a three year-old feels like to someone in full time recovery. That might afford him some clarity about his indifference to his life situation. The symbiotic nature of the relationship between Dante and Tonia will be a challenge for both of them. In the past, Tonia's love addiction has left her defenseless against his needs, wants and control. Her fear of abandonment has left her unable to create real, sustainable boundaries or to hold healthy anger. Tonia's best chance for real traction in recovery is that she is scheduled to go to The Meadows in February for Survivors week—a weeklong retreat that helps address family-of-origin issues, ages zero to seventeen.

This process is going to take a long time. Dante's ambivalence about the relationship, combined with his newly de-activated sex addiction, make a prognosis for success highly guarded at best. I am an eternal optimist and I believe in miracles. More shall be revealed…

JANUARY 22

MY NEW GROUP

During the past ten years, I have started fourteen men's groups. Theory and concept are easy; making each group work is the tricky part. As soon as I get five or six new clients amenable to recovery who can self-identify with the label sex and love addict, I start a new group.

As part of our contract, each man understands that he will have to see me individually once every two weeks, attend at least two SLAA meetings a week, and commit to this process I call "recovery." It is definitely labor-intensive, and it is not easily sustainable. Most guys who walk into my office are in so much pain, the easy conclusion to make is they would be willing to go to any lengths to save their marriages or their jobs, or to avoid arrest and to get well. Yet some have such distorted thinking that they believe the process will be only slightly more intrusive than "take two aspirins and call me in the morning." The breaking of an elaborate denial system takes time. They come in with thick shields of armor. One of my alumni aptly said of me that I was the OB-GYN of SLAA: I birth people into recovery.

My latest group called "New Wednesday" started with five guys on September 2. I always set the group schedules in two-month increments. Of the eight Wednesdays in any two-month period, we have six groups. The groups run from 6:30pm until 9:30pm, but I make it very clear from the start that if someone is emotionally bleeding at 9:30, we're not leaving. We seldom end on time. On the two bye-nights, the group is instructed to get together without me. They can meet for dinner, see a movie, go bowling, or just hang out at someone's house. The need for intimacy doesn't stop because the group has a night off.

This group got off to an unusually difficult start. We started with only four men: Ned, Clint, Larry and Will. The fifth, Edgar, was already in inpatient treatment at KeyStone. By the third week, we added a sixth man when Dante returned from KeyStone and joined the rest of the men. Unbeknownst to the psychiatrist who referred him, porn was just the tip of Dante's behavioral iceberg.

It says in the AA Big Book that "We are people who would normally not mix." This group is that quote personified. Age range was twenty-nine to fifty-four. All four were college grads. Two were educators; one was a tech guy, and the other worked in the criminal justice system. One had been married for twenty years, another for ten. The third man had been married for only eighteen months, and the fourth guy was engaged for the first time in his life at the age of fifty-four.

One man was bi-racial; the others were white. Their behaviors ranged from procuring prostitutes to compulsive masturbation with porn. One man acted out on the job with a co-worker. None of these illegal behaviors—prostitution is illegal in forty-nine of the fifty American states—involved minors.

They also came from every corner of our geographic area. One man lives on the other side of Puget Sound, a ferry ride away on an island. Another lives on the other side of the Cascade Mountains, two hours to the east and through a mountain pass that often shuts down in winter. This group was going to be a challenge. The man who lives only twenty minutes away has cataracts and has difficulty driving at night.

As for their levels of addiction, all of the men in the New Wednesday group exhibited behavior that was going to get them dead, arrested, fired or divorced. With one exception, all the women in their lives had caught them, and for all of these men life had become unmanageable.

For each of the men in this group, the activating event that drove them to seek help had given their spouses very large hammers. The sad part is that when a woman gets thrown into the role of mom and cop, there is absolutely no room in the equation for wife, friend or lover. That's the true cost of doing business with an untreated sex and love addict. Just ask the wives of the disgraced politician Elliot Spitzer, the President of France Francois Hollande and the recording artist Robin Thicke.

By the fourth meeting, our KeyStone man, Edgar, had come home. I had spoken to Edgar often during his time there and I was keenly aware that it appeared he had not turned the corner on the surrender/willingness spectrum. Surrender is a key indicator of initial change and of things to come. In the philosophy of ending active addiction, I think you have to surrender to win.

Edgar's life had blown up in mid-August before this group started. Edgar's new wife—number two—of seven months found out that her Mr. Right was really Mr. Right Now. Edgar had a penchant for prostitutes that predated her. Not surprising that she didn't know much about him: they married four months after meeting. Ah, the power of love at first sight. Dr.

Patrick Carnes, who wrote the seminal book on sexual addiction, *Out of the Shadows*, calls this situation "courtship gone awry." Unfortunately, Edgar's wife never took the time to think through terminating the marriage. She was on her way out the door before he made it to my office. I never did meet her.

Edgar presented in an extremely unstable state. He was weepy. He could not eat or sleep. He couldn't concentrate at his tech job. He was falling apart. Edgar glommed onto a variety of men in NMS looking for immediate relief. Within a week, he had found one of my NMS guys who was a great sponsor. To say Edgar was leaky emotionally is an understatement. I had some real concerns about his well-being and safety. After talking to several of my KeyStone guys and having no real place to put himself after his wife threw him out, Edgar decided to go to treatment. Looking back, I believe he wanted a haven to run to instead of a place to find treatment and healing.

Upon Edgar's return to group, he talked in detail about his thirty days in inpatient experience. I challenged him on some obvious distorted thinking, which was coupled with a very apparent rampant self-will. Edgar had decided to find a roommate to help defray costs at his new place. He insisted it had to be a female. Edgar would not for a second consider living with a man, much less a man in recovery.

Edgar was one of the few men who came out of treatment pretty much the way he went in. Within two weeks he had fired me, his sponsor and his group. Through the course of the next few months, Edgar's attendance at meetings declined and his phone calls waned. Last I heard, Edgar had relapsed and was again involved with the sex industry, this time without the buffer of a wife. No one in recovery has seen or heard from Edgar in months. This is a powerful illness. What a waste of thousands of dollars— and another sad example of a man's self-will running riot. Once again, this is a disease that tells you every day that you don't have a disease. I will keep Edgar in my thoughts and prayers.

In week six we added another man, Roy. Four months before coming to my office, Roy's wife of ten years had found him with a woman from the sex industry. This was not the first time. Roy had been caught acting-out by his wife four years previously. Like so many men in that spot, Roy ate a lot of crow, put his tail between his legs, stayed banished to the couch, and waited for the tornado to pass. All the while, Roy professed love for his spouse, apologized repeatedly, and promised it would never happen again. He sought no counseling, no help, and just planned to wait her out. That's a prescription for disaster. This behavior is symptomatic not just of bad behavior but of a long-standing pathology. It comes with its own life and cannot be self-willed away. It is not an error in judgment, but, again, denial is a bitch. To make it an acronym, DENIAL stands for Don't Even kNow I

Am Lying.

Before Thanksgiving we added another man, Wayne. Wayne was thirty-five and never married, but had been living with his partner for seven years. He had gotten over his fear of commitment—driven, really, by his guilt—and set a wedding date for June. Wayne's partner had known about the porn for a long time. Early on, like most men, Wayne was able to groom her and bring the porn into the bedroom. But Wayne's fiancé was getting more and more annoyed with his porn use the older she got. Wayne couldn't stop and his partner knew it, so he went looking for help. Wayne thought help would be brief—something like reading a book or two. Boy was he wrong. What Wayne's intended bride didn't know was that he had acted out with other women. Whoops!

What Wayne never expected was that his four dalliances with real, live women would have real, lasting consequences on his marriage plans. I challenged Wayne strongly on the first day. I asked him bluntly if he could understand the difference between when a woman gives a man consent to be sexual and when a woman gives informed consent to be sexual. I was crystal clear. He was putting her life at risk, and she didn't know it. By lying about his behavior with other women, Wayne was taking his betrothed "hostage."

I told him he would have to do an orchestrated disclosure, detailing his acting-out behavior. This should not be done at the kitchen table. Serial disclosure under duress is just not healthy for either party, even though oftentimes the woman doesn't know it. I could see that he wanted to clear his conscience by what I call verbally vomiting on her. I implored him to wait. The pressure of the upcoming wedding was driving his behavior. He believed like so many men that he could control his universe. He was wrong. He had zero capacity to stay self-contained. He verbally puked all of his sins all over her at their kitchen table. She was devastated beyond words, left as road kill without any support.

In December we added two more men. Both were computer professionals, not uncommon considering I'm located in Redmond, Washington. Charles came first. His wife had caught him on the computer. He called me thinking life as he knew it was ending. I asked him how long they had been married and how many children they had. He responded with ten years and three kids. Then I asked if he was out of the house and he said no, just on the couch.

I assured him that she wasn't done with the marriage yet. I've seen women be done. It's usually fast and clean: out of the house, change the locks, get the best lawyer possible as soon as possible—not to mention get to the bank first. She did none of those. She was hurt, but at the end of the day she wasn't going anywhere. I told him to come see me. He also had emotionally vomited on her over the course of a few days. As a result of his confessions he wasn't emotionally safe from her wrath. But he lacked the ability to set boundaries, to lay down rules for fair fighting. Most of these men are not very strong, especially when confronted by their partners. They suffer from Mr. Nice Guy syndrome, except, of course, when it comes to their sexual acting-out. There is nothing nice about betrayal.

The second was Owen, who is forty-five, has three kids and is fifteen years into a marriage that has been in trouble for years. His wife knew enough about his behavior that she was demanding full disclosure. She was chasing and chastising him around the house, room to room, with the proverbial rolling pin. He called me one Saturday in a panic. I told him to leave if she did not stop. I told him to say he would be back in thirty minutes and then he needed to return exactly when he said to keep her abandonment issues from jumping in her face. He did this twice before she relented. I'm a firm believer that we teach people how to treat us. He was trying to set a boundary, something he had never been able to do.

Owen joined NMS by jumping into the deep end of the recovery pool. Within a week he had a sponsor (the one that Edgar fired), and was reaching out for support within the fellowship. Even though his spouse wanted no part of this, I had a good feeling but I was wrong. I didn't see the depth of her dysfunction.

Going into the year, the new group was now at nine. In the third week of December, Larry and Will went together for Survivors week at The Meadows. Both absorbed a ton about what their lives had been from birth to age seventeen.

Clint was the weakest link. He had made it to only five groups out of the twelve meetings so far. He was not attending many SLAA meetings, had no intention of getting a sponsor, seldom, if ever, made a phone call, and was everyone's least favorite go-to-guy when it came to making contact. He had not come to see me in a month, and he was orbiting NMS and recovery at more than arm's length. I asked him to come in and bring his wife. To my surprise, they showed up.

It was clear the dynamic between them was toxic. She was "twenty-seven going on twelve." She had little or no inner resolve to set a "Deal-Breaker." Her need to be with a man superseded her need to be safe. He had vomited on her enough of about his behavior to make even a semi-mature woman cringe and back away, but she was unable to do that. The system within their marriage, coupled with their general unwillingness to do the work made him a bad fit and not workable for NMS. NMS men have a deadly disease. As I encourage them to lock arms in the row boat for life, the last thing they need is someone sitting with his feet up, unwilling to row.

I first tried to get Clint's wife's attention. I drew on my whiteboard a large circle with the word recovery in the middle. I drew an umbilical cord extending to a small circle on the end of the cord. That is, I had a small planet orbiting a larger one. I explained that sooner or later the cord will be stretched and will break, setting the small planet adrift to float away into space and into the ether of addiction. She wept quietly while I spoke. She was so petite, reserved and overwhelmed by the spot she was in. There she was, just another young bird with a broken wing selected for use and abuse by a sex-addict partner. She never really stood a chance. Poor baby didn't have a prayer or a clue. Within a month I suspended him from NMS for January and February to give him time to decide if he truly wants what we have. I haven't heard from him since.

That leads us to this week. I finally had all eight men in the same room at the same time. Between Dante, who had been to KeyStone, and Larry and Will, we now had three men who had done a significant amount of recovery and could push the dialogue. Seven out of eight had sponsors, went to meetings and were making calls. Roy will probably never get a sponsor and is only really visiting NMS. As the New Wednesday group entered its fifth month, it was beginning to coalesce. With two more spots to fill, I could begin to turn up the heat. Let the games really begin…

JANUARY 29

SELF-WILL RUN RIOT

This disease is like a hurricane roaring its way through the lives of the people addicts claim to care for the most. The sheer absurdity of the situation is beyond normal comprehension. I get to experience this insanity first-hand and in person on a daily basis. The best part is that every once in a while from the devastation of addiction comes a miracle. I can never really tell whose marriage will make it and whose will not. I am not clairvoyant nor do I have a crystal ball. In the end, it's in God's hands and on God's time. My job is to "suit up and show up."

When Sam came to me almost eighteen months ago he presented as a soft-spoken yet firm man who was seldom in need of help. He is autocratic by nature and very competitive. Basically, he wants what he wants. He became his wife's entire universe and was the keeper of her "okayness." She lived a life of quiet desperation with a very small voice for a very long time. She was reared to be that kind of woman.

On the acting-out scale, his behaviors rated nine of ten. That scared me right off the bat. The most amazing part was it appeared that he had never had any real consequences. The cold truth is that he should have been dead, in prison, divorced, unemployed and HIV positive. Yet none of these had happened. He was one of the men I recommended go to inpatient treatment during our very first visit. He pushed back when I did.

His presenting issue appeared to be panic attacks. That state led him to seek psychiatric help, where he disclosed some of his sexual behavior. That led him to me. He was honest and direct when I asked him questions no one had ever asked him. In the middle of his calm mannerisms was a lack of sincere remorse coupled with no real apparent sign of fear. He could show sadness while his rage was well-hidden.

He was amenable to joining a men's group and going to 12-Step meetings. He jumped in hard. His one constant pushback was inpatient treatment. His entire way of living was in his head. Life was directed by measuring the world one person at a time. It was all cost-benefit analysis.

His home was ruled by male privilege. He acted unilaterally and dominated his wife. My first job was to try to get her some support. Getting her into a women's group was a challenge. Hilarie did a great job trying to get her to be introspective about her life before and after she married. Based on her cultural background, her religion, his hermetically sealed secret life, and her twenty years with this man, to say she was guarded would be an understatement.

She finally did join a women's group, but to date she has not bonded with any of the women, nor does she with any regularity use them for support. Her church relations are guarded due to the shame she feels about her husband's actions. She is virtually locked inside her own head.

As the need for change was finally catching up to him, (one of his girlfriends called his wife), his willingness to look at going to inpatient treatment became greater. It took more than a year, but he finally went. The next hurdle was disclosure.

It was brutal. She was aware of only five to ten percent of his behavior. She was devastated. Working with women in our community, she finally mustered enough courage to ask him to not come home upon leaving KeyStone. He was fortunate to have a man in our program who offered him a place to stay. Thus began their ninety-day "no-contact".

Because he has three kids, he had to go home to pick them up for visitation. She had a job working outside the home and traveled out of town several times a month. That created a need for him to go home for child care, so there was a soft "no-contact." By and large, it was a pretty clean. The three months—and still counting—of not being at home prompted him to explore some of his feelings of grief and loss. Getting unhooked allowed him to finally feel some fear. But for the most part, he was still up in his head trying to manage life with all the pawns that play in his game. Two days ago, they sat in my office face-to-face for the first time in ninety days, the first time post-disclosure and post-KeyStone.

She was composed and professionally dressed. She came with a notebook and some questions. She was prepared. He presented a bit unkempt and was open to whatever came his way. I started by re-assuring her that she would set the tone, not him. In my room, she would not be bullied; she would be safe. She remained skeptical of the process even though Hilarie was there.

I asked him to share with her, in detail, what his recovery has been. He has been to ninety-two meetings in ninety days. He has been making at least three phone calls a day, excluding calls to his sponsor. He has not acted out on his bottom-line behaviors, and he has been attending my weekly group.

It has been very labor intensive, but then again there is no such thing as a convenient recovery. It just doesn't work like that.

She started asking him questions. Some were healthy and some were not. Women in the middle of betrayal will often ask questions that, for their own best mental health, they would be better off not knowing the answers to. Yet pain and not having done their own work lead them down that slippery slope. Questions like; "Was she blonde? Were her breasts bigger than mine?" Those questions should not be answered or asked, now nor ever. Only harm can come from going down that road. The last thing a woman needs is another "Kodak Moment" in her head of what his betrayal looked like. It's a lose-lose situation. It's bad enough that she was devastated at the time of disclosure, but I was damn sure not going to let it happen to her again. She was very matter of fact. She didn't shed a tear or show emotion at all. She could have been reading from a grocery list. She was very detached. In the end, she was willing to meet with him again in my office. I left the time frame up to her. To my surprise, she set the next appointment for twelve days out.

Just to be clear, she did not serve him with divorce papers. Nor did she curse him or rail at him. For a woman in that much acute and extreme pain, she did a great job of containing her rage. But given her background, I was not surprised. After she left the room, he and I began to process the session. I was pleased with the session. She was still in the game. The only thing he had experienced for two hours was that she hadn't looked at him once. That's a feeling he needs to hold on to for a while. Now, he was finally feeling some fear. His shame prevents him from acknowledging hope and, for now, that's fine. It keeps him humble.

~

January's highlights underscore the need for "Getting Honest." Honesty is at the epicenter of getting well. Without rigorous honesty the disease of addiction will win. Our watch word must be: go far, stay still and dig deep. It is a must that people in recovery be free from deceit. And just think, we still have eleven months to go. Sitting back to reflect on this month gives me pause to conclude just how devastating this illness is and to take stock of the enormity of the task at hand. I have often wondered if my passion is a curse.

February

~

Hope

FEBRUARY 5

THE STORY OF SHANE

I call him my hero. Yes, it is a little tongue-in-cheek but, in an endearing way, it is my truth. Shane turned ninety-two in January. Yes, I did say ninety-two, and he has been with NMS for just over two years. Conventional AA wisdom has an apt expression for Shane "if left untreated, it always gets worse." Shane is the poster child for that line. He's my hero because he keeps coming back!

Shane walked into my life like all the others: as his life was in crisis. His marriage of fifty-four years had ended five years before with the passing of his wife, whom he met at nineteen while an underclassman in college. The activating event that catapulted Shane into NMS was not spouse-driven. Her death did not give him a permanent get-out-of-jail-free card from any consequences.

He had been wintering at their home in Arizona, when he suffered a mini-heart attack and crashed his car, all very non- life threatening. The accident landed him in the ICU for a while and his two adult children rushed to be with their wonderful and loving father to nurse him back to health. It was during his stay in the hospital that his sons—ages fifty-two and sixty-two—while doing some house cleaning and paying his bills, came across the truth about Dad. They found his secret life.

They were shaken to the core. They not only found his extensive porn stash but they found a list of every time he had purchased a sex-industry worker. Dad liked whores. Ouch! They started to focus on his comings and goings. It appeared that dear old Dad had gone so far as to buy a Porsche for one of his lady friends. When that "relationship" went south—meaning she split—he hired a private investigator to find her and get his car back, which he eventually did. His life was a mess. His children were his hammer. That's a first for me.

As he sat in front of me for the first time, I found him to be lucid, smart, witty and honest. Again, I asked him questions no one had asked. The first thing I wanted to establish was some kind of time line. His current behavior clearly predated the death of his wife and, to be succinct, his laundry list of behaviors predated his wife entirely. This guy was hard core and had been in it for more than seventy-five years. I must admit I was taken aback. I had never worked with someone in his eighth decade of still very active addiction. I knew from the start that this would be interesting.

His son had drawn a line in the sand: The addiction had to go away or he would no longer be welcome in his life, which included his grandchildren and family events. He was a cancer survivor and knew that additional stress in his life could no longer be tolerated. The thought of being cut off from his family drove him into my office and into recovery. I also knew this was not going to be easy.

Shane was a doctor by schooling and a wealthy businessman by profession. He was the grandson of a high ranking political figure and the son of a doctor. He grew up as a legacy child and went to private schools while being raised on a daily basis by hired help. Dad was a workaholic and Mom a socialite. His was an upper-crust Protestant family with minimal sense of God and limited participation in church. They had a ton of table manners and a social life that revolved around the yacht club and playing golf and piano, all without any real warmth or affection.

By the age of sixteen and already away in college, Shane had gone with some schoolmates to a Mexican brothel for the much-anticipated, rite-of-passage "first lay." He came home with a case of "the clap" and was forced to leave school. Both parents came to get him and drive him back to Seattle. During the two-day car ride home there was absolutely no conversation about the clap, his morality or the ramifications of having to leave school.

Young man Shane learned two great lessons that day: There is always a way to clean up a mess, and in our family we practice a very simple rule of don't talk, don't trust and don't feel. It's a common thread in all addictive families. That life lesson would serve his addiction well for the next seventy-six years.

He was born just after WWI. Let's put that into context. He was a child when Babe Ruth hit sixty home runs and at the start of the Great Depression. As a teenager, he saw FDR elected president. When he was a young adult, our country entered World War II and he enlisted. After the war he went to university, then to medical school, and got married. His bride was a virgin. He claims he told her about the gonorrhea, but other than that there was never any honest dialogue concerning sex. He remembered how she would go sailing with him before they were married and how great she looked in her two-piece bathing suit. Once married he never saw her in the swimming suit again and he could never get her back on the boat. She obviously knew how to close the deal. Their first child was born post-WWII. He decided early on not to follow his father and grandfather into the practice of medicine and instead Shane ventured into business, where he was very successful. He lived a life of privilege.

In 1950, a friend of his wife, unbeknownst to him, saw him in an embrace with a woman who wasn't his wife. Upon receiving this startling news, his wife declared that his behavior could only be attributed to his relationship with alcohol. So forty plus years ago Shane went into Schick Shadel for a ten-day treatment and a few follow-ups to cure his drinking problem. For the next seventeen years Shane didn't touch a drop. His womanizing and sexual acting-out, though, continued unabated.

He was great at compartmentalizing his life. He never acted out on the job or with women in his very large social circle. He did, however, love the low life he could find in the old days on Pike Street in downtown Seattle. Once he saw his older brother coming out of a topless club. Neither man ever talked about it.

He had a thirty-year affair with a woman he met as a young man. During this time, she married and had children, as he did, but the casual sex never stopped. She was an invisible friend with benefits long before the expression gained currency. No one in his life knew she existed. He lived this dual life pretty much guilt—and certainly consequence—free.

In 1960, he was involved with a lady of the night. He often created pseudo-relationships with these prostitutes, using them emotionally as well as sexually. Never once did he consider leaving his wife for any of these women. His money was always his calling card to affection, time and attention. Being Mr. Altruistic was easy for him. He would repeat this nice-guy game over and over. This time it almost got him killed. She was "owned" by a pimp and she wanted out. Shane rented her an apartment and tried to get her out of the life.

Her pimp threatened Shane with physical violence if he didn't get out of her life. Shane rented her a place through his regular real estate broker, who happened to leave a voicemail on his home phone. When his wife heard the message, she drove through an ice storm across town to knock on the door and find her husband relaxing with his hired help. Shane followed her home believing the marriage was over. But she never said a word. She never banished him from the house or to the guest room. She just rolled over in bed for a few days and that was that. Bless her heart, and I hate speaking ill of the dead, but she had reacted to his behavior just as had his parents when he was sixteen. He had married the world's best co-dependent.

In the late 1960's, after seventeen years of not drinking, while on a flight from Seattle to Asia with his wife sitting next to him, he ordered a drink. And again she never said a word. He thought he was cured. By the time they arrived at their destination he was drunk, and he pretty much stayed drunk on and off for the next thirteen years, all the while keeping his business going, acting like a great family man, and never getting a DUI. By 1980, his adult child, with the help of his wife convinced him to do real treatment this time. So into Lakeside-Milam Recovery Center he went, and to this day he has not had a drink. His sex addiction was not addressed.

He attended AA for years. He learned the language and the jargon well and fit in. He never had a sponsor nor did he do the steps. He loved the social aspect and stopped drinking. To his credit, he never did any thirteenth stepping—sexual acting-out with a newcomer—in the program.

Shane and his wife were not sexual at all for more than thirty years of their fifty-four-year marriage. They just stopped trying. And all that happened in utter and complete silence. She was a bride of the 1940s. Divorce was not in her vocabulary. While she was ill and dying, he attended to her dutifully, like a life partner should. He was holding her when she passed away in her mid-eighties. His ability to create two distinct worlds amazed me.

Shane is still driving at ninety-two, though he recently sold his car. He is still very much a man's man, forever keeping up with sports, theater and politics. He still possesses a full head of white hair, walks with a spring in his step, and thinks he's sixty. He lives alone in a prominent senior retirement center where he lived for many years with his wife before she died. He has friends there whom he has known more than sixty years. Every week he entertains his five hundred-plus housemates by doing magic tricks. I kid him that when he dies his obituary will read like the Who's Who of the Seattle upper-crust. When I probe about why he does recovery and what he wants out of it at this late stage of his life, he simply says, "I want to know who I am when I die."

Shane could not stop his behavior. Every time he felt lonely he described it as horny. At length, I was able to get him to identify the right feeling. His actions were so brazen that he would have a prostitute come to his apartment in the retirement community, and then if he liked her—and he seemingly always liked her—he would invite her to lunch in sight of his peers and never give it a second thought.

About eighteen months ago, Shane went to KeyStone for thirty days. He was their oldest client ever. As reported to me, his time there was not well-used. He had a hard time getting in touch with real feelings. Within six weeks of coming home, he was arrested on a solicitation-of-prostitution charge. At his hearing it was revealed that he had a prior arrest from about twenty years ago. He didn't remember. He was given six months' probation and ordered to do twenty hours of community service.

I made him tell his children about the arrest. He needed to be known. Neither of them was happy, but they stood by him. When they asked me what I thought, I honestly said that I believed the very best we could hope for is "harm reduction," a concept developed at the University of Washington by Alan Marlatt, director of the university's Addictive Behaviors Research Center. As described by the university's College of Arts and Sciences, the concept offers an alternative to zero-tolerance or abstinence-only programs.

Shane's recovery has been spotty, but given the circumstances I really can't expect more. He has gone through three sponsors, all NMS guys. He can't show up consistently. He has been resistant to do the reading or the writing. He started out attending weekly SLAA meetings, but his attendance fell off as his car went away and his motivation waned. However, he loves coming to group and social events.

Shane's Monday group settled down at seven men. Amazingly, that group is my first NMS group in which every man has done some kind of inpatient treatment and six had gone to KeyStone. They function on a very high level of accountability and honesty. Some friendships formed in group that I believe will last a lifetime.

Stan, Kevin and Kelly are in that group along with Luke, Keenan and Harry. Since that group began meeting more than two years ago, it has been facilitated by Gavin, who is from my Tuesday night group and has four years in NMS. In the ten-year history of NMS, I have had seven men run different groups for me at different times. I realized early on when NMS started to grow that I needed to delegate and that this model could be run by others. There were just "too many days and not enough Jays" for me to do it all myself.

I tried initially to find licensed counselors interested in doing this work, but I just couldn't find a good fit. The confrontational nature of what we do along with brutally honest and frank talk about sexuality eliminated many. Needing to find suitable help, I decided to try peer leadership. These men had longtime sobriety, were well known in our recovery community, and had the mettle to challenge directly. Two of these peer leaders have taken to this work, have gone back to school to become Chemical Dependency Professionals (CDP), and are working in the field. Peer counseling seems to work for NMS group work. I still see all the group members one-on-one.

Shane has been willing to go to any lengths to get to group. He has even taken public transportation. One of the men will always step up to drive him home. His dedication to the group is noteworthy even though he still has a hard time making phone calls and staying connected during the week. At this week's group, he got honest about "falling in love" with his latest escort (or as I always insist he call them "sex industry workers." He hates when I use real language). His group did a great job holding a mirror up to him. When he falls he usually falls hard and that translates to losing money.

His distorted thinking can get him into a lot of trouble. Once he connected the dots, he committed to cutting off relations with this new flame, to come to talk to me about it, and to start going back to meetings. He followed through on all three.

Whatever one might think about this stately old gentleman, he is a picture of large contradictions. In the middle of our session he stopped to take a call from his twenty-six year-old granddaughter who lives out of state. She was recently married and Shane walked her down the aisle. Her dad, Shane's oldest son, had died suddenly many years ago, and Shane has stepped up to take his son's place in his granddaughter's life. This young woman knows most of her grandfather's story and still loves him unconditionally.

I listened to his side of this wonderful, endearing conversation. As far as most people know, he's just a wonderful senior citizen living out a wonderfully rich, rewarding and moral life.

Dr. Carnes, in *Out of the Shadows*, wrote in 1983 about the Four Core Beliefs of a male sex addict. Paraphrased, the first is "I am basically a worthless person"; the second is "No one would love me if they knew me"; next is "I'm never going to get my needs met if I have to depend on anyone else"; and lastly, "Sex is my most important need."

I have a sense that some of these core beliefs are lessening somewhat inside Shane's heart. The men have time and time again demonstrated their unconditional love for him, while his family is getting to know the Shane his wife never knew or never wanted to know. As he watches from afar, men and their spouses work through these issues and he often wonders "what if?" What if she were alive and we were much younger and we showed up for this work? What if?!? It says in the Jewish Talmud, "That which cannot be rectified must be endured."

I find Shane fascinating to work with. He provides me with details of a life time of acting-out behaviors with seemingly no real down side. He gets to teach me about the agony of regret and for that alone, Shane is a blessing in my life.

FEBRUARY 12

THE STORY OF MATT AND SOPHIE

This one hurts to write, it just plain hurts. The social psychologist, Erich Fromm (1900-1980), wrote in his 1966 classic *You Shall Be As Gods* that "Every evil act tends to harden a man's heart, that is, to deaden it. Every good deed tends to soften it, to make it more alive. The more man's heart hardens, the less freedom does he have to change, the more he is determined already by previous action. But there comes a point of no return when man's heart has become so hardened and so deadened that he has lost the possibility of freedom." Those words haunt me, especially as I write about Matt and Sophie.

This past Tuesday, I watched Matt, a man I have known for almost five years, sob uncontrollably in our group. Matt was finally experiencing the consequences of his actions. I had prayed this day would never come. We all worked so hard to prevent the preventable, but in the end we are all autonomous. There are no victims, but there is definitively collateral damage. No one can be denied their misery or their desperation—wives and children get swept away in the debris, appearing to the addict to be nothing more than collateral damage. But I'm getting ahead of myself; let me set this up for you.

My Tuesday blended group is now my senior group and their time as a working NMS group will close at the end of June. Matt has been with me the longest of any of the six men left in this Tuesday blended group. He started with an initial Saturday group of ten men. He came to NMS because he thought he had given his wife of ten years an STD. They had a nine-month-old son at the time and he was on the ledge of despair. It has been a long and bumpy ride since then.

The five other surviving men in the blended Tuesday night group are a mix of two other groups. The five of them have seen and experienced a lot during their time at NMS, and each has grown immeasurably and gained tremendous insight. All five today have protracted sexual sobriety.

Gavin and Ben had experienced long sexual abstinence and emotional separation from their spouses at the beginning of their recovery journey. They joined NMS still in long-term relationships, more than twenty years for each of them. Both marriages were on the brink of dissolution when we met. Today their marriages are fluid, stable, honest and open. A couple of years ago, Gavin and his wife welcomed their first child. Gavin was forty-one. We like to think of that child as a miracle baby.

Ben was the father of many children with an equally addicted wife in total denial. They survived all those years due to an unwritten, non-verbal, non-aggression pact. He let her gamble, take prescription pills, and socialize with men, and she was okay with him addictively looking at porn, under-earning, and being emotionally unavailable to her and the kids. They were both co-conspirators.

She is the only wife I have ever met who claimed that she really didn't mind if her husband looked at porn and that his involvement with porn had no bearing on her own body image or self-esteem. That's an interesting statement coming from a mother of five children, three of them daughters. Ben and his wife were the living example of "quid pro quo." Their dysfunctional lives were masked to the outside world by their ability to present as a pious family with a strong connection to a fundamental religion. Theirs was a true case of everything that glitters isn't gold.

One hundred days of an inpatient treatment center for her, plus a ton of 12-Step recovery work by him (plus showing up for those kids while she was away), and today their marriage is real, transparent and vulnerable for the first time. They have become the latest gatekeepers—respected leaders revered for their recoveries—in our NMS community.

Ellis is the third surviving member of the original group along with Gavin and Ben. He also is a member of a fundamental religion. He came to me as his second marriage was imploding because of his porn use and flirting activities. He worked hard to stop the behaviors. He worked hard to get honest about who he is. But most of all, he worked hard to learn how to feel. In the beginning, he could talk about sadness, anger, pain and hurt, but he did those feelings with an ever-present smile. He was shut down and drowning internally in a marriage with someone who was equally as damaged.

Ellis had four young children from his first marriage that ended when his first wife had to be long-term committed for mental health issues and he pulled the plug on the marriage. In the next ninety days, Ellis "interviewed" eight women for marriage, all from church, before selecting a woman five years his senior who had a checkered past, no means of support, and five children of her own. He thought they would be "The Brady Bunch." He was wrong. It was a classic case of the magical and mystical thinking of an addict. It was another classic case of quid pro quo, sex for economic security. At the nine-month mark, that marriage was falling apart.

After a long time of living apart (an agreed upon "no-contact"), while doing recovery and then coming back together to see what was truly there, Ellis finally had the courage and clarity to call it a day. As much as I believe in marriage and the nuclear family, I supported Ellis in his divorce. His wife's recovery effort was minimal and not sustainable. The marriage needed to end.

Today he is raising his three kids alone, staying sexually sober, and not actively looking for a new wife. He attends SLAA meetings, does step-work with his sponsor, and does sponsoring himself. He is fully connected to our NMS community. His life is full and rich. He shows appropriate fear when he thinks of dating again. Now that's a miracle. He finally learned to see his distorted thinking of the past when he believed that "the next one will save me."

During the life of our blended group, two other original members had started with us. They were Noah and Frank. The nucleus of those five men who came from a hard-working group set the tone for how this blended group would work. Toby and Evan came from an original group of eleven men. They came to this blended group with a third man, Cory, who after a year left the program and left recovery altogether after a series of minor acting-out episodes.

Cory's wife had been the hammer in the beginning but refused to do her own work. Cory, like so many of the men whose wives refuse to do any of their own work, often began to feel as if he were being pulled apart. Simply stated, she went from being the hammer for recovery to being a disincentive. The stronger Cory's voice became in sobriety, the more equity in the relationship he tried to demand, and the more Cory's wife raged. At the two-and-a-half-year mark of stellar recovery, Cory's wife was still treating him as if he had acted out last week. As a result of this conflict Cory relapsed with several episodes of masturbation without porn. It was clear to us that his imbalanced and un-repaired sexual life had never been addressed in his marriage. He was unwilling to separate or even move out of the bedroom, but the relapse episodes continued.

In a twenty-second voice message after almost three years, Cory quit NMS. He didn't have the courage to come to group to find closure with the men who had supported him for so long. Cory simply took his ball with his tail between his legs, and went home to mama. It was another sad commentary of the power of this illness and all the different manifestations of how it presents itself in a man's life. Cory never learned how to be a man in a man's world. In the end, his wife won as his untreated love addiction was killing him.

Toby and Evan, by contrast, have stood the test of NMS time. Their original group was one of the most dysfunctional groups I have ever had in NMS. They never coalesced. I believe that joining with Gavin, Ben, Noah, Frank and Ellis forced them to "shit or get off the pot" about recovery. With these five men there was no get-out-of-jail-free card. It was suit up, show up, and they needed that accountability. The five's work ethic became this blended group's work ethic and because of that, in short order, they functioned really well.

Toby came to me by way of Ben. They have known each other for a long time as members of the same religious community, and their wives have been best friends. Ben took a risk one day in early recovery and shared with his friend Toby his struggles with porn and his involvement with NMS. After overcoming some initial fear, Toby shared that he might have the same issue. Ben encouraged Toby to call me and he did.

Our first visit was almost our last. It also could have been the quickest session I ever had. Ben had given me a heads-up about his friend. So I wasn't going into it as blindly as Toby was. After he sat down and got settled, I asked him the same question I ask everyone who sits in my office: "What brought you here today?" His answer was clear and concise. "I look at inappropriate websites." To his amazement, I got out of my chair, extended my hand, and thanked him for coming in, telling him that the session was over at no charge. He was dumbfounded by the strength and quickness of my response.

Then I looked Toby in the eye and calmly said that I was not going to spend the next two hours talking to him in code. My response might seem odd or even hostile but the truth is that I knew what he meant and I also knew that his answer was a nice, sanitized way of describing something ugly. Toby's language was soft and kind and gentle. I told him, "there is nothing antiseptic about looking at men ejaculating into every orifice of a woman's body." Words are very important. After he closed his dropped jaw, I asked if Toby was willing to start again. He said yes and we did.

A more telling example comes from a client I had about five years ago. While on vacation with his wife and two year-old son, this man got arrested for solicitation of a prostitute on a late-night stroll alone near their hotel in La Jolla. The trip was to celebrate his wife's fortieth birthday. When the local police called and informed her that she would need to gather bail money for her husband, she collapsed in hysterics, all in plain view of her baby. When I finally met him some months later and asked him the same question, his response was, "I broke my marriage vows." Get my point?

Since that first meeting with Toby, he's learned to get transparent with his actions, thoughts and words. He and his wife spent more than a year living separately in the same house while caring for a special-needs adult daughter. They came to the table with a great sense of urgency coupled with a desire to go to any lengths to heal. Toby has had continuous sobriety for well over a year. His wife has gone to Cottonwood, joined SLAA, worked her own steps, and has a sponsor. They are a delight to work with.

Evan was referred to me by an NMS alumnus named Caleb, who happened to be in Matt's first group. They had known each other through a church camp. Evan was in a thirty-plus year marriage with a life wrapped around church and family. Their marriage, like many others, looked great on the outside. Inside, the marriage was riddled by anger, resentments and a complete lack of trust. Evan's addiction to porn and masturbation had deadened his heart. His wife lived in a constant state of righteous indignation and contempt. Finally, Evan decided to seek help. With much reservation, he chose a non-Christian-based program. He was willing to be willing. She was not.

For Evan, "putting down the porn" and stopping masturbation was not all that troublesome. His real issue was and still continues to be the marriage. Not only did Evan's wife choose not to participate in recovery, but she did not value his personal 12-Step work. First and foremost for her, she rejects the program because it's not Christ-based. I believe an even greater underlying reason exists: All the walls in their marriage are her personal walls. Evan's wife is in a "death do us part" marriage and divorce will never be an option for her. She is willing to live in this insanity forever, so she has no reason to be introspective at all. Like Cory's situation, Evan's wife is a disincentive to his recovery. To be clear, the women do want their husband's behavior to stop. They just don't want their husbands to change and gain equity in the relationship while stopping the behavior…

Almost two years ago, things got so contentious at home that Evan made a unilateral decision to move out of the house for a relationship time-out "no-contact." Evan's wife freaked out. Her first ploy was to try to have sex with Evan for the entire weekend before his move. They had sex but he still moved out. At work at lunch time on his first day out, Evan's wife had his favorite gourmet meal delivered. She had never done that during their entire marriage. Evan ate the lunch but did not respond. About day twenty of the "no-contact" Evan's wife had their eighteen year-old daughter call him to say that Mom had set a place for Evan at the dinner table and that he should come home. Evan held serve and did not respond.

We had planned to have the couple meet on day thirty in Hilarie's office. I was quite sure Evan's wife would not be comfortable in my office. I thought there might be an outside chance she would show with Hilarie. She refused. The "no-contact" continued.

On day forty-five, Evan received an urgent call from their adult married son who lives on the other side of the country. The call said that Evan's wife was having a nervous breakdown. That got Evan home. To this day, I have never seen him happier or healthier than he was during those blessed forty-five days of a "no-contact".

That night Evan moved back in, he had several healthy demands that his wife agreed to. First, they would have to see Hilarie for couples counseling. Second, she would have to join a women's group. And last, they would abstain from sex until the marriage healed.

The very next day they both showed up in Hilarie's office in the morning and Hilarie went over the agreed ground rules. Four hours later Evan and his wife were sexual followed shortly by the other two "demands" never materializing. So much for boundaries! Evan's wife knew after more than thirty years that sex was her currency and sex was Evan's most important need. It only goes to prove that if "Nothing changes, nothing changes."

This program is about sex and love addiction. The sexual acting-out is clear and easy to articulate. The love piece is a horse of a different color. To this day, Evan's lack of internal or external boundaries is killing him. He lives in a state of quiet desperation in which his every action is geared to appeasing a wife who cannot be placated. It's a lose-lose. The love addiction dynamic is so mercurial in nature, so hard to see, and so destructive to the human soul. All the while Evan has had stellar sexual sobriety. It is difficult for me and the men in his group to watch.

Evan, Toby, Ben, Gavin, Ellis, Frank and Noah. These are the men, the entire cast of characters, who are in Matt's recovery world. They are neither angels nor demons. They are just a group of men each with their own story, struggles and challenges, each dedicated to healing and helping each other. That gets us current to this past Tuesday with what was seemingly the culmination of Matt and Sophie's five-year effort to resurrect a marriage and change the inevitable.

The two of them are so cute together. Matt and Sophie appear as the perfect couple. They work together, have fun together, co-parent well together, and each one claims to be the other's best friend. The only problem is that Matt lies, deceives and manipulates. Matt also likes to dabble in the sex industry.

When they showed up five years ago Matt and Sophie both had a burning desire to get through this quickly so they could go back to their perfect life with their beautiful little baby. Matt joined my Saturday morning group and Sophie joined a women's group.

Even in the company of sex and love-addicted men, Matt had a hard time completely giving himself to this very simple program. He went through several sponsors and had a really hard time making it to SLAA meetings on any consistent basis. He hides behind work and often would say he was "overwhelmed."

In group, whenever Matt would get pushed hard he would retreat into three basic strategies. His first ploy was anger. Once, early on in group,

Matt got up while reaching a breaking point and slammed his clip board on our table in the middle of the group room. As the board shattered, flying into many pieces, the rest of the men in the room recoiled at the rage. I didn't flinch. I asked him, "Are you done?" Then I calmly told Matt to clean up his mess and sit down. He complied sheepishly.

Matt's second and most common strategy was victimhood. It played out in myriad ways and reminded me of that old Flip Wilson routine: "The Devil made me do it." The AA slogan for that is the poor me's: Poor me, poor me, pour me another drink. It was an easy place to retreat to.

The last item on Matt's "to do" list was the subtle, seldom-manifested and often veiled cry about suicide. The world would be so much better off without him: His wife, his daughter and the entire planet in general. Matt used all three on his wife during their fifteen-year relationship, and one of them always worked. Until now.

Matt tried to stop acting-out, he really did, but the compulsion never left and he never really got any hard-core distance from any of the wide range of behaviors. At the one-year mark, Sophie found his online account that included dating sites with a profile he had created claiming he was divorced. Nothing like looking for a new wife when you already have a wife, to help rebuild trust in a challenged relationship. That's distorted thinking.

Neither Matt nor Sophie were open to KeyStone as a treatment option right from the beginning. Sophie was never willing to kick him out of the house or even out of the bedroom. Matt had never really had a hard consequence for his life-threatening behavior.

At the two-year mark Sophie found Matt's porn. The electronic world was problematic for him, yet he didn't do much to build in any safeguards. Once again feathers got ruffled, and hurt and mistrust were again the order of the day as back to square one in recovery he went. He never, ever got honest on his own. His behavior only came out as a result of getting caught. This time Matt was open to going to The Meadows for Survivors week.

Matt's childhood trauma was massive. He was exposed to porn at an early age. He was abandoned multiple times by his father and moved on numerous occasions. He was raised in a house with his mother and two sisters. He was never able to bond successfully with males. When Mom sent herself back to school to help her family, Matt again felt abandoned. The Meadows helped him gain new insight, yet his inability to trust anyone and to become transparent never went away. With each and every new acting-out came a new disclosure.

In the summer a couple of years back, while on vacation with his wife and family, Matt used Sophie's laptop to access porn. The blatant nature of this behavior made it appear as if Matt believed he were "ten-feet tall and bullet-proof." In the end, he always got caught and only then would he get honest.

The following May, while Sophie was trying to pay the cell phone bill online, she discovered thousands of text messages sent and received by Matt to unknown numbers. That information piqued her curiosity and the forensic unraveling of the truth began. At first Matt denied it by blaming the phone company. He went so far as to call them in front of Sophie, demanding that they correct the error. As reality set in, Sophie demanded Matt go to KeyStone. The recovery meter was at three years and counting and they were back at square one again. Before Matt left, he could only acknowledge that they were his texts, and, yes, they were to sex-industry workers, but he maintained that no face-to-face encounters had happened. His group of sex-addicted men did not for one second buy the story. No one in our NMS community bought the story.

Matt caught the red-eye back East. He was driven to the airport by one of his group members directly after group ended. During group, we offered him another opportunity to get honest with us before treatment, but he stuck to his original story.

Three-plus weeks later Sophie was at KeyStone for disclosure and the truth came out. To no one's surprise, Matt had lied. At KeyStone she asked him to move out of the house for at least thirty days. Matt became indignant, believing that he had the right to be home. Sophie was now finally willing to give him a hard consequence and he didn't like it.

Sophie by trade was a psychologist. Her training and expertise did not serve her one bit in this life experience. When it came to sex and love addiction, she was just another hurt wife feeling betrayed beyond words. As Sophie started to heal and to do her own work, I offered her an opportunity to work with some of the newer women in NMS. Sophie accepted the chance to expand her base professionally. Before accepting, she talked about the opportunity with Matt and he signed off on it. She was thrilled at the chance. Every Wednesday night she ran a group while Matt stayed home to care for their now three year-old son. What we didn't know was that his alone time was being used to act out.

Matt later talked about how Sophie being gone on Wednesday nights rekindled his feelings of abandonment that he felt when his mom went back to school. He made up a story about how, now that Sophie was working more, his emotional safety was threatened.

As so often happens with the women connected to our men, Sophie had a difficult time finding anger. She could access pain, hurt and sadness pretty easily, but anger wasn't on her emotional landscape. She was the embodiment of that bromide that says little girls are "sugar and spice and everything nice." Once Sophie heard her third disclosure (the third was at KeyStone), she finally found and held her anger. With that anger came a "Deal-Breaker": If Matt acts out again with another human being in any sexual way, the marriage is over. Sophie finally said it and I believed Matt finally heard it. He stayed out of the house from June to December, finally coming back in time for Christmas—to the delight of their son, now five.

The reconciliation process, consisting of couples coaching and individual work, was done very slowly. We did not put it on "spin dry" to speed it up, the reconciliation process was painstakingly slow. Matt went to ninety meetings in ninety days. He started for the first time in his three-plus years to put pen to paper and do step-work. Matt was staying connected to the men in his group while some semblance of order was returning to their lives. The prognosis was finally looking good. The whole NMS community had a sense of hope. The family Christmas photo looked like episodes of *Father Knows Best*, *Leave It to Beaver* and *The Cosby Show* all wrapped up in one.

What we didn't know was that Matt had already started to slip in October, two full months before he moved back in. It was electronic porn. The pull of this "delivery system" is unbelievable for someone with a history of sex addiction. Access to the Internet is available 24/7. It's effect is like an endless supply of crack cocaine for a coke addict. Additionally Internet pornography is not your father's *Playboy*, it's now industrial-strength. It provides an endless supply and enormous variety. This is the new reality of the modern age. As it says in the AA Big Book, "There is no defense against the first drink," kind of like when an alcoholic walks by a bar and sees a sign in the window that reads, "All you can drink for $1."

In February, just two months after Matt's moving back in, Sophie found women's names and numbers on a slip of paper in a pants pocket she was going to throw into the wash. Sophie's tendency was not to micromanage or snoop. I am sure she wasn't looking for it. When Matt came home Sophie confronted him and, like a good dope fiend, he went instantaneously into a song and dance about how he found it while cleaning out his car and was going to get rid of it but had forgotten. Sophie brought the event to her women's group, members of which in turn told their husbands, who in turn brought it to our men's group. The story just didn't make sense.

As one of the men said, if it had been him, he would have ripped the paper into small pieces, flushed it down the toilet, and called his sponsor, his group and his wife. With Matt, none of that happened. Again, if Sophie had not found the paper, none of us would have known. In the end, the event just passed; no further action was taken and life proceeded on.

Of all the NMS men, Matt created a divide between programs, sponsor and us. His sponsor was a Sex Addicts Anonymous (SAA) guy and did not integrate at all with the SLAA community. Nor did Matt interact with any of the NMS men even though several of them attended SAA on a regular basis. Matt liked playing "The Blind Men and the Elephant," that children's story about the blind men who only could feel a single piece of the elephant thus never getting a true picture of what they were touching. Matt's compartmentalization and need for secrecy proved to be his demise.

The following November came still another relapse episode. Sophie had misplaced her iPod. For most people this would not be cause for alarm, but for the spouse of a sex addict it is. All kinds of illicit behavior can be downloaded onto an iPod. It had been missing for at least three weeks and she had looked everywhere. Sophie began to wonder if someone at her job might have stolen it.

One Tuesday night in December during group, Gavin asked Matt about something that was glowing in his bag. We all were well aware of Matt's bottom-lines against using electronics for prurient purposes. Gavin was the only one who saw the glow. Matt made a lame excuse and we moved on. It never really registered with me. On the drive home, Gavin called Matt and confronted him in a more forceful manner. Matt stayed true to the con. Then minutes later Matt called Gavin back "Getting Honest" about the iPod.

The story was that Matt had found it that morning while cleaning out the car and was going to give it back to Sophie, yet all day he had not called to tell her that he had found it. The story made it seem that he had it for only about twelve hours and during ten of those he was working. Sophie got this version of the story only after Gavin and Matt had talked. Once more, getting caught seemed to be the only way Matt could get real. This time, Sophie told him to leave the house. The entire NMS community was abuzz. The fear this kind of information creates in the women in the program is amazing. Everyone including Sophie believed that this time where there was smoke there was fire. This time, she demanded a polygraph test.

They met soon in my office and when Sophie informed Matt that she wanted him to take a polygraph test he didn't flinch. She set the test for a week out. In the meantime, he was not staying at home. Even with his men, Matt once again held to his story. A day before the test, he asked to meet with Sophie in my office. She was braced for the worst and armed with resolve, a result of her own recovery.

With a direct question from Sophie and a tearful answer, this marriage was over. "Did you act out with another woman?" Matt couldn't look at his wife and answered sheepishly, "Yes." Sophie jumped out of her seat, leapt into the air, and shouted at the top of her lungs: "Fuck, fuck, fuck, Matt… I'm done!" She stormed out, slamming the door. Sophie's outburst was so loud, the management people from the floor below came running up to see if everything was okay. As Sophie left the room, Matt broke down. He went right to veiled threats of suicide, sobbing how Sophie and their son would be better off without him. For the next hour, I tried to talk Matt off the ledge. I can't adequately convey the drama and intensity of the situation. The only words that fit here are from an Italian proverb: "Traduttore,

Traditore," meaning "to translate is to betray."

They managed to get through the holiday season fairly well. Sophie was great at dividing time for Matt to spend with their son. As part of her work, she added to her list of bottom-lines "Never having sex with Matt again." She needed to say it out loud. She has such capacity for forgiveness—and Matt knew all the buttons to push—that I wondered if he would be able again to wear her down emotionally so that she would take him back. With the help of her women's group, she emotionally held serve. Going into the New Year, Sophie had resolve.

Matt sprang into action and upped his recovery program in hope of saving his marriage. He was so badly looking for an external enemy to blame. His mind went in myriad directions. He believed he needed trauma counseling, so he found a trauma counselor. In our group meetings, I tried to focus on sobriety. The truth is Matt needs to be sexually sober for himself, his son and his general wellness. Sobriety was not about Sophie anymore, yet Matt held onto hope for the relationship.

Sophie did not run out and get a divorce attorney, nor did she seal the bank accounts, change security codes or change the house locks. Her main focus was to get their son counseling and to form a plan on when and how to break the news to a precocious five-year-old. At a joint session with a child psychologist, Matt caught Sophie off guard, asking her to wait eight or nine months for him to heal as a result of this new counseling. Sophie didn't know how to respond. She said she needed to think about it.

In her own NMS group, Sophie was steadfast. She was not open to another reconciliation. "Four disclosures are all I can take," she said. Sophie's self-worth and self-confidence were sufficiently strong that even the thought of being a single mom wasn't throwing her back into fear. But she needed to clean this up with Matt.

As Matt sobbed in my group this week, he shared that earlier that day he had taken a walk with Sophie and she had told him that she had begun filling out divorce papers. Sophie was not willing to honor his request to wait eight or nine months.

Watching Matt's pain pour out was difficult for all the men to watch. The AA Big Book calls that "irreconcilable demoralization." We had been on this journey with him a long time. This marriage did not have to end this way. The insanity of this illness is hard for most non-addicts to comprehend. This illness is a killer, yet it does not come uninvited, and all the while I still believe it can be placed in a state of remission.

I wish I could have done more to avoid this outcome but I know that's my own magical thinking. My first thought about Matt these days comes from an AA quote from the Big Book, "Those who do not recover are people who cannot or will not completely give themselves to this simple program, usually men and women who are constitutionally incapable of being honest with themselves." The book goes on to say that it's not their fault; they seem to have been born that way. In reality, Sophie did not divorce Matt but Matt's behavior, coupled with a lack of honesty, disqualified him from the privilege of being Sophie's husband. Sophie got well and Matt did not.

Flying under the radar of the chaos, sadness and trauma of the day is the cold, hard fact that their little son just had the worst day of his young life and he doesn't even know it. Now there's a painful gift that will keep on giving…

FEBRUARY 19

THE POINT OF DISCLOSURE

They walked in together. I didn't ask if they had driven here together. I had suggested to him, as I do all the men, that they arrive separately. She had never been in my office before. During the course of their year of participation in NMS, I could sense that she didn't really want to engage with me much and I respected that, but today was different. She had demanded this day because of pressure she was getting from the women in her group. I believe she would have been just as content to forget the entire thing.

Nine months ago, when Kirby walked into my office for the first time, his wife Eve had "just" found him looking at adult porn. Catching him looking at porn triggered a huge response. Her overriding emotion was fear.

Sixteen years before, just shortly after the birth of their second child, Kirby had been arrested for exhibitionism. But Kirby was an anomaly; he would do the behavior once every two or three months at the height of his addiction, just infrequently enough to tell himself that he was okay. Even his exhibitionism was measured. Dr. Gene Able, one of the national experts on the topic, states that for every time a man is arrested, he has already done the behavior two hundred times. That was not Kirby's story.

Kirby entered into a plea agreement with the court that called for him to complete successfully two years of a sex offender's treatment program in order to avoid being incarcerated. In addition to the get-out-of-jail-free card, Kirby also would have the offense expunged from his record. Knowing the gravity of the situation, Kirby was a model student. He and his wife worked overtime to believe that the event would come and go, and life was wonderful.

From the time she caught Kirby with porn until he showed up in my office, Eve had managed to squeeze from him every detail of his behavior that she thought she needed to know. This unhealthy, serial disclosure was done long before he hit my door. As Kirby started his work with me he was intent on getting an "A" in recovery. Compliance had worked in the past. He willingly joined my New Monday group, got a sponsor, and started attending meetings. What Kirby didn't expect was that the work I asked him to do would force him to feel. Eve, on the other hand, grudgingly went to see Hilarie. She agreed to join one of the women's groups but was adamant that she didn't have issues of her own. She was willing to attend, but she made it very clear it was only to support her husband. Other than this "little" sex issue, Eve claimed, they had the best of marriages.

As Kirby shared with me about the arrest sixteen years ago, and I pressed him for details beyond his comfort level, several things became evident. The most glaring fact was that since that event, neither Kirby nor Eve had shared that piece of their life with anyone on this planet—not a sibling, best friend, college roommate, clergy, no one. I can't communicate how powerful that fact was. The two of them had buried their shame deep. Kirby's porn use unearthed it all.

The second fact that jumped out was that Kirby, even after two years in an offenders program, had little or no awareness of the genesis of his behavior, nor was he aware how his behavior of sixteen years before was connected to the porn. It appeared that the aversion therapy model for the exhibitionism worked; Kirby had had no other episodes of exposing himself, but the treatment didn't leave him with no real insight other than to keep his pants on in public.

As with so many of the NMS men, Kirby had a very narrow bandwidth of authentic emotions that he could easily access. He presented as a mature man in his mid-fifties who was successful, affable, funny, smart, giving and willing to listen to others. What Kirby could not do was acknowledge fear, sadness or any unpleasant feelings at all. His upbeat, almost Pollyanna-esque, persona masked his inner self from the world and from himself. For Kirby, life was beautiful. He had a great wife and wonderful family and not a cloud in a forever-blue sky. Oh, yeah, except for this dirty, little secret. At the end of the day, Kirby's wife was a co-conspirator in the myth.

About six months ago Eve was ready to quit her group. I only found out because Kirby shared it in his group. The women in Eve's group didn't have a clue about her intentions. When I pressed Kirby on how he felt about the possibility of Eve leaving, he acquiesced to her needs while having a hard time stating his own. His stance so typified most of the men I deal with; they seek harmony at any cost.

It had been only a few weeks before that Eve had shared with Hilarie that their troubled teenage daughter had recently been date raped. I can only imagine the rage and anger that an incident like that might invoke in a dad. Later that week, when Kirby was in group and he did his weekly check-in, he failed to mention that heinous act. When I pressed him if there was anything else of note from his week that he wanted to share with his group, Kirby drew a blank. The fact was that Kirby was not withholding, he was not keeping a secret from these men, and he was not lying. He simply had put the event into his "away box," and, for all intents and purposes, it had never happened. As we processed the possibility of his wife leaving her group, I refreshed Kirby's memory about that incident and pointed out how deeply compartmentalized he kept his life. So did his wife. Their system was so closed. That's so unhealthy.

A week later, while I was doing my bi-monthly women's workshop, I asked Eve directly, in front of the other attending women, about leaving group. Eve gave a meek ambivalent answer. I told her if she could find one or two or three women outside NMS with whom she was willing to be totally honest about every aspect of her life that I would support her leaving group. I knew Eve never would, and she stayed. Later that week, Kirby said he believed that Eve remaining in group and seeing Hilarie was a good thing. Hurray for small victories.

Kirby had seen other men in his group go through disclosure. One of these men, Dean, had done it with his partner and her counselor. Dean's partner was so hurt initially that she demanded Dean do disclosure immediately in their living room, which I stopped. It takes a lot of written work to get it right, to be thorough and forthright. The AA Big Book calls it a "searching and fearless moral inventory."

I also stopped Dean's disclosing in private because his partner didn't have a support system in place and she was unwilling to join our program. She had a sense that there was more to Dean's story than she knew, but in reality she had no idea. In time, and mostly due to his strength of conviction about not doing disclosure in a non-supportive environment, Dean's partner found her own counselor along with a women's group and started getting the support she needed. After fourteen months of Dean in recovery she was sufficiently ready to receive Dean's formal disclosure. Today they are coming out of an extended "no-contact".

Norm, another man in Kirby's group, had a difficult time stopping behavior that led him to realize that he needed to at least leave the bedroom, if not the house. Norm was reluctant to leave his home because they had two small children, ages four and one. His wife had joined Hilarie's group but, like Kirby's spouse, repudiated loudly any link to her own dysfunction. She knew most of Norm's behavior beforehand as she had been able to do the "rolling pin around the house" routine enough times to beat the information out of him. That's a concept I like to call "serial disclosure."

As Kirby watched these men from his group do their work and his wife experienced the value of disclosure on the women's side, Kirby began to see that formal disclosure would be a beneficial experience for all involved. With much anticipation, this was the week.

The reason I suggested they come in separate cars was simple—Kirby and Eve are so enmeshed that they would rescue each other from any unpleasant thoughts and feelings. My thought was if Kirby and Eve each came alone they just might have an individualized reaction to a joint life experience. Without the created space, her experience would become his and vice versa.

After a few pleasantries, I repositioned Kirby and Eve in two chairs about two feet apart and facing each other. I sat on the couch to the side of them directly in the middle. I had Kirby tell Eve exactly how many sets of eyes had looked at his letter. I wanted Eve to see what an open system looked like. This was not a didactic exercise created in a vacuum. Kirby had been challenged to be fearless beyond any level of honesty he had previously imagined. I instructed Kirby to read slowly and to look at Eve as he went. I told Eve to not process the information on the fly and, at the end, that Kirby would give her a copy of the letter that she could keep. Eve had a hard time staying still. Her eyes wandered as Kirby began. She stroked her own hand in an attempt to self-soothe. Her eyes started to well up long before Kirby got to any of the "meat-and-potatoes." Kirby's voice was cracking almost from the beginning. Since he began his work with me, I haven't seen Kirby cry. We had touched pieces of Kirby's soul he did not know were there. He was being vulnerable and that was new behavior for him. Kirby's new-found emotions added to Eve's discomfort.

After many rewrites, Kirby was finally ready to get started. Even though his wife was holding his feet to the fire for looking at porn, I had wanted Kirby to start his disclosure letter with his arrest. For years, whenever the topic came up, Kirby had referred to being arrested as the day he got a "citation"—as if it had been a ticket for jaywalking. Kirby's language about the arrest had historically kept them both safe. Now I wanted him to paint a real picture of his transgression. Everything does look worse in black and white. Exhibitionism is an ugly behavior. To be sure, sitting in a car with your pants down to your knees masturbating to women while exposing makes porn look benign. I wanted Kirby and Eve to feel what they should have felt sixteen years before.

I wanted Kirby to talk about how devious he was. About how when he received the phone call from the police to come in for "The Chat," he had to rearrange his workday. About how when he had come home from work that day and Eve had asked how his day was, Kirby had lied. I wanted Eve to hear how, for several weeks, Kirby had managed to get to the mail box before she could find the court date information. I wanted Eve to hear how for several months, while Kirby was attending a weekly sex offenders group on Tuesday nights, he had told Eve he was working late and she believed him. Most importantly, I wanted Eve to understand and hear that Kirby had been arrested, not "cited." It was more than a littering ticket and, if he had not gone when summoned, the police would have sent a squad car to their house, handcuffed him in front of family and neighbors, and taken Kirby away.

After Kirby finished reading, I asked Eve what she was feeling. All she could say was, "I just don't understand why." Staying in her head and not feeling the blunt force of Kirby's words protected them both. I told Eve that Kirby is who he is because of his childhood as an army brat who went to eight schools in twelve years, whose father was a drunk and whose mom took refuge in religion. Such a disjointed upbringing was a big part of why Kirby became who he became. I wanted Eve to hear, that for a few years before they met, Kirby had been a police officer in a large city. Kirby had witnessed terrible events that were never therapeutically processed. The only thing he did to feel better was change careers. Out of sight, out of mind, but the "Geographic Cure" did not make the post-traumatic stress disorder go away. Most of all, I wanted Eve to understand that this is not a condition Kirby can outgrow. He needs recovery today, tomorrow, next week, next year and forever, just like every other addict. With recovery, the prognosis is good; without it, Kirby's history says he will repeat the behaviors.

Eve quickly regained her composure. I gave her an assignment for our next session, in two weeks. I wanted Eve to write a cost letter, point by point from Kirby's disclosure letter. Several of Eve's women's group members told me Eve had started writing her cost letter a week before disclosure, but she had been encouraged to stop. Eve so badly wanted to fax this in. The assignment was simple but difficult: When you did _____, it cost me _____. The only way to get through the pain was to "Name It and Claim It" before discarding it. Eve just wanted to get it all behind her ASAP.

I cautioned Eve not to stay in the sadness nor to trivialize the truth, but to find some anger about the lies, mistrust and betrayal. Kirby needed to see Eve angry to help him break his own denial system, while Eve needed the anger to allow Kirby to continue doing recovery. Eve had to work hard not to paper over this as she had in the past. I also told Eve that, at some future point, when their personal finances are more in order, Kirby would need to go to The Meadows for Survivors week. I was planting a seed. It could be so easy for them to go back to "Business as Usual" after the immediate crisis has passed. Now the ball is in Eve's court. Kirby showed up in integrity, vulnerability and transparency. I am proud of him. My goal and hope for Kirby and Eve is that this time their reconciliation is real and not held together with a tube of Krazy Glue. Time will tell...

They really are a nice couple and they do truly love each other, but love is not enough to combat this disease. As the AA Big Book says, there are three pertinent ideas: That we were alcoholics and could not manage our own lives, that probably no human power could have relieved us of our alcoholism, and that God could and would if He was sought ... and to seek is a verb, an action word.

As we go forward in this recovery process we are all keeping a good thought. As they say in AA, "More shall be revealed."

FEBRUARY 26

LUNCH WITH CRAIG

I see four clients a day. My hours are 10am, noon, 2pm and 4pm The clocks in my office are set five minutes fast to ensure that I get at least a quick lunch and a snack break. For some strange reason it seems to work for me. As a result I seldom have time to schedule anything else during my workweek. This week was different.

To date, NMS has "graduated" over forty men. They are not cured but, for the most part, they have restored their lives to some sense of normalcy. After surviving four years in NMS together, these men go their separate ways. Many of their relationships remain. I see most of them at our annual NMS events, such as our five movie nights per year, NMS Summer Softball/BBQ Picnic, our December holiday party, or our yearly attendance at Seattle Mariner baseball and Seattle Storm WNBA games.

Thirty of the alumni are still active members of the greater SLAA community. As senior members they sponsor, lead meetings, take phone calls from newcomers, and attend the yearly SLAA Men's Retreat. I see these men pretty consistently. I love seeing these men and keeping up with their lives. Our bond is strong and sincere.

During the past few months I noticed that one man, Craig, was showing up to meetings and events less and less frequently. I asked others if they had seen or heard from Craig and their answer was a disturbing no. It appeared he was falling off the grid. Not a good sign. Craig had graduated from NMS in June a couple of years ago and had never strayed too far from the program. Six months ago, Craig had lost his job as a graphic designer and, at the same time, he learned his wife was pregnant with their first child. That's a lot of pressure.

Two weeks ago I finally saw Craig at a meeting, his first in a long time. He said he was so glad to be there. Craig could acknowledge that he was feeling overwhelmed. At the end of the meeting, as we hugged I said, "Let's do lunch." I jokingly added that it would be my treat and when Craig gets a new job he could return the favor. He called the next day and I set aside a noon slot to spend some time with Craig.

It has been more than five years since Craig first walked into my office. He was a frightened young man of twenty-seven. He was a man of few words. More than just shy, Craig seemed afraid. His longtime girlfriend had found his porn stash and his well-compartmentalized double life was starting to unravel; Craig was falling apart.

Craig was from the Midwest and had moved here for a job shortly after graduating college. He is a first-generation middle son of immigrant parents who came to America to obtain higher educations. His dad became a well-respected lawyer, and his mom was trained as a paralegal but worked as a homemaker instead. Craig's brothers followed Dad into law and remained in close proximity to their parents. Craig was the black sheep. He did not go to law school and instead moved to the other side of the country.

Craig came from a devoutly Catholic family, attended parochial schools, and had been an altar boy. He continued to go to church weekly as an adult in Seattle. Craig had a strong religious sense of right and wrong. When his sense of morality collided with his private sexual behavior, Craig felt ripped apart. When his partner learned about his dirty, little secret, his sense of shame overwhelmed him. Sitting in my office for the first time, Craig was lost.

Getting Craig to string together more than a few words was hard, yet he was honest. I could see his social awkwardness and how difficult it was for him to be vulnerable and expressive. He had difficulty making eye contact. Shame seemed to drip from him and, to my amazement as I probed beyond the porn and the masturbation, Craig was a virgin. Of all the men I had seen, this was a first. He was different. This was going to be interesting. A virgin sex addict!

As with so many of the men who walk in my office, Craig said his primary concern was not the addiction, but losing his relationship. His partner was twenty-three and her family background was the same as his. Craig's girlfriend was still living at home but spending a lot of time at his place. As he explained it, their sexuality had an adolescent air to it. They did anything but intercourse, even though she was not a virgin from a prior relationship. They acted "as-if" the sex they had was not sex. I gave Craig my definition of sex for future reference: "sex is any behavior you wouldn't want your partner to do with someone else." How about that for leveling his playing field about the reality of his, "wink, wink," definition of sex?

Craig claimed that the fact that his girlfriend had been sexual with someone else didn't bother him, but I didn't buy it. The more we explored the relationship, the more it looked like most of the other ones I had seen in the program—riddled by an imbalance of power in which the man doesn't have the voice to claim equity on a daily basis. It's the constant curse of the Mr. Nice Guy, and Craig is his poster child.

After a few sessions, Craig disclosed that his girlfriend would be moving to Canada indefinitely to care for an extended family member. It was Craig's intention to commute on the weekends. I pushed back on his thinking and he didn't like it.

In week number four Craig came in at his appointed time but remained standing. He mustered enough courage to tell me he had come to say goodbye and that he wasn't going to work with me anymore. Now it was my time to hold up a mirror. I asked if his girlfriend trusted him yet around the porn and, of course, the answer was a resounding no. As I started to strip Craig of his defenses and our dialogue continued, I asked Craig to take off his coat and sit down. He hesitated but complied. To this day we joke about that.

I had been slowly uncovering the main dynamic of Craig's family. His father was a powerful attorney who is held in high esteem in the work place. Yet it was his mom who had wielded the power in the family. Her need for control had squashed Craig's spirit. Mom was a narcissist. She tried to orchestrate his life to meet her world view. Craig had had enough awareness of this dynamic to move far away, across the country. For him, that was an act of pure survival and pure rebellion. Craig's story developed like a chapter from John Bradshaw's *On The Family*, and—surprise, surprise—his partner today resembled his mom in every way.

It was clear to me that Craig needed to avoid buying into his girlfriend's idea of doing what I was calling the I-5 Shuffle, which translated into giving yourself away to meet someone else's needs. In the middle of our heated exchange, Craig asked what I wanted for him. My direct and concise answer amazed him. I wanted Craig to stop his addicted behavior, find his voice as a man, make peace with his own sexuality, get connected to men to learn intimacy instead of trying to find it in the arms of a woman, and, most of all, I told him I wanted to dance at his wedding. We made a deal that day: Craig would do a thirty-day "no-contact" with his girlfriend and continue working with me. It was a start. To his credit, when I told him not to leave before the miracle, he didn't.

As is often the case with men in the program, Craig's love addiction was way stronger than his sex addiction. He was able to stop the sexual acting-out behavior before walking into my office, but his need to have a girlfriend and to be partnered was another story. When Craig's girlfriend moved to Vancouver he had an easier time with the "no-contact." The more work Craig did in recovery, the more willingness he had to stay apart. His girlfriend refused his invitation to come see me; she was adamant that this was solely Craig's issue. Hers was not an uncommon stance for a younger woman—especially one without children.

At the four-month mark, Craig was able to write a full disclosure letter in hope that his girlfriend would be willing to come in to the program. Craig had heard through his church grapevine that she might be dating someone else. Within six months Craig had put some closure to the relationship and was settling in as a single man in recovery.

Craig was a member of my first Tuesday night group that lasted from 2004 through 2008. I designated that group as my "Superstar Group." Those Tuesday night guys did more to put form to NMS than any other group I had. They were the face of NMS for those four years.

The age range of the original ten in the Tuesday group was twenty-seven through forty-five. That is a small gap. Three men were married and one guy was living with a partner and her son from a previous relationship. Three other men had been divorced prior to joining NMS. One of the men was an inpatient candidate right from the start and had chemical dependency issues as well. He was gone before the first month was up. Another man didn't want to take a break from his serial monogamy and he was gone by month three. At the end of the first year, we had settled in at eight members and only two of them were married, both without children. This lack of family obligations gave these men time to bond inside and outside of my office. It was wonderful to watch.

Three months into the existence of this group, a member in his late thirties, Sean, lost his teenage daughter to a congenital heart defect. In the face of this tragedy, these men, who suffer from a severe Intimacy Disorder, all stepped up to walk with their recovery brother through his grief. That event, the death of a child, more than any other single event helped meld this group into a unique and special group of men.

Craig was finally in an open system with men he could trust, and he thrived. His next life lesson was to create boundaries with his parents, which really meant his mom. When Craig made his weekly call home, it consisted of two minutes with Dad then the phone would pass to Mom for the real dialogue. We had a lot of work to do.

Craig's biggest hurdle was to create and hold healthy boundaries around his parents. He had tremendous fear of his mother's negative judgments. Craig's need to please her was dwarfed by his need to avoid conflict. He needed to learn where he started and where he stopped.

I have come up with a simple, but I believe accurate, construct about how the avoidant addict is created. Let me explain. When a man as a boy had been raised by a raging parent, he learns he is not emotionally safe to be authentically known. He responds to his fear by building compartments within his life. He develops an internal resolve that he never wants to exhibit the kind of rage he has witnessed. As a life strategy, he develops a passive persona. Having never seen appropriate anger modeled, he can only "do" passive. He, therefore, never learns how to do appropriate anger. He becomes someone who seeks harmony above all else. This is an interesting concept that gives us food for thought. Craig's mom was abusive to him emotionally and physically. He just wasn't safe around her.

The same strategy and processes are used when it comes to the ability to confront. Men who grow up with a criticizing parent never want to be that "wagging finger" as an adult. In response to that internal fear, they swing to the opposite end of the emotional spectrum and become passive, skipping past the healthy ability to confront someone and to hold others accountable for their behaviors. This dynamic is the driving force in love addiction. Untreated love addicts cannot show up honestly in a relationship, and inevitably they "shrink-to-fit" in any partnership. Their mantra when given a directive by their perceived criticizing partner becomes "Yes, ma'am, boss, sir" followed by a salute. The imbalance of power within the partnership becomes wider as life unfolds. The hidden sexual acting-out re-enforces their need to be compliant.

The origins of this conflict-avoidant man show up in his inability to be assertive. Growing up with an emotionally aggressive mom leads him to move to the opposite end of the scale; he settles into a life of unmet needs and unexpressed feelings. His fear of being aggressive leads him to become passive, bypassing the healthy human trait of being assertive. The ability to demonstrate appropriate assertiveness is a necessary life skill for a man; it enables him to compete in the world. Craig's internalized feelings of rage became eroticized the more he connected his passivity to the good feeling of an orgasm. It didn't take long for the template to be embedded in cement.

Any man depleted of the ability to access anger, to confront and to be assertive goes through life feeling inadequate, insecure, alone and afraid. Acting-out becomes a mask, a coping mechanism, and his "drug of choice." His insides never match what he sees on the outsides of others. His internal system is designed for failure while his outsides look pristine. This is where Craig started.

Sitting among sex addicts was harder at first for Craig. He felt the same guilt and shame as the others, but he had a twisted sense that he was even more broken because he was a virgin. Initially, some of the other men had thought things like "Come back when you have a real problem." For men who had been acting-out in more egregious ways, Craig's behavior looked and felt benign. Yet his brokenness was evident to the other men and he integrated well into the group.

His core group of Hugo, Neil, Troy, Quinn, Cain, Walker and Sean stayed together for almost two years. The sheer volume of time they spent together was incredible. With group work, SLAA meetings, fellowship and bye-nights, they really bonded. It was amazing to watch Dr. Carnes' Four

Core Beliefs in all the men start to evaporate as time went on. Like Craig, Hugo, Cain, and Quinn also let go of relationships based on addiction. They partnered for a wide variety of non-healthy reasons and in recovery these relationships were not sustainable. That's not to say the women were at fault, but what I am saying is that these men partnered for all the "right" wrong reasons. It's an interesting concept; Carnes calls it "Courtship gone awry." As each man found his voice in his aloneness, he developed the capacity to be rigorously honest and set new standards for healthy relationships.

Neil and Walker were married men without children. Their marriages were the most important pieces of their lives even thought their spouses were totally running the show. The women would say "jump" and the men would reply "How high?" These men were painfully emasculated and love-addicted within their marriages. It was often hard to watch. Their love issues were every bit as strong as their sex issues. Through the course of their NMS experience, both men lived outside the home attempting to find slivers of sobriety, sanity and self-worth. These slivers never really appeared.

The women my men partner with are equally un-treated in their addictions, yet because of the sexual acting-out the men get the designation as the "Sick One" in the partnership. The system is very symbiotic in nature.

Troy and Sean were both divorced. Troy's divorce started before he joined NMS and was finalized early in his recovery. He had a ton of shame, guilt and sadness for breaking up his family. I met Troy's ex-wife once, just before the divorce. Sitting in my office, she was crystal clear that she was done. I tried to push her a little, but she was ice cold and had a huge shield of armor up. I can't really blame her. In trying to get Troy's wife to reconsider for a moment, I told her that whenever she finally divorced him she would be divorcing a "stranger." Troy didn't really know who he was and his wife definitely didn't know him either. Considering they had two small girls, I thought I might have an outside chance of getting her attention. But she never flinched. Troy's wife walked out the door and never looked back. As it turned out, Troy would go on to do great recovery work and really repair his soul from the inside out. He became an excellent dad to his two girls, now teen-aged. Within four years, Troy was partnered with a wonderful woman who knows his entire sexual history and loves him for the man he is today. It just goes to show that "One woman's trash is another woman's treasure."

Craig, meanwhile, started to go deep inside his family of origin. He eventually distinguished between what was real and what was part of a TV fantasy he bought into growing up with a "Donna Reed" type for a mom or the forever surreal world of *Ozzie and Harriet*. Once Craig could see that everything that glittered wasn't gold in his family he could start to make sense of it all. It truly became a case of take what you want and leave the rest. His conflict involving the commandment to honor thy mother and father caused him a huge amount of unrelenting turmoil. In the end, Craig came to understand that he could see his parents for who they were. Not as mother and father, but as human beings he did not have to vilify in the process. Craig was becoming his own man.

One of Craig's other great challenges was how to come to grips with his concept of God. His version before recovery was given to him by his family. It was juvenile in nature. Craig's God was extremely conditional, punishing and unforgiving. Combining that concept of God with a strict adherence to scripture concerning the sin of masturbation made his guilt seem endless. Craig struggled to find space between him and a child molester. The shame he experienced far exceeded the nature of his behavior. As time went on Craig developed a mature relationship with a Higher Power of his own understanding. He was growing up in front of me and it was a gift to witness.

A huge piece of the glue for this NMS group was music. Hugo, Cain, Neil and Craig had, at one time in their lives, made music professionally. Craig is a classically trained violinist. The violin was connected to Mom however, and to her push for him to be world renowned. The more work Craig did in recovery, the more he found his passion and gift in music. When the four men played together, it was heaven; it was the music of recovery.

Craig took another growth opportunity when he joined Toastmasters to work on his fear of public speaking and his innate shyness. It was an excellent, safe venue for him to practice developing this new muscle. Craig's new stretch really blossomed when he shared his life story at an open speakers meeting of SLAA. He invited some friends from outside his recovery community to attend. Craig's shame was lifting.

After about eighteen months of sobriety and stability, Craig started the process of "intentional dating." I am a firm believer that for sex addicts not to get caught up in the swirl, intensity and rush of an early romance, they have to have some rules to protect them from their own nature. With his guidelines in place, Craig took the scary step of dating. With the scrutiny of ten men in recovery, and armed with the "rules for dating," he ventured out and eventually met a woman through his church. This deliberate course gave Craig an opportunity to select a partner and not merely settle for someone just because she liked him. This was a new paradigm for Craig, as it is for all recovering sex and love addicts. This approach protected him from himself and increased the odds that this relationship would be better. Craig was doing this relationship in a way I call "cards face up."

By the three-month mark Craig was introducing his girlfriend to his recovery community and taking appropriate risks around self-disclosure. The more this woman learned, the more she fell in love with him. Craig's recovery and past relationship history did not run her off. She was able to see the man he was over the boy he had been. At the one-year mark of the relationship they got engaged.

In September 2008 my wish came true. My wife and I danced at Craig's wedding. What a blessing it was for me to bear witness to the power of recovery through grace and redemption. This is a very simple program, yet very hard to do. Craig's entire men's group was there along with his sponsor, who is an NMS alumnus. The intimacy that Craig never knew before had been created.

Against the backdrop of our relationship and our work together, lunch with Craig was going to highlight my day. We caught up with how he was doing around his search for work. Even though Craig has been unemployed for a while, he was still upbeat. He was looking in different directions and contemplating going back to school. Craig was getting excited about the prospect of being a dad. I learned about their pregnancy at our holiday party in December and I announced it right then to the NMS community. The baby is due this June. What a blessing!

Since his group ended in June 2008, Craig has struggled to stay in close contact. Without the regular group schedule, life seems to get in the way for everyone. Some guys find ways to stay connected. Hugo, Troy and Neil joined the ManKind Project (MKP) New Warriors program the weekend before Craig's wedding. Quinn had decided against participating in MKP mainly to concentrate on his son, who has Asperger's syndrome. The lack of connection is taking a toll on Craig emotionally. He knew enough to start trying to reconnect. I was an easy stop along the way.

In the middle of my workweek full of constant new drama and trauma, it was wonderful to break bread with a former client who has become a friend. This passion of mine is more than a job. My cup runneth over with blessings. For the most part, all of this brings me immeasurable pleasure, joy and fulfillment.

Thus ends February. Time is flying by and there is never a dull moment. I'm still energized by my New Wednesday group that is now at eight men. My New Monday group is now eighteen months-old and some of the miracles of recovery are starting to come true for those men. The Monday group that Gavin runs is pretty stable as they enter "stage two" recovery. My oldest running group, also on Wednesday, is winding down towards a June graduation. They still have the turmoil of the impending divorce of Matt and Sophie, but the rest of the men are solid in recovery and are facing their challenges from places of mental health and emotional maturity. All in all, I can't complain and, heck, it wouldn't help if I did.

~

February is all about hope. Without hope, despair would engulf those affected by this illness. Without hope, relapse is inevitable and all would be lost. With hope anything is possible and our experience tells us miracles can and do happen.

March

~

Faith

MARCH 5

DEMONS AND ANGELS

Demons

Sex and love addiction is a fatal illness, yet it does not come uninvited. It is chronic in nature, progressive if left untreated and is potentially fatal. This truth jumped into my cup once again in March of 2008.

It was just after New Year's 2008 when I received a phone call from a man who needed to see me quickly. I moved some people around and got him scheduled the first week in January. His name was Marcel and he was a few days out of Lakeside-Milam, an inpatient treatment center where he had just completed a twenty-eight day stay for his cocaine addiction. As fate would have it, while he was there, his group counselor was a former member of NMS and had been a group facilitator for me. I had pushed this man to pursue a career in counseling and it was during my watch that he went back to school to become a CDP.

I make up that, as Marcel did his work around his relationship with his drug and alcohol counselor, what he saw was this co-occurring disorder. During Marcel's stay in treatment, his counselor couldn't really do anything to address Marcel's sex and love addiction. It's one of the drawbacks of doing only a traditional chemical dependency treatment program, but Marcel's counselor did have the good sense and wisdom to refer Marcel on to me upon his discharge.

Marcel definitely had the amped up, "speedic" persona of a coke addict. He talked a million miles a minute and had a hard time staying on point, but he was honest. I knew from the moment we met that Marcel really had gone to the wrong treatment center, and that's not a knock on Lakeside, but he needed a higher level of care that they could not provide. They are very good at what they do. Marcel was just beyond their reach but they didn't know it.

Marcel was in his late forties and married with four kids. He was a college grad, very successful in business and seemed to have it all. There is a riddle in the chemical dependency business that defines the power of drug addiction very well and it goes like this: "What do you get the richest man in the world, who has everything, for his birthday?" The answer is "crack cocaine, because a year from now he won't have that dilemma anymore," he would have lost everything!

Dr. Arnold Washton, MD, a leader in the treatment of cocaine addiction, wrote a paper in 1991 entitled "The Link Between Cocaine and Compulsive Sexuality," in which he clearly states that relapse is inevitable when the sexual compulsivity component of the addiction has not been addressed. This is true even with cocaine addicts who have put together a year or more of sobriety from the drug, because there is still a high likelihood that the sexually acting-out behaviors are still continuing. The two addictions, at least for men, are forever joined at the hip. Editorial comment: I still cannot believe that drug treatment centers do not deal with this reality two decades-plus after the research was first published. Now, back to Marcel.

Marcel had lost his twenty-eight days of sobriety soon after leaving treatment, and the coke took him back to escorts and the sex industry. All the while he was obsessed with returning to his wife and kids. Marcel had been living out of the house since right before going to treatment, yet he and his wife were talking several times a day and that wasn't a particularly good thing. All the while there was no counseling going on. Simply stated, they were just two broken souls trying to figure this mess out on their own.

I knew the day I met Marcel he needed more help. I started to talk to him about either going to KeyStone or to The Meadows for their thirty-five day inpatient treatment program for poly-addicted clients. My main focus was trying to keep Marcel safe and to get him more help. In the beginning I was seeing him two times a week and I dropped him in the middle of NMS even though I did not have a group to put him in. The men of NMS responded in a big time way with time and attention. Marcel was also going to a 12-Step meeting every day, either AA, CA, or SLAA. We had a plan.

The drug treatment did nothing to address the shame Marcel was feeling about his years of infidelity. His wife had caught him cheating several times throughout the course of the marriage and she did know about the substance abuse. Most men who get caught and do "Hammer over the head" type of disclosures in the living room never give it all up. They only give up what they believe their spouses can handle. The core belief of "You wouldn't love me if you knew me" runs the show. Marcel's wife only knew about fifty percent of what he had done.

The drug treatment center also didn't come close to dealing with

Marcel's history of being molested as a child and the resulting trauma. Dr. Carnes has a great slide he shows in one of his workshops that I'll never forget. At the top of the hand drawn cartoon panel there is a sign that says "ABCD Drug and Alcohol Treatment Center" and there is a circle of chairs in a group room. Sitting in the circle is an obvious clinician with clipboard in hand and only one client. In the extreme top corner of the cartoon is a mass of huddled bodies as far away from the chairs as possible. The caption under the picture reads, "But you told me to be honest!" Drug and Alcohol Treatment centers are not designed to deal with sexual trauma and offending behavior.

The cocaine led Marcel to the extremes of being either very high or very low. In his high state he could see that the light at the end of the tunnel doesn't have to be a train, but in his low state he could only see the blackness of the tunnel and an abyss at the end. I was scared for Marcel and I told him so. Whenever I asked him if he would do self-harm he would say "No way, I love my kids." He came out of the drug treatment center in the care of a psychiatrist and on medication.

At the end of February we had our every two month movie night and Marcel showed up. He was up and down all night. He could not stay still and yet he didn't leave. I knew Marcel had been using, but I wanted him in the NMS community. Only a few of my men had any knowledge of cocaine addiction and could see it; the rest just assumed he was a man in early withdrawals around his sex addiction.

All Marcel could focus on was that he had done some snooping and was positive that his wife was having an affair and was planning to leave him. Marcel finally decided that going to KeyStone was a good idea. He called and got a bed date but it was two weeks out, they were maxed out. I got on the phone to them and they bumped his bed date up to eight days. Now all we had to do was hold serve. Marcel's obsession concerning his wife grew exponentially worse every day. I could hardly get him to focus on anything else. I was just trying to contain him. My only goal was to get Marcel to KeyStone. His love addiction was kicking him in the butt. He was in close contact with Dirk, Earl and Eliot. All three of these men had gone to KeyStone and two had struggled with substance abuse at some point in their lives. They got it. I saw Marcel on the last Friday of February and he seemed stable enough, and again he took a no self-harm pledge. Then on the following Monday morning, I got a call from Marcel's wife.

I had never spoken to her before. Since Marcel was out of the house and she was extremely angry with him there was no point to try to push that meeting. Her voice was a bit shaky when she introduced herself. I was caught off guard by her call. She said, "I'm Marcel's wife and I'm calling you because he spoke highly of you and all you were trying to do for him." Then she was silent for a moment and after a pregnant pause said in a very soft voice, "Marcel is dead." I could tell she was trembling. I told her to take a breath. She did. I asked her if she was willing to talk about it and she said yes. She continued, "Marcel didn't answer his phone for a few days and I started getting concerned so I went to his apartment, I knocked on the door but he still didn't answer so I called the police, I had a very bad feeling." Her voice calmed as she told me that the police came to do the wellness check and went in first. They tried to stop her from following, but she ran in to find him hanging. I was numb hearing this tragic news and she started sobbing again.

As if the story couldn't get any worse, she continued on. She had become obsessed about what Marcel's last hours might have looked like, so she started checking with everyone and everywhere. Her curiosity took her to his cell phone and she saw that he had made five calls from 1:30am and 3:30am on the night he died. She called all five numbers. They all belonged to prostitutes.

Marcel's wife called again the next day to tell me when and where the memorial would be. I wasn't going to be able to go but I passed it on to all the NMS men. The bounce around the NMS community was lighting quick and took a high emotional toll on everyone who heard. Last week this man had sat in Movie Night with us and now he was dead by his own hand.

Don't tell me this disease isn't fatal. I had to call KeyStone where my client Kelly was expecting Marcel any day. I spoke to the staff first before I told him. At least Kelly was in a safe place to process it.

Earl went to the funeral and spoke briefly to Marcel's wife and saw his four kids. How about that image as a "Kodak Moment!" Earl reported that there were over 400 hundred people in attendance. The man was loved. No mention of how he died was made. The next day I saw the obit in the newspaper. What a great guy. This is a treatable illness. Words cannot explain the profound loss I feel.

I took the memorial handout and had it framed. It is on my wall in a black frame. I take it off the wall from time to time if I think Marcel's death could be of service to someone else. Every March I take it down, pass it around and talk about him. This past March I was with my new guys. You could hear a pin drop after I shared the story. I will not let him be forgotten, at least not in NMS.

I only knew Marcel for two short months, but he has had a lasting impact on me and on my program. Marcel's life and death only serve to reinforce my belief that whenever I am talking to an active addict I have to approach it as if this might be the very last time we talk. Sad but true, I must never forget the fatal nature of this illness. Marcel, also sadly, drives home the reality that you can't deny anyone their desperation and, that if an individual decides to be desperate, no power on earth can stop them. It's a hard pill to swallow. May he rest in peace.

Angels

On the day I received Marcel's obituary, I also experienced the joy of what we do in NMS. Walking back into my office building after dinner, I was mentally getting ready for that evening's group work. I knew I was going to pass around Marcel's obituary and drive the point home what a bad outcome looks like. Just inside my door, I saw a glowing woman with a huge smile who was waiting to see me. I was shocked at first and then warmed by her presence. Out of nowhere there she was—Taja.

It's been twenty-one months since I have seen Taja last. Her time here in the women's side of NMS was intense and exhausting. She had started, like all the other NMS women, working with Hilarie first, and then joining a women's group. That was almost three years ago. Taja's marriage was falling apart and she was the epitome of what's described on page 68 of the SLAA Basic Text, namely "whatever power is usually involved in making sound choices in our sexual and emotional behavior did not reside with us." Taja wasn't even in the same ball park in regards to sound and rational. Her life was completely being run on self-will and her addiction had, as Dr. Carnes likes to call it, hijacked her brain. In her marriage Taja was the sex addict, she was the designated "Sick One" and she was the one who needed to get fixed. After talking with Hilarie for less than a full session, Hilarie suggested that Taja see me.

Taja was very bright, aware and head strong. She carried herself with the persona of a man, yet she was very much a woman. I established from the start that I would be dealing with her with the same directness that I do with the men. Taja said she was up to the challenge. Her presenting behavior was going to get her "Dead, Divorced, Fired or Arrested." She needed to be confronted in a way that she could accept, so healing could begin. Soft, kind and gentle was not going to work with Taja. We were a good fit.

Taja was born and raised in India. She had a womanizing father, a no-voice mother whose only voice was directed at trying to control her daughter. Taja and her mother clashed every day. Taja was molested by an extended family member when she was very young and when she told her mom she was instructed to never mention it again. It was going to stay a family secret along with all the other family secrets. Taja's dad had another family somewhere else yet no one ever mentioned that either. Life for Taja as a child was unsafe and chaotic, and what she learned growing up in that patriarchal society was that men can do whatever they want. Taja had observed much and learned well. She knew how she would be.

Taja married a very nice, kind, mild mannered man who was totally submissive due to his own domineering mother. When he met Taja there was something very familiar in her behavior to him. He never really stood a chance.

Taja and her husband were apart for a while back in India before they got married and she cheated on him and he knew it. In spite of the apparent stop sign, their relationship continued. Taja's husband was teaching her how to treat him and she was making the most of it. Once they were married Taja got a job with a software company. She couldn't wait to leave India, her family and the constraints of that male-dominated society.

Once in Washington State, Taja flourished in the workplace and started a series of affairs with co-workers. She would never lie about being married or about her intention to not leave her husband. Taja used her sexuality as currency both in and out of her marriage. The final straw was almost getting caught having sex on the job with someone she managed. This situation finally gave Taja a small glimpse that something might be amiss. To pour salt on her husband's wounds, her affair partners were either African-American or blue-eyed American, both deemed an added cultural insult. Taja really couldn't have come up with a bigger "Fuck You" in her husband's mind than that. That's when she came to me for help.

Taja honesty made her fun to work with. We processed her life in detail—from her father's infidelities to her molestation. I pushed Taja to look inside and go deep and she did. About the nine month mark I did some subtle arm-twisting to get Taja to go do Survivors week at The Meadows. I had her commit to not calling home or any affair partners while she was at the retreat. We processed every night her experiences of the day. Taja was finally getting in touch with what the AA Big Book calls "stock in trade and saleable goods." She was learning which part of her to keep and which part to discard. Taja came home ready to do life "Eyes wide open" for the first time ever.

Taja had been very vocal since she was a little girl that she didn't want to have children. She saw children as an encumbrance to her freedom. Kids would certainly get in the way of her sex addiction. Taja also had the core belief that she was worthless and she believed that she would be a bad mom if she ever had children. We rolled up our sleeves and went to work. I started with God. I was clear that we had to attack the Four Core Beliefs and for that Taja had to get some sense of a Higher Power. Without a belief that there is a God and that her God could be forgiving, Taja would never be able to get past her shame over her sexual history. She pushed back initially when I talked about prayer and meditation but finally gave in and became "willing to be willing."

Taja was also going to two women's SLAA meetings a week. She historically never had any use for women. Now, for the first time in her life, Taja was bonding with females and talking about her past shameful sexual acting-out. When she read her life history in her women's group all the women were crying. That's the day Taja's heart started to open up.

Over time Taja saw that she had a gift to pass on to children; it was the gift of recovery, it was the promise of healthy children being raised by healthy parents that could break the multi-generational family addictive cycle that she was raised in. Taja came to believe it was possible for her to become a good mother.

The next step was to repair a very broken marriage. Taja's husband didn't have a voice in any arena of his life and was totally repressed from any real emotion. He was co-dependent but was not open to doing his own 12-Step work. I did manage to get Taja's husband to talk to some of my MKP Warrior alumni and he was open to doing that. After about nine months, Taja's husband completed the MKP initiation weekend and his life started to change. He learned how to set boundaries, he learned how to state his needs and, most importantly, he finally had a "Deal-Breaker." If Taja cheated on him again he would leave the marriage. Over the course of the next year the marriage started to heal.

At the NMS Holiday party three years ago, we had three pregnant women there in full glow. Taja and Gavin's wife were soon to become first time moms. Both women had been very vocal about never wanting children. Obviously both women changed.

Twenty-one months ago Taja had twin boys. I had a picture of her holding them in the hospital on my bulletin board for the longest time. The overwhelming demands of caring for twins pushed Taja to leave group but she never forgot her recovery roots. She was in the area on this March 3 and decided to stop by in hopes of seeing me. Taja's smile was ear to ear. Her boys are growing up in a recovery home with a sober Mom and a Dad with a voice. Taja and I exchanged email addresses and she promised to come to our annual NMS Summer Softball/BBQ Picnic in August and bring the boys. That would be wonderful.

Now I was beaming ear to ear. Some of the men who arrived early saw me talking to a woman they had never seen before. As she and I hugged and parted she thanked me for giving her the life that she now has. I told her that was God's doing, not mine.

Walking into the New Wednesday night group with three men living out of their homes and a ton of turmoil going on in every one's life, it was good for me to balance the sad story of Marcel with the powerful redemptive story of Taja—both of which happened on the same day. This is my life in real time.

The Demon and the Angel: which end result will it be for all of them? It says in the AA Big Book that the "freedom of choice has been restored." Time takes time.

MARCH 12

RELAPSE AND RIPPLES

My older Monday group that Gavin runs for me is now down to seven men. Six of those seven have been to inpatient treatment at KeyStone and the seventh man did Survivors week at The Meadows. In all the years of NMS I have never had an entire group where everyone has done some kind of supplemental treatment (KeyStone, The Meadows, etc.). For the most part these men have been crisis free for a long time. Two of the marriages have been somewhat repaired after the men were out of their homes for eighteen months. Old man Shane still has periodic brushes with the sex industry, but the length, width and tenacity of that behavior has, for the most part, abated. We understand the concept of harm reduction when it comes to Shane. Keenan has the occasional slip up—most likely due to living in a very unhealthy marriage. For the most part, the Monday group is experiencing smooth sailing. This week however, things changed.

Against the back drop of the low level sound of elevator Muzak, we heard the alarm go out loud and clear, "Clean up on aisle three!" Unlike the grocery store mess that disappears like it never happened after employees show up with their buckets and mops, this mess does not go away that easily.

I tell the men all the time that their feelings will not kill them, only their behavior will. Thoughts and feelings will pass. I jokingly ask each one if they can remember a past day when they were really happy. When pushed, they reflect back to a moment in time with a slight smile on their faces and say resoundingly, "Yes." Then I bluntly respond, "It passed." Following a pregnant pause, they awkwardly laugh as I make my tactical point. As simple as it seems for most people, addicts have the mental construct backward and inside out. Addicts believe that their "feelings will kill them," while their "behavior will save them." Now that's an example of the insane and distorted thinking of an addict for sure.

Kelly had over two years of immaculate sobriety. He maintained his sobriety through tremendous adversity, consisting of but not limited to, a very contentious divorce, a less than equitable parenting plan, a year of spousal support to an ex who is cohabitating with the man she cheated on Kelly with while they were married. To deepen the wound even more, Kelly was arm-twisted into volunteering for a yearlong domestic violence program. Kelly also begrudgingly moved across town to be closer to his only child, and through it all he stayed sober, until now. What a miracle it was!

The silver lining is that this week's relapse was nowhere near his behavioral bottom of two years ago. None of Kelly's current behavior will get him "Dead, Arrested or Fired." Kelly doesn't have to worry about "Divorced" any more. So after fighting such a good fight for so long, what went wrong? That is a legitimate question for sure. Let's explore it more.

Kelly came from a large family in New York with a ton of craziness. His dad was a policeman who died on the job when Kelly was twelve. After his dad's death, Kelly's life only got worse. He managed to finish college and then fell into a job at a tech company. This work was never really Kelly's passion, but like so many techies, whenever they are asked what they do for a living, they answer with where they work, not what they do. Kelly's external identity came from the company.

As Kelly's life was falling apart, his job remained stable. The moniker of a well-known tech company was Kelly's external anchor throughout all of his work life and especially throughout the chaos of recovery. About nine months ago, as the industry started making their first ever layoffs, Kelly started to get scared. He did talk about it and he was confident that his job wasn't going away—and initially it didn't. As his company's reorganization progressed, it became clear that Kelly's safety net was going to go away. His fear of economic insecurity started to increase.

Again, Kelly was only marginally talking about his situation. In one of our sessions, we talked about Kelly trying to keep his fear "Right-sized." Addicts think in black and white and it's easy to get into a place where you believe the sky is falling. Kelly was in an anxious state of catastrophizing— our conversations were full of Kelly spelling out worst-case scenarios. About a month ago, the anxiety got so intense he saw a doctor to get anti-anxiety medication—and it did help in the short term.

As Kelly's fear of economic insecurity increased, he began to emotionally spiral downward as he struggled with life after divorce. The marriage legally ended a year ago, and Kelly had been separated from his ex-wife since before I met him. Like most newly single men in recovery, Kelly closed the sexual spigot tight when he came into NMS. His acting-out had been life-threatening and it was also connected to drugs and alcohol abuse. In one fell swoop he put the "Plug in the Jug" with everything. After almost two years of living in a box it was time for Kelly to stretch.

Just before New Year's we started to talk about the practical concept of "healthy masturbation." The goal is to take a very shameful historical behavior and normalize it—of course without porn or in any other toxic manner. Whenever they get to that point in recovery, the men get scared. I believe their fears need to be addressed. It would be unhealthy for any man to live in a permanent state of sexual and social anorexia. In fact, that's just as unhealthy as sexual acting-out. In this regard, I believe that sexual addiction is more like an eating disorder than a chemical dependency. A person with an eating disorder has got to learn how to eat healthy and in balance. If they cannot learn this new behavior, their addiction is certain to return. Men need to learn moderation and balance in all areas of their lives.

An adult human being is supposed to live their entire adult life without ever having to smoke crack cocaine or even having to get drunk. No adult is supposed to live without ever having healthy sex and love. In this arena, SLAA does have the goal of teaching recovering people how to "Drink like a gentleman"—a concept that does not exist in AA for sure, nor should it. I believe healthy masturbation is the first step towards "Drinking like a gentleman." It's just not healthy for a man to go through life scared of his penis and his own sexuality!

Kelly was aware that he was not ready to try dating. His work life was up in the air, he still had several months of spousal maintenance to pay, and his domestic violence classes were not ending for another six months. Kelly was more than fine with the thought of not dating. He often expressed gratitude for not having a spouse, as he was constantly watching the endless pain and conflict of the coupled men in this group.

With great trepidation, Kelly tried "healthy masturbation." With this, I always warn men about what I call the "Boomerang Effect." Healthy masturbation can backfire. All I mean by this, is that once the spigot of orgasm has been reopened, the addict will want to go back to that "feel-good" place fast and often. After all, it's been a life-long habit. As the SLAA Basic Text clearly explains, the main reason people act out is to "Lessen pain or augment pleasure" and often they revert to old habitual sexual behavior.

Healthy masturbation is defined as no more than once every seven days and without any external stimulation. Other boundaries include not using the behavior when feeling "Hungry, Angry, Lonely or Tired" (HALT). Masturbation is also not to be relied upon as a sleeping pill. We also encourage men to call another man and talk about it. We have to work hard at taking the toxic shame away—including euphoric recall. There is a level of mindfulness required when adhering to these boundaries.

Kelly's initial experiment with healthy masturbation went well, but within three weeks he had done it twice in two days. The challenge had arrived. Kelly's response was to go back to NO masturbation; he said it wasn't worth it. I was fine with his decision for now, but internally I could see he was starting to come a little undone by it all.

Then last week, Kelly had to attend a funeral for a co-worker's three year-old daughter who died suddenly. Kelly's child is six. The slippery emotional slope created by that experience started an internal downward spiral. It also brought up all of Kelly's family of origin feelings because when Kelly was four he lost a sister to meningitis. That grief had never been processed. The way Kelly talks about it now, was that after the death of his sister, his father was never around. Internally Kelly was abandoned twice. Kelly was being flooded with more feelings than he could process minus addictive distractions. He was on emotional overload.

The next day Kelly got on Facebook and contacted an old girlfriend from high school. Then he went to craigslist looking for love in all the wrong places. Before Kelly actually hooked up with anyone, he pulled himself out of it. Within twelve hours he was telling his truth to all of his men. With the help of the men in his life, Kelly was able to dust his ass off and start again. He recommitted to attending ninety meetings in ninety days and he is grateful he got a reprieve. Even though Kelly did break some of his bottom-lines, he did not go back to square one. The rest of this week we are staying in very close contact. In the end, I'm proud of Kelly and that his recovery did not fail him. Sometimes it's hard to see the gift.

Like always, when a prominent person in NMS relapses, there is a ripple effect throughout our community. Kelly had to share it with his two sponsees and give them an opportunity to fire him. He did so courageously and they both didn't or wouldn't fire him. We truly are a program where we don't shoot our wounded or eat our young. Both of Kelly's sponsees could still see his wisdom and value and chose to keep the relationship as is. All the men in NMS with less than a year of sobriety got scared. Kelly was and is a gatekeeper and is rock steady in the NMS community. Then the chatter spread through the women's side of the program, leaving fear swirling about and doubt in its wake, echoing through multiple relationships. It's kind of like when you throw a boulder in a still pond. Two things happen—the boulder sinks and ripples go out in all directions.

Kelly is definitely not back to square one but his recovery and ego did take a hit. The fear of life without a partner or the flip side of life with a partner began to rent space in his head. I gave Kelly lots to work on and much to think about. I know Kelly, like so many of the men, had been checking his mail box for the letter that would say that this entire addiction/recovery thing was one big clerical error, but the letter never came, nor will it. As it says in the fourth edition of the AA Big Book on page 417, "Acceptance is the answer to all my problems today." Kelly stood up in the recovery row boat, and it's definitely rocking, but the good news is he is not alone.

MARCH 19

COURAGE TO CHANGE THE THINGS WE CAN

Every once in a while, someone walks into my office that I just know in my heart arrived there not by accident or dumb luck. Call it divine intervention, or serendipity, or whatever—but there are no mistakes.

Two years ago, a young (by my standards) thirty-one year-old man walked into my office struggling with porn addiction. His wife had found out and demanded that he seek help. There is nothing at all unusual about that scenario, but there is more to the story. Harry was the father of two small boys, had married his college sweetheart and was a boys' basketball coach at an area High School. The more I probed, the more I started to connect the dots. Harry's dad was a small college coach who, in my past life in the basketball world, I had crossed paths with marginally. I couldn't pick his dad out of a line up nor could his dad of me but we were connected. Our paths had crossed. The more Harry shared his story with me and the more I pushed, the more I saw how basketball, Dad, Harry's marriage and sex addiction were all connected. The two of us pretty much had an instant bond and that bond continues to this day. I feel blessed that I have a chance to mentor this young man.

The thought of being part of the NMS extended family initially excited Harry. Having an arena where he could be honest about his shadow side gave him hope, but as much as he was drawn to NMS was as much as his wife was not. This was a prime example of that eternal marital conflict of "I want my husband's behavior to stop but I do not want him to change." This was clear from almost day one. Harry and his wife lived in a closed system and she liked it that way. However for Harry, living in a closed system was killing him.

I met Harry in August three years ago, the week of the annual NMS Summer Softball/BBQ Picnic. I encouraged him to come and bring his family. As a former college basketball player and general all-around athlete, Harry had not played softball in a long time. He also told me that his wife had played in college, so Harry was jazzed when he left my office. That Sunday at the appointed place and time Harry showed up with his family in tow. His wife was not a happy camper. She stayed next to him like white on rice.

The women of NMS were, as always, very welcoming to Harry's family. We had face painting for all the little kids plus a ton of games and lots of food. I could tell early on that Harry had no ability to just mingle with the men or to just go play. Harry's caretaking of his wife was off-the-charts compared with other men who were in that same new life experience. His "okayness" was directly connected to her "okayness," and she was not okay. When it came time for our picnic picture, Harry had to really coax his wife to bring their boys and stand still. I tried to engage her as I do with all the wives I meet for the first time. Harry's wife was virtually on the edge of crying the entire time we talked. She presented like a shy androgynous fifteen year-old at Daddy's company picnic, not as a mature thirty-something year-old mother of two.

Harry's personal trauma index, as defined by Dr. Patrick Carnes, was very high. In a thumbnail sketch, Harry's parents got divorced when he was in grade school and his father was a high school coach. Harry's mom was a hospital administrator. For some strange reason, the kids were divvied up as a result of the divorce and Harry went with Dad while his younger sister went with Mom, both living in different towns. Harry's dad was obsessed with basketball, giving all his time and attention to his career, and Harry was the epitome of a latchkey kid from age thirteen on.

Basketball was and still is the only area where Harry and his dad meet for dialogue. Harry's job in that house was truly to be seen and not heard. Harry retreated to practicing basketball, porn, masturbation and alcohol. His dad never came to Harry's games in high school because Harry's dad's team was playing at the same time, and of course Harry understood. Meanwhile, Harry's mom could not be alone and was always in a new relationship. When Mom and Harry did connect Harry got to be her surrogate husband. Harry was privy to the part of his mom's life that no adolescent son should be given access to. Harry's job was to take care of his mom and try to make her okay. He learned that lesson well and married a woman who needed him to do the same task. Harry's role as the "caretaker" was killing him. He was a mess and no one knew it. He presented as a choir boy, crew cut and straight laced, and in most regards he is that guy, except of course for the dark side.

Harry's dad moved up to coaching college, which then demanded even more of his time and attention. When it was time for Harry to choose a college, there was no doubt about it—Harry was going to play for his father. Harry loved the college, but his basketball experience was less then successful. He quit as a senior but stayed in school. By that time Harry had found a girl whose father had abandoned her as a preschooler and whose mom was an active marijuana addict. As I often say, my men choose who they choose as partners for all the "Right wrong reasons."

Then, when Harry was in his early twenties, his mom was murdered. When I had met Harry he would use the word "died" when he spoke of his mom's passing—he would never say "She was murdered."

After working with Harry for about six months I sent him to The Meadows for Survivors Week. While he was there he used the hotel's computer to access porn. Harry is the only man I've sent to The Meadows who acted out while there. Touching the pain was too intense for him. Even though on our scale Harry's acting-out behavior of "just porn" seemed benign enough, I knew he was a "YET" away from blowing up his life. He was just a "Wink and a smile" away from looking at porn on the job, having an extramarital affair, or visiting prostitutes, just to name a few.

In many AA halls in America, you can find a small 8x10 framed three-letter word hanging on the wall. That framed word is "YET." It's a point of reference for the guy who shares in a meeting that his drinking wasn't that bad because he never lost a job because of drinking, or that he has never been divorced because of his drinking or had never gotten a DUI. Those statements of fact are always followed up with the word "YET." This was really true for Harry. He never cheated on his wife, accessed the sex industry or spent money at a strip club, YET!

Also in our work, Harry was able to get clear and honest that he did have a desire to coach in college. He was so shut down emotionally that he could never even allow himself to dream of that. I pushed Harry hard to recognize that part of himself that wanted to dream and live on a larger stage. Harry began to get excited about the possibilities. The more he started to dream, the more his marriage started to rock. Harry's developing dream was not part of their implied marital contract. Harry had presented himself as a man who wanted to coach at a little high school, live in a nice appropriate house near the school, raise his two kids and never push the envelope. His new dream was starting to get in his wife's way.

Harry was really struggling with his sobriety, including alcohol. He would get to ninety days and relapse. Even though Harry had only had sex with one female in his entire life, that being his wife, the thoughts in Harry's head were very dangerous. The pain in his heart was pervasive and his Intimacy Disorder was still huge. Harry had a hard time bonding with the men in his group, showing up for events or even returning phone calls. Harry's wife did not have a real "Deal-Breaker" around his porn use and the cycle was continuing. She actually wanted him to drink, although she wanted to control time, amount and frequency. Most of Harry's drinking these days was at his wife's family gatherings. She didn't want Harry's abstinence to be noted by her family, yet she didn't want him sloppy drunk either. It was a source of conflict to be sure. I knew Harry needed more. I knew he needed to go to KeyStone.

With a lot of advanced planning and a huge push on his wife, Harry decided to go to KeyStone for thirty days. He had a clear understanding that the trauma in his past needed to get addressed and flushed out. He also understood the power of his "YETS." During the past year I would cut out articles of athletes and coaches whose sexual misconduct made it into the newspaper and show them to Harry. I was trying to get his attention and I did. He had willingness to do this intensive recovery work before he started to pursue his basketball dreams. Harry came back home from KeyStone the day before our annual picnic and showed up again with his family in tow to be welcomed back in to our NMS community. It was so great to see Harry. His wife wasn't particularly happy that his first day back after a month away was being spent with NMS, but she and the kids came. Since KeyStone Harry has been sexually sober—until now.

This March is Harry's third basketball season in recovery. Historically, pre-recovery, Harry acted out almost daily in the same way as many alcoholics drink. This is referred to as "Relief Drinking." However, this season Harry stayed sexually sober. Also, during this time Harry established a "no-contact" with his father. With the internal push to achieve, coupled with pressure from home and his work, Harry's participation in recovery started to wane. He was serving way too many masters to stay sane, safe and sober. All the men in his group and his sponsor saw it coming. Harry's basketball schedule stopped him from coming in to see me, yet we talked a lot during the season, mainly about basketball. I even went to see his team play three times. I planned a NMS outing night at one of his games and twelve men showed up. Harry was truly moved that these men would come and support him.

Harry would call to seek advice about conflicts with his Athletic Director or some player's parent who was annoyed at him as the Coach because their son wasn't being treated as if he was Michael Jordan. That comes with the territory of high school athletics. Harry doesn't do conflict real well and he has a real hard time advocating for himself. His first instinct is always to "shrink-to-fit" and be a caretaker. Mom taught him well. Harry would say things like "I feel slippery today" but that was the end of the recovery talk—he felt he just didn't have time for it. Recovery wasn't convenient for sure and it got shoved to the backburner on Harry's priority list, but no one bothered to tell his addict, which was doing pushups in the parking lot waiting for him to be desperate.

As soon as the season was over Harry went into a dark place. It was very reminiscent of how he remembers his dad curling up on the couch with a blanket for a couple of weeks after his season had ended. Harry's wife, meanwhile, has been sitting on a "Honey Do" list, and now, without Harry's scheduled practices, scouting trips and games, he's lost his "Get out of the house" card. Proximity does breed contempt. Harry's inability to have difficult dialogues or uncomfortable conversations was killing him.

Once again the inequity in Harry's marriage brought up feelings of being "less than." Whenever he would broach the topic of his dream of being a college coach, which would entail, in all probability, moving away, all Harry's wife could say was no way. Harry felt trapped. All these feelings reached an apex within three days after the last bounce of the ball, and he retreated to his historic coping strategy. With his head hung low, feeling a ton of shame, Harry came into group and told the truth. Nine months of sobriety were gone. His wife's first reaction was about the KeyStone fee being a waste of money. She just didn't get it. Harry's wife believes that all he has to do to stop acting-out is to pull a Nancy Reagan and "Just Say No."

We all circled the wagons around Harry. It's one of the good parts of recovery. We are all like soldiers in the foxhole of life. Harry made an appointment to come see me and he committed to going to ninety meetings in ninety days. He told his wife it was only a thirty-in-thirty. Harry is so afraid of conflict. His wife didn't see the point. There is an expression in AA that seems relevant here, "Anything you place in front of your recovery you will lose." As long as Harry seeks harmony in his marriage above all else, his sobriety will be tenuous at best.

I got a call from Harry today. He and his wife are in San Jose watching the first round of the NCAA Men's Basketball Tournament and he is dreaming again. He did go to a meeting today—even on vacation. Harry still has a huge mountain ahead of him to climb. He has to find his voice inside his marriage, which will not be easy given that his wife is not doing any of her own work around her life issues. He has to stay focused on his dream and to do the necessary leg work that might make that dream materialize. All the while Harry must remember that nowhere is it written that he HAS to be a basketball coach; the world doesn't owe him that job— he will have to work for it.

Harry must also work through his issues with his dad to create healthy boundaries, if possible remembering that his father is NOT in recovery and probably will not change. Finally, Harry must remember that without putting his personal sobriety and recovery first, none of this will be possible. It certainly is an uphill climb. I do have faith in Harry. His group and sponsor have faith in him. Now if we could only convince Harry that he's worth it, that would be a miracle! Stay tuned; more shall be revealed…

MARCH 26

THE PROCESS OF RECOVERY

I am a teacher first and foremost. I teach recovery, sobriety, emotional maturity and discipline. My classroom is my office and my lab is my group room. Like most teachers, I would like to believe that my prodding and pushing will lead my clients towards a better life. The component of the NMS program I truly love the most is giving formal lectures on the basic tenets of addiction and recovery. Sadly, because of all of the life's dramas and traumas going on around me, I do not get enough time to do. My newest group stayed still long enough this week for me to take the time to give them one such lecture. It is always fun for me to watch the light bulbs switch on for them as the men discover some facet of this process they had not previously connected with before.

I have a series of eight workshops that I present in group, usually during the first two years. The material is a compilation of all the learning I have done since getting into the recovery field in 1994. During the beginning phase of my professional career, I had a lengthy run as the Education Director for a large Psych/Addiction Hospital in Houston, Texas where I was responsible for creating and implementing a school that trained Mental Health Professionals. As part of that job, I had to find capable instructors for the academic course portion of the program. That led me to sit in on workshops and presentations of many of the top experts in Houston. Along the way, I picked up a lot of knowledge I have since synthesized into my own coaching bag of "Tricks of the Trade."

My new Wednesday group started in September so it is six months old. We are still adding new clients, so the group lecture piece has been slow in coming. The lecture I did this week was presented to eight men. One man was absent and I still have two open group spots left. My newest man is just three weeks in and I still have to find the time to catch him up with the two presentations I have already done. I find it's important to have everyone on the same informational page.

This week's workshop is called the "Process of Recovery." All addicts are event orientated. What I mean by that is each and every addict finally comes to recovery as a result of an "Activating Event"—a DUI, a sexual harassment charge in the work place or a wife finding a porn stash. The men understand the concept of an event. What they do not have the ability to initially see is a sustainable recovery process that develops over time. The internal and unspoken watch word of every addict is, "I want what I want when I want it, and I want it now." That kind of mindset, or as some might call it, hedonism, doesn't leave much room for the internal patience necessary to wait for a process to unfold.

There are four stages in the Process of Recovery. I start out by stating as clearly as possible that this is not a linear process that has a predictable trajectory through it. In fact, this process is very liquid in nature as the addict can flow through all four sections in any order and in any moment. The conventional wisdom of AA is that yesterday's recovery does not buy today's sobriety. The four stages move, they are fluid.

The first stage of this process is the stage people are in the day just before the activating event. This first stage is "Denial." No one checks themselves into rehab the day before they get a DUI or overdose or get caught by their wife, only the day after at best. I go on to teach the acronym DENIAL (remember, that stands for "Don't Even kNow I Am Lying"), and I start a spirited conversation asking the men for illustrations about how they lied to themselves during the multiple decades of living with this malaise. To a man, they tell stories of believing in their hearts that they could manage their own addiction at worst and, at best, make it go away based on their unaided self-will. That's the true distorted thinking of an addict.

Denial is what makes any addiction sustainable. Without the active presence of denial, healthy men, when confronted with living proof that their behavior had negative consequences, would be able to do a "Self-Corrective Action Plan." Whatever the singular behavior was that caused them pain would stop, and would go down in their own personal life story as just an "Error in Judgment"—a single anecdote in a lifetime of mental health and emotional maturity. As an addictions coach, my mantra is always "Keep Your Eye on the Disease." Denial can crawl back into any addict's life in a heartbeat. If addicts understood that basic truth, there would be no relapse.

Stage two of the Process of Recovery is "Admission." Admission is the addict's verbalized acknowledgement that they have a problem. That usually happens as a result of some kind of negative consequence. It says in the SLAA Basic Text at the bottom of page 119 and top of page 120 that "it would be tempting to conclude that everyone coming into the program would get recovery since they are usually coming in with acute pain." The text goes on to state that "often time's that is not necessarily the case even for those who express the most relief when they first come in because they seem to forget their pain after the immediate crisis has past." The point I try to drive home is that being in "Admission" is not enough.

The indication of when someone is in this stage is easier to hear than to see. An addict will always give themselves away if you listen closely enough. Sooner or later in their speech you will hear them unknowingly string two simple words together that will give them away. Those two words are "Yeah, but…" You'll hear statements like, "Yeah, but" you would drink too if you were married to my wife! "Yeah, but" you would need a release if you had the stress of my job! "Yeah, but" "Yeah, but" and more "Yeah, but." Addicts believe that the reason they do whatever they do is always external.

This is a tragically flawed belief system. The AA Big Book said it best on page 101, "His only chance for sobriety would be someplace like the Greenland Ice Cap, and even there some Eskimo might turn up with a bottle of whiskey and ruin everything! Ask any woman who has sent her husband to far distant places on the theory he would escape the alcohol problem."

Stage three of the Process of Recovery is "Acceptance." The stage of "Acceptance," as it says in the SLAA Basic Text on page 68, does not come from strength or courage but from the certainty of the dire consequences of what will happen if action is not taken. This pro–action movement in recovery is a unilateral decision and must be done with or without the consent of a wife or lover. I have had men clients who have put themselves on a sexual fast from their wives because they realized the toxic nature of their own sexuality. A pre–recovery life strategy of needy sex, make-up sex, sex as proof of not being abandoned, sex as proof of being attractive, sex as a coping skill for problems and sex as currency has got to stop. That level of "Acceptance" is difficult to achieve.

The last stage of the Process of Recovery is "Surrender." Simply stated, surrender means willingness to go to any lengths one day at a time to get well. This includes going to ninety meetings in ninety days, getting a sponsor, becoming sexually sober no matter how much your addiction tugs at you, developing a manner of living that demands rigorous honesty, finding a power greater than yourself, accessing a 12-Step fellowship and finding professional assistance. This work is labor intensive and never ending.

At the end of this workshop I asked the men to do their own assessment of where they thought they were in this four-stage process. I was impressed with their collective honesty. Several of the men were able to get honest about still holding on to control in a particular area of their recovery, mostly around partnership, which is to be expected with less than only six months in recovery.

Once again, this academic piece proved to be a good use of our precious group time. It is good for these men to get some kind of global view of where they are and where they are going. We made a good dent today in their awareness, but like it says in the program of AA, "awareness without action is useless," kind of like knowing that your car is out of gas and being unwilling to get off the couch, walk down to the filling station and buy some gas, dammit!

This week's group was a nice break from the drama and trauma of nine newcomer men's lives. Next week we are back in the trenches. So much for rest and relaxation…

~

The focus of March is faith. March concludes the process of sharpening our pencils. Faith gets us to the jumping off point towards doing the real work. The New Testament says: Faith without works is dead. I say awareness without action is useless. Faith is the active ingredient that gets one to finally move, that leads to a belief that is not based on proof. Our community provides the men who want it with enough of a safety net to finally put one foot in front of the other, all without knowing the outcome. Faith turning into action is a beautiful thing to watch.

April

~

Courage

APRIL 2

EMPATHY: SAM

Almost three months ago, I wrote about Sam, his inpatient treatment at KeyStone and his now very estranged marriage. Sam's "no-contact" period with his wife had begun and we all were waiting for the post-disclosure storm to pass.

I can honestly say that within each separated couple there are two opposite thoughts and feelings, both a desire to run away and never look back and, at the same time, a desire to re-partner. This internal conflict is always intense, but with Sam this dynamic was more on the outer edge of the bell curve than with most couples. I believe that the degree of difficulty in any reconciliation is directly proportional to the amount of new information the spouse is given at disclosure. For Sam's wife, the amount of new information and the pain that came with it was one of the most extreme I have ever experienced in NMS.

During the past three months, Sam's wife had developed uncontrollable panic attacks that bled into her work and had on occasion debilitated her to the point of being unable to do her job. With word of each new panic attack, Sam fell into a deep dark hole connected to his sense of shame and guilt. Sam has a burning desire to rescue his wife from her pain while knowing full well that he is the last person on the planet she will allow to be nurturing to her. It's an odd paradox for sure.

Except for some email contact concerning the children, their "no-contact" has been tight. Sam and his wife have been in my office together at the thirty-day mark so he could just tell her what his recovery has looked like during their "no-contact." At that visit, Sam's wife was unimpressed with his recovery and did not make eye contact with Sam at all. Her contempt for Sam was ever present. After that meeting, Sam was devastated, yet I reminded him that she did make another appointment so she was "Still in the game."

Their next meeting, on day sixty, was much more intense. It was time for Sam's wife to read him her "Cost Letter"—a detailed account of what she believes Sam's behavior has done to her. As Sam's wife began to read her letter, I almost stopped her. Most women in our program review their cost letter with Hilarie, their group or their sponsor to insure that they stay focused and that the letter is not just a "Husband Stomping" exercise. Sam's wife did none of that and her opening portion was honest and brutal, but unnecessary for the process. If Sam's wife had not shifted to a germane point when she did, I would have stopped the reading, but she did get back on task as she continued. As brutal as her letter was, it was how Sam's wife ended her letter that got my attention. She ended with a verse from a spiritual book that read "Have patience for the afflicted." Sam was such a mess at that point that I was sure he had not heard the verse, so I asked Sam's wife to read it again and she did. Sam struggled to find hope in her hopeful verse.

The next assignment was for Sam to take his wife's letter and write an empathy letter that sincerely acknowledged point-by-point the harm he caused her. The empathy letter is not in lieu of a Ninth Step letter of amends that Sam's wife will receive at some point when Sam gets to Step Nine in his 12-Step work. Sam agreed to do the letter and his wife made another appointment to receive it. Sam still could not allow himself to find hope.

So here it is at day ninety and Sam and his wife, along with Hilarie and me, are ready to hear him read his letter. I asked Sam how many people had been part of his process and he said three—which for NMS is a small number. I have not seen Sam alone in my office in over a month and had not been privy to a preview. In the week leading up to this meeting, Sam had been playing life a bit too reckless for my taste, putting his finger way to close to his addictive flame.

Last week was their wedding anniversary and Sam was alone sitting on the "Pity Pot" of his life. Sam didn't share his thoughts and feelings with anyone, all the while acting "as-if" he were "Ten-foot tall and bulletproof and had an 'S' on his chest." Sam started down the slippery slope of addiction, finally pulling himself up just before the abyss. As they say in AA on page 24 "We are without defense against the first drink" the same is true for a sex addict and a click of the mouse leading to a porn site. Sam had come just that close to acting-out. For an addict, the internal pressure that comes just from dealing with life on life's terms can sometimes turn fatal. It's a difficult concept for a "Normie" to comprehend.

Sam started to read his letter. He and his wife were two feet apart and facing each other. I instructed Sam's wife to look at him, and for Sam to pause and look at her. Before the end of his first paragraph Sam was crying.

Sam's wife remained well-armored and unemotional as Sam read. He meticulously addressed every point his wife had referenced in her Cost Letter. Sam was truly feeling the harsh reality that their long marriage was a sham. I urged him to not stop reading. Sam plowed through despite the pain.

In the end, Sam's wife shared that she has seen him say he was sorry this intensely before and that she could not distinguish between those other times and now. That was a reality check for Sam to hear how good he had been at managing her reality before recovery. Those "I'm sorry's" were always manipulative. I could see his little squirrel wheel working in his head trying to do a cost/benefit analysis as to where his wife was concerning her willingness to try to reconcile. That internal mechanism is so difficult for an addict to shut off. I urged Sam to stop trying to figure his wife out and to just stay "present to the process."

The next traditional step is for the spouse to write a Forgiveness Letter but I was sure that wasn't happening any time soon. Without mentioning it, I went to a creative "Plan B." I talked about where we needed to go, explaining the concept of "Healing Time" to them. The acronym for "TIME" is "Things I Must Earn" and I explained to Sam that we cannot put that on a spread sheet or in a power point presentation; it will happen when it happens or it won't. As Ringo Starr once said, "Time takes time." I needed to find a creative way of stretching Sam's wife back into contact with Sam while continuing to give her a sense of safety and control—the two things she had never felt in her marriage.

To move the process along I asked Sam's wife if she was willing to just talk to her husband on the phone for thirty minutes a week, with each of them taking turns making the weekly phone call to ensure equity. With some reservations, she said yes. I explained to her that inside of the "no-contact," she will never be able to learn to trust Sam and that her view of him would only change with proximity. She got it. Sam's wife did have one question which was, "What if I have nothing to talk about?" I replied she should let Sam carry the conversation. He was concerned about his ability to show up in the weekly call minus his addictive distractions. This included trying to manipulate his wife into letting him back into her heart. Both of their questions illustrated the depth of their personal fear about reconciliation. These fears are real and based upon their history.

I reminded Sam and his wife that this might be a good time for them to individually find their own faith as they venture down this challenging path towards reconciliation. We set another appointment for three weeks later. This time Sam was able to experience some hope. However, any reconciliation is going to take a long time because Sam's wife's wounds are so profound and Sam's illness is so embedded in him. Yet I also believe what it says in the AA Big Book on page 60, "God could and God would if

God was sought!" I reminded them both that "to seek" is a verb!

So here we are at the quarter mark of the year and the new personal journeys in recovery are starting to take shape. The older NMS stories are adding new chapters consisting of experience, strength, hope and the promises of new life.

In the AA book *Daily Reflections*, for March 2, it reads, "Hope to not be discouraged, I trudge the road of happy destiny." I hope you are enjoying your time on this road.

APRIL 9

SUDS

SUDs #1

In the world of chemical dependency the topic of relapse and of relapse prevention is of great importance. One of the leaders in this area of the addiction field is a man named Terrance Gorski who has developed a model that is used in almost all CHEMICAL DEPENDENCY treatment centers in America. One of the focal points of Mr. Gorski's program is to try to get the addict to understand and recognize the concept of the SUD. Simply stated it stands for Seemingly Unimportant Decisions. Gorski maintains that addicts, historically, do not have a good handle on their own emotional landscape and therefore are seldom aware of relapse before it happens yet what we do know is that relapse always happens long before the moment of indulgence.

Mr. Gorski also talks about becoming aware of what he aptly calls the BUD Signs (Building Up to Drink), kind of like learning to identify all the pressure points along the way long before the first drink, porn site or call to the escort. As simple as it might sound, this skill of learning how to take one's own emotional temperature takes a long time to be honed. The SLAA Basic Text on pages 112 and 113 goes into great detail about the signs that indicate withdrawal is over. The first of these signposts reads as follows: "we were now quite seasoned at dealing with temptation on a regular basis. Those situations which had been so transfixing in the earlier phase of withdrawal were easily, if not always comfortably handled." Most people reading this relate to it in only sexual ways. The ability to drive by a strip club or a prostitute on the street and not stop or do a U-turn is the picture that comes to mind. That overt challenge is the obvious First Step in sobriety. Passing on photos of Sports Illustrated swimsuit models that pop up uninvited on the CNN website is just one of many of life's little situations we must learn to face in sobriety.

As time goes by and those situations become less threatening, the next challenge is seeing people, places and situations that occur in our organic life with that same level of awareness and caution. That "muscle" takes a long time to get developed. This week, two of my men were staring down the barrel of the addict's gun around this kind of challenge.

Let's do a review from the last chapter. Sam has been living out of his house since his return from KeyStone in September. He and his wife met in my office for her second cost letter. She had written her first cost letter while her husband was in KeyStone and because of timing that letter was written and processed pre-disclosure. As in most cases, the new information that came out at KeyStone proved to be the most hurtful and damaging, so it is a necessary step toward reconciliation to have her do the entire cost letter again, but this time squeezing the entire sponge dry. Everything looks worse in black and white. It's tantamount to vomiting after a meal that gave you food poisoning—you want to get it all out.

She railed at him. It was hard to hear and harder for him to swallow, but he did get through it. The next time they met in my room, Sam got to present his empathy letter. With tears and snot coming out of every orifice he struggled through it. She received it with a very dispassionate response, not quite like he was reading a grocery list but not much more either. She was obviously still very hurt and very guarded. Her comment afterwards was that she could not tell the difference between this "heartfelt" show of empathy and other times she had caught him, when he went into an immediate barrage of the seemingly worthless "I'm sorry." She just couldn't tell the difference!

The next step in this process, by prescription, is for the spouse to write a "Forgiveness Letter." I knew in my heart that there wasn't a snowball's chance in hell that she was ready to forgive him, even a little, so I went to a Plan B.

I shared with them that to continue in this "no-contact" prevented her from ever seeing and experiencing her husband any differently, and I told him that at the epicenter of this process is the concept T.I.M.E., ("Things I Must Earn"). He got it. I asked her if she would be willing to talk to her husband once a week for thirty minutes on the phone, and she said yes. As they parted he was somewhat buoyed by this turn of events.

And now for the SUDs, which stands for Seemingly Unimportant Decisions, but also includes conversations and feelings. Two days after our meeting was Sam and his wife's twenty-second wedding anniversary, and of course it was the first one with him out of the house. Sam's emotional "okayness" started to slip, but he did not recognize the power of that event nor share his thoughts or feelings with anyone. At the same time, in the work place Sam's coworkers were off at an out-of-town conference that he was not selected to attend. Sam's position at work has been tenuous at best and he made up all sorts of stories in his head around why he didn't get invited to go, none of which were good. Once again Sam failed to share these thoughts and feelings with anyone. At work on Thursday, in an empty office, he started down the slippery slope of addiction on his work computer. Sam was thinking about who he would have to make amends to when and if he got to his Ninth Step and he started to search for previous acting-out partners. All this was based on a private conversation he was having in his own head. It's a bad internal neighborhood for any addict to visit, and whenever they go there alone they usually get mugged! This time was no different.

After work Sam went to the Thursday night SLAA meeting and never said a word about his struggles to anyone. After the meeting he got a car ride home from one of his recovery buddies and still he didn't say a word. He was way deep in the bubble and could not recognize it. This notion of the bubble was developed by Dr. Patrick Carnes as described in *Out of the Shadows*. As plainly stated as possible, the bubble is when the addict becomes so transfixed in the pursuit of his own addictive pattern that he loses touch with his surroundings and with the potential consequences of his intended behavior. In chemical dependency counseling, this process is referred to as "Drug Seeking."

Once Sam got back to the house where he was staying with another recovery brother and found himself alone, he again got back on the computer. This time he accessed clips of young Asian women kissing who were wearing bikinis, telling himself all the while that it was not porn and that they were over eighteen. When his roommate came home, he stopped the behavior and finally went to bed, never talking about his behavior or his emotional pain. It was all one series of Seemly Unimportant Decisions.

This week in the Monday night group, the dam broke surrounding all of the events and emotions Sam was experiencing. Even with Sam having been here for over a year and a half and with his forty-two days in KeyStone, he still wasn't able to connect the emotional dots of the facts of his behavior. He never saw it coming. Then Sam's denial kicked in and he claimed he didn't need to reset his sobriety date. His stance was solely based on how his wife would react if she heard that news. Sam's situational ethics and the bar he was setting for himself in this process seemed to be connected solely to her. Sad but true.

The joy and hope Sam felt over his wife agreeing to break the "no-contact" (if only for thirty minutes a week), the fear he felt connected to work that is tied to economic insecurity, the sadness he experienced spending his wedding anniversary alone out of their house and their marital bed, combined with the everlasting shame he continues to feel over the hurt he has caused his wife due to his behavior: all these feelings provided the backdrop for the perfect emotional storm. Without accessing his safe harbor (his program) he was dead in the water, and he never saw it coming! All that time he was Building Up to Drink (act out). The outcome was inevitable.

SUDs #2

I have a template for how this "Recovery" thing is supposed to look. I have a good understanding of which elements are optimal and which ones are not. But just because I know the recovery plan doesn't always mean it gets implemented. I tell my clients all the time that this is not the world according to Jay, this is God's world and it works on God's time not mine.

When last we checked in on Dante and Tonia, they were in a "no-contact" that started when he returned from KeyStone. Dante and Tonia were both still struggling with being apart. Dante's guilt and shame drove him to want to fix Tonia's pain today. Tonia's neediness drove her to want to give Dante a free pass on his behavior so he could come home and, she hoped, life would be wonderful. In their saner moments they both understood the distortion of that mutual mind set, but this is an insane disease.

Their "no-contact" was messy from the beginning, mainly due to having a toddler, and their need to communicate about child care. A piece of that is real, but most of the time a couple can work around that obstacle and create a healthy separate space. Dante and Tonia's attempt was not so clean. In the middle of the first thirty days, Tonia went to the doctor to have a lump in her breast checked. That event changed the essence of this recovery process. Over the course of the next month, Tonia was diagnosed with Stage II breast cancer.

Initially Tonia was steadfast that she had all the support she needed and did not need Dante to assist. As the reality of the cancer became clear, Dante began to bargain to be back in the house. Even before the final diagnosis was known, Dante claimed he would be willing to be in the house in the spare room while Tonia was saying she was fine with him not there at all. I jokingly told Dante that he would be fine if she let him sleep in a tent in the back yard!

As things progressed Tonia began to waver. I constantly told her that it was her call. I believed that her cancer trumped the "no-contact." I brought the couple back into my office for a sit down. It was there that Tonia made a request that Dante move back in. They both stated that it would be best if Dante slept in the spare bedroom and I agreed. We talked about the need for sexual sobriety. As they left, we were all on the same page—or so I thought. Within three nights they had intercourse. Dante's sex addict and Tonia's love addict hijacked their brains again. As the pair disclosed their behavior to me, Dante was ambivalent and Tonia was upset. Her need to get an "A" in recovery was stressing her out and they both felt validated just because they had had sex.

As it says in "The Problem": "we took from others to fill up what was lacking in ourselves, first addicts then love cripples." The internal Yin and Yang fight that Dante and Tonia go through is interesting to observe. My position is, and always has been, that I do not want to be the arbiter of anyone's sex life. I did want them to understand, and they both admitted, that Dante would not be in the house—let alone back in the bed—if Tonia had not been diagnosed with cancer. Their unique situation was not meant to be a "free pass" to be sexual again.

I went over again what a "Rolls Royce" reconciliation would look like. I emphasized that each and every one of the individual steps is in place for a well thought-out reason—not just as penitence for bad behavior. I told Dante and Tonia that my goal for them was to resurrect this partnership built on a bedrock of openness that could withstand the winds of life for a lifetime. Once again they found their willingness to take suggestions. The couple agreed upon a sexual fast that could only be re-negotiated in my office—in the light of day, not in the throes of passion in the middle of the night. They needed to be intentional about their sexual behavior. After all, Dante and Tonia are both sex and love addicts.

Fast forward to last Saturday. Every Saturday Tonia leaves early in the morning for a day of recovery with her support system. That day renews her strength and her commitment to this process. Every Saturday Dante stays home with their toddler and wallows in loneliness and self-pity like a little lost puppy, whimpering as its master drives away leaving it behind for the day. This Saturday the SUDs got to him.

Soon after Tonia left for the day, Dante received an email from his boss calling him on the carpet for some unfinished work. The tone of the email left Dante feeling vulnerable and inadequate. His answer to those feelings was to do nothing. Soon after the email, Dante decided to call his oldest two children, who live in another country, and whom he abandoned when they were still in diapers in order to be with Tonia. As Dante tells the story, all he heard during that call was his kids asking for toys, and his ex-partner screaming in the background about how she needs more support money. As Dante's outer shell hardened, his inner self took on all of the feelings of guilt and shame that have haunted him all of these years. Dante's answer to this emotional onslaught was again to do nothing. He went all day sitting in his own pity pot doing what they call in AA the "Poor Me's." Eventually Dante got on the computer in search of false comfort. By orbiting porn sites disguised as celebrity sites, Dante managed to convince himself that his behavior wasn't all that bad. His thirty days in KeyStone and all of his recovery was forgotten, as Dante drowned in an ocean full of feelings he never saw coming. He had set aside all his work and all his new knowledge as he was catapulted into the "Bubble of Addiction."

It says on page 105 of the SLAA Basic Text, "No matter how powerful your thoughts and feelings are tugging at you to continue indulging, you cease acting on them. It is at this point when you finally stop that really signals the start of your recovery in SLAA." How about that for clarity? After about an hour of getting lost in his addiction, Dante came out of the bubble and stopped the behavior, but still didn't make a "reach-out" call.

Later that night when Tonia came home and she and Dante did their nightly check-in, he failed to get honest and the secret festered. The next day Dante awoke and acted as if yesterday never happened. The couple spent the day together and felt close. In their couples counseling session on Monday, Dante said Tonia had worn a "sex addict blouse" on their day out together. Tonia laughed at the description of her blouse, stating that she had lost weight recently and was feeling good enough to wear a blouse that she had worn many times before—even in the work place. Ah, the "phenomenology of perception!"

Dante shared with me alone on Monday, before Tonia arrived at my office, the events of the past weekend. Later on Sunday as Dante was feeling triggered by what he perceived as Tonia's sex addict blouse, he asked her to sit on his lap. She agreed and did. They started to kiss, then agreed to stop. Later that night at their check-in, Dante failed again to disclose what he had done on Saturday. By Sunday, he had started to share Saturday's transgressions with some men in the program, and by Monday he got even more clarity and got honest with them.

Dante and Tonia were in my office that Monday for Tonia to do a new cost letter—based this time on the information she received from Dante's disclosure at KeyStone. Before I let Tonia begin, I gave Dante the opportunity to tell her what happened on Saturday. He stepped up and told Tonia what he had done. Tonia's reaction was real anger and disappointment, but she still hadn't gotten an integrated account of the events of the weekend so she could process it. I asked Tonia point blank if Dante had disclosed at their nightly check-in on Saturday about his computer behavior earlier in the day would she have agreed to sit on his lap or kiss him on Sunday? Tonia's answer was a resounding no! I pushed her to identify her feelings and she said she felt betrayed. Tonia was pissed and Dante was numb. Tonia decided to push through and still read her cost letter in spite of this new information.

The cost letter was real and it hurt. Tonia knew a lot about Dante's behavior before KeyStone, but the new information she received in Dante's disclosure was that several times during their ten-year relationship, whenever Dante went back to South America, he would be sexual with the mother of his children, to whom he was technically still married. That data point was devastating. To add insult to injury, Tonia also learned that Dante would engage in webcam sex with this woman when Tonia was out or even while she was asleep in the house! How about that for a "Kodak Moment."

During Tonia's reading, Dante was walled off and didn't show any emotion. I believe he was still emotionally reeling from Saturday's binge and his subsequent disclosure to Tonia. At the end of our session, Tonia asked Dante to not sleep in her bed that night and he agreed. Again I believe that if Tonia had not had cancer, and was not doing an intensive cancer therapy that left her sick and in need of help, Dante would not be in that house. I guess this isn't a "Rolls Royce" reconciliation—but it's the one they have and will have to do.

Once again, the first and foremost point of it all is that the events and feelings of the day—loneliness, plus an email from a boss and a hard conversation with his family back home—all led to some very strong legitimate feelings that were not expressed in a healthy way and got turned inward into eroticized rage. This is an old habit that is hard to break. The SUDs strike again, and as my buddy Mark would always say, "Learn, Learn, Learn."

APRIL 16

TALE OF THE TAPE

One of my best memories of my 9th grade had nothing whatsoever to do with school. It was a cold night in New York City on February 24, 1964. I was sitting with my father listening to the radio, straining to hear every detail of the Sonny Liston vs. Cassius Clay heavyweight championship boxing match. As the final introductions were being made, I was busy studying the "Tale of the Tape" printed the day before in the *New York Post.* "Tale of the Tape" is the side-by-side comparisons of each fighter. Height, weight, age, win-loss record, arm reach, fist dimensions, shoe size and so forth are all spelled out in intimate detail. Almost everything you would need to know to pick the winner is there, every category, except the two most important ones—heart and cup size! At the end of the day, it was those missing ingredients in the "Tale of the Tape" that seemed to make the biggest difference in the fight—as I believe is the case in life.

Charles sat nervously waiting for the group to begin. I wasn't paying much attention to him. In recent weeks Charles had been in what I call "Exit Strategy Mode." We have all experienced it before. It's when a client is caught between a rock and a hard place. Sometimes I jokingly call this the "Gumby syndrome." It's when the "Nice Guy Addict" who does not have any internal strength (heart) or fortitude to create any boundaries (cup size) gets pulled apart. The NMS community is pulling him from one side while his very legitimately angry untreated spouse pulls from the other. At the end of the day the wife almost always wins. Earlier I described Charles' panicked phone call as the wheels were falling off in his life, followed by his immediate relief after finding NMS. Over the past three months it has become clear to me, and to all his group members, that Charles' wife was "Writing his treatment plan." She is his Higher Power. That's a prescription for disaster.

Before we get into this story I want to make it clear: I hate porn! That's my truth. Porn skews a male's sexual arousal template—especially when he starts watching it as a pre-pubescent boy. Porn separates the concept of sex and love and conditions viewers to objectify the female form. Porn erodes the concept of monogamy, exploits females through violence and drug addiction, and in some cases de-criminalizes and thus normalizes the concept of rape. So often, in porn movies, no, No, NO turns into yes, Yes, YES! So I get the contempt most healthy women have for porn and the internal harm it does to them—not to mention how they feel if they believe their children might be at risk of seeing it. I get how knowing their spouse looks at porn affects their body image. It is really difficult for a forty year-old mother of three to feel good about herself when her husband watches air-brushed twenty year-olds, with 44D's and no stretch marks. I really, really do get it, and my feelings about porn have nothing to do with religion, God, or hellfire and damnation.

Porn is a major factor in Charles' situation. Right from the beginning, I found the dynamics in Charles' marriage and his wife's response to his behavior a bit odd. In fact, it was disproportionate to what we have seen in ten years at NMS. Charles came into NMS with a "Honey Do" list from his wife. High on that list was "Go to church." The odd fact was that, for their entire relationship, they never previously went to church. Now they were suddenly attending as a family every Sunday. Charles' wife also demanded that he attend a 12-Step group at church, which took him away from his recommended SLAA group. As I tried to connect Charles with a sponsor, I had a great man in mind; Luke has been in NMS over two years, has the same history of acting-out as Charles, is in a long-standing marriage, and who, by the way, is also a pastor. I thought this match was a no-brainer. Low and behold Charles' wife didn't like this idea at all. She thought that a recovering sex addict should not be in the clergy, and furthermore that all of the men in NMS were "perverts." She dug her heels in. That was our jumping off point.

Charles' wife saw Hilarie for a month or so, and she attended the women's group three times, but she said she couldn't relate to all those "sick women." In short order Charles' wife was gone, driving down the road with both of her hands firmly planted on the steering wheel of both of their lives. Whenever we had a bye-night Charles was not "allowed" to attend. She didn't see the value in Charles hanging out with "perverts." The more the men in Charles' group understood the reality of his life, the more they challenged him. The more Charles was challenged, the more his internal weaknesses showed and the more his boyish smile couldn't protect him from the truth.

Three times during the four months Charles was in group, he and his wife had been sexual. Despite the fact that Charles had been sleeping on the couch and we had tried unsuccessfully to get him to set a bottom-line of "No sex with his wife." The truth is that Charles' wife was using him somewhat like an overcoat. When she was "cold" she would go to the closet and put him on and when she wasn't he would stay in the closet. Not a healthy position for a man to be in, but Charles was powerless over his wife's demands. One time at a group meeting, Charles had me stand next to him with the clock behind us so he could use his cell phone camera to prove where he was, what time it was and who he was with! No control issues there!

Each time Charles' wife called him into the bedroom "to talk" while she was under the influence of the hypnotic drug Ambien, they had sex. The next morning, Charles' wife would be outraged over "his behavior" while maintaining plausible deniability and no culpability for herself. I bluntly called Charles a predator to his face in group. One of our group members is a medical doctor and this man suggested a list of other sleeping aids that would not leave Charles' wife at risk. Of course she got outraged when Charles suggested changing medications. Ah, the beauty of a "Catch-22!"

Charles cancelled his last three one-on-one sessions with me, citing work commitments, while telling group members I was driving a wedge between him and his wife. In reality, what I wanted for Charles was to find a way to increase the size of his cup and to "Grow a Pair!" I wasn't surprised when, at the beginning of group, Charles asked to read something. He fumbled with a piece of paper and ultimately didn't even open it. Charles said that this was the hardest thing he had ever had to do and then announced that he was leaving group. You could see the fear dripping from Charles' face. He said the same thing everyone who is in that spot says; they will keep in touch, still go to meetings and that nothing will change. None of these end up being true—most departing men spout the same sentiments as they walk out the door.

My comments to Charles were two-fold. First, I asked him if he had discussed this decision with his sponsor Luke. Charles gave a veiled answer. I asked him again, this time even more precisely, "In the past three days have you told Luke that you have decided to leave NMS?" To that question, Charles sheepishly said no. I was not surprised. Charles formed a private conclusion based upon a private conversation in his head. I'm sure when he announced his decision to his wife he got an "Atta boy!" and a pat on the head, plus a roll in the hay that night—with or without the Ambien!

Next I made a statement. I said I supported Charles' decision to leave, and that every human being is autonomous. I told him that NMS is not a good fit for him because our level of transparency is not for the faint of heart. Then I told Charles straight-faced that I respected his right to be wrong, but also hoped that I was mistaken. I thanked Charles for coming in to do this face-to-face because I would have expected no more than a voicemail from him. I wished Charles well and then he left. The group stayed silent.

Every man had seen it coming. They each had tremendous fear for Charles in the future around how he could stay sane, safe and sober while being held on such a short leash by such an angry and controlling woman. At the end of the day, Charles' wife won—kind of. Chances are, over time, Charles will fade away from his group and recovery and we will never know the outcome. Although the very next day, one of the guys told me they had spoken to Charles earlier in the day and Charles shared that his wife had gotten into his computer and read the disclosure letter he was writing for me. So much for boundaries! I will keep Charles in my thoughts and prayers. As I have said so many times before, I have tremendous empathy for children who are afraid of the dark and little or none for adults who are afraid of the light!

Dr. Brené Brown, a researcher of shame at the University of Houston, often says that the definition of courage is to be able to tell the story with a whole heart. Dr. Brown adds that a key component of shame reduction is the ability to be vulnerable, which she defines as the willingness to do something when there is no guarantee. I believe that most of my men are so love addicted, so relationship addicted, and crippled by this un-named illness that they can never muster enough courage to push back on their wives at all, on any issue, because these men believe that to do so would threaten the sheer existence of the relationship itself. It is excruciatingly painful to watch. Charles was one of those men. The outcome of this phenomenon, Dr. Brown concludes, is that people of this ilk learn to numb their vulnerability. Charles had certainly learned that skill and strategy well, years before he met his wife. I wish him well.

Years later, I had a new man in my office who had previously done work in a more offender-based recovery program. This man shared that he knew a former NMS guy in that program, who talked all the time about his wife. It was Charles. This man told me that Charles and his wife had gotten a divorce. With the ending of the marriage, Charles left the other program, having already found a new "Ms. Right." I just listened as I redirected the conversation back to this new man. None of this information came as a surprise to me. I never get any delight in being right. When I am right, somebody is bleeding.

APRIL 23

THE YIN AND YANG OF
SEX AND LOVE ADDICTION

They moved to the Seattle area two years ago. They met, married and raised a family in the Southwest for many years, but an immune deficiency disorder forced this couple to get out of the heat and relocate. On the surface they appear as a happy couple who lead a life of enlightenment—but that was on the outside.

Keith called me about eighteen months ago looking for some assistance with his three decades of sexual acting-out. This was not his first foray into problem solving. Keith had been a "seeker" for many years, but could never really stop, what the SLAA Basic Text refers to on page 72 as, all "courses on the menu" when it came to his sexual compulsivity. Keith had a large appetite. I was drawn to Keith from the beginning. I gravitate to strong men who can take a shot across the bow and not run and hide. Keith has inner resolve. We never did talk "in code." Right from the beginning I was able to shoot straight with him, not having to pander to the usual high level of sensitivity that often accompanies the stereotypical sex and love addicted man.

Keith has been a leader in an international men's movement that helps men focus on the four Jungian archetypes of what it means to be a man. These concepts were advanced in the 1970's by author Robert Bly. Keith was able to access his own King, Warrior, Magician and Lover. Despite all of this inner-strength-building work, his sex addiction never went away. Keith shared with me a story about how, years ago, he shared in his support group that he might be a sex addict—shocked by Keith's admission, two men quit the next week. As free as Keith thought he was to talk about this part of his shadow side, at the end of the day, his sex addiction scared even men who claimed to be "evolved."

In 2001 Keith found his way to Sexaholics Anonymous (SA) and Sex Addicts Anonymous (SAA). Those experiences became another failed attempt at fixing the problem. Keith gravitated to the sickest people in the room and ended up acting-out with a couple of them. Acting-out with people you meet in meetings is a reality in all 12-Step programs, but as I have observed in SLAA it is a rare occurrence, especially among heterosexuals.

For seven years Keith saw a PhD therapist on a regular basis. This therapist did help Keith with aspects of his life. Unfortunately the therapist's lack of knowledge concerning sex addiction was evident to me when Keith shared that his therapist didn't see the harm in an occasional "blowjob" while traveling for work. That story made me cringe, but then again it wasn't until the 1970's that psychiatrists were finally prohibited from having sex with their clients, convinced that it was a therapeutic tool of the trade!

When Keith married Elaine, she had a good amount of knowledge of his sexual history but, as happens so many times, she ignored the red flags that would have stopped a healthier woman. Elaine knew Keith had a history of acting-out with men and of having multiple female sexual partners, yet she thought he was her best candidate for a healthy life partner and to be the father of her unborn children. She saw enough of his resume and decided to hire him in spite of what it said. I call that phenomenon "Reading the white instead of the black."

During their twenty-plus year marriage Elaine would find out about Keith's acting-out, erupt into rage and anger, move to uncontrollable sobbing, only to paper over her emotional distress and start the whole cycle over again. At one point about ten years ago, Keith made a commitment to Elaine to remain faithful in their marriage. Every morning before leaving for work, Keith would say out loud to Elaine, "I'm not going to betray you today"—and he wouldn't. But over time the addiction would win out, and Keith's answer to his internal fight would be to leave the house early before Elaine woke up so he wouldn't have to lie to her. Now that's distorted thinking for sure.

In 2005 Keith discovered the Internet and quickly started to drown in porn, both written and photographed, all the while believing that it was an improvement because he was no longer involving himself with others. The SLAA Basic Text addresses such distorted thinking on page 72. This new course of the menu that he considered "Steps Forward" cost Keith countless hours of life both on and off the job. When he shared with me his recovery history, all I could see was a classic case of "Harm Reduction" without any lessening of shame, guilt or remorse. I told Keith that there is another way, a real solution beyond harm reduction—a solution that might set him free. Keith had willingness to jump into the deep end of the pool.

Lord willing and the creek don't rise, next week Keith will have a year of continuous sobriety from all of his bottom-line behaviors, but that's next week, not now.

Elaine was reluctant to join the women's group but after a short time she did. It took another six months for Elaine to see her own sex and love addiction. She also had the courage to get a sponsor and start going to meetings. Elaine had been faithfully seeing Hilarie while exploring her past. As Elaine and Keith both sat in groups with men and women who were going through the disclosure process, neither one was in any big hurry to rock that boat. After a while, it became evident that we had to get the show on the road. Keith committed to writing his life story so he could begin to get a handle on the full breadth and width of his addiction. He also successfully completed Survivors week at the Meadows which helped him break through his denial system. Around this time, Keith began to focus on his sexual history during Elaine's watch. To quote the American singer/songwriter Paul Simon, "Everything looks worse in black and white." Two weeks ago it was time for his formal disclosure.

It was hard to get Keith and Elaine to drive separately to the session. Their level of enmeshment is very high. They have the ability to withstand intense emotional battles and then act "as-if" everything is fine. Hilarie and I both demanded that they drive separately.

Elaine braced herself as Keith began to read. Soon she was reduced to a puddle of tears. When, as Keith disclosed to Elaine that he had sex with several of her former employees of both genders years ago, she lost it. Elaine went into a blind rage. In an instant she backed her chair up as far as it would go, screaming "Fuck you Keith, FUCK YOU…" only to sit back down with her knees to her chest, sobbing again. It was painful to watch. All the while Keith worked overtime to not react. After he finished reading, we all just sat there for a while in the silence of the moment. Then Hilarie in her calm and steady voice started to gently probe Elaine about her thoughts and feelings.

Keith was planning to leave for the weekend to do a men's group training and the time apart was needed for the both of them. Elaine said that Keith could come home tonight but she wanted him out of the bed. The oddest piece of this grueling two hours was that Elaine wanted and asked for a hug from Keith before they left my office. She initiated it and held Keith in a full body hug for at least two minutes. I could see Keith's confusion by it all. As they parted, Elaine agreed to come back in two weeks and read a cost letter. Yesterday was that day.

I didn't see Keith in group on Monday night because they had a bye-night. Keith did call me over the past two weeks, so I had an inkling of how they were doing. Elaine had had a session with Hilarie and read her cost letter to her group for feedback. On Wednesday afternoon, just before

Elaine's group was to start, I saw her in the hallway and she was unusually bubbly. Elaine looked at me and asked if I had spoken to Keith this week. She then proceeded in a very school girl like way to blurt out that she and Keith had sex! I was floored. We had a brief thirty-second conversation. I listened to her justify why the sex was a good thing. I knew right from the start that Elaine was in her "Love Addict." I only had time to ask her one question. I wanted to know where her rage of nine days before had gone. It seemed like the only appropriate question at the time. Elaine was surprised by my reaction and question and was unable to respond. Love addicted women often times use "Sex as Currency" against abandonment. It's a flawed strategy.

In Elaine's group she was adamant that the sex was healthy. She had a hard time hearing feedback from the other women that she was in her love addict. To top it off, all this happened while Elaine was writing a cost letter about all the hurt, pain and betrayal Keith had caused her! This is the insane and mercurial nature of this illness. On page 10 of the SLAA Basic Text it says "But physical craving for relief of tension would warp my resolve, and I would find myself with her again."

Yesterday was cost letter day. We spent the early part of the two-hour session talking about the sex. Keith and Elaine were now able to see that maybe sex wasn't the best decision, considering all the emotions going on, but that was water under the bridge. As Elaine began to read her very eloquent letter, neither one of them was very emotional. To my surprise she only really referenced three or four exact pieces of Keith's behavior in her letter. Most of what she read was just a low level oozing out of her overall feelings. It was only at the end that Elaine started to cry, when she started to wonder if she had the ability to get unhooked from Keith; this was the first time I had heard either one of them say that out loud.

Elaine was starting to get that something needed to change. Without knowing it, she was parroting the SLAA Basic Text on page 73 when it says, "this was not willingness that came from strength, but from the certainty of the dire consequences of continuing on in our addiction."

We finished the session with an open-ended conversation about the possibility of a "no-contact"—just the possibility. As our session ended, Elaine left to go back home and Keith headed to the Thursday night SLAA meeting. He had committed to write an empathy letter in another two weeks. We set the appointment and intention.

After the Thursday night SLAA meeting Keith was surrounded by the men in his group. Keith got to experience some real, powerful feelings as he started to sob. It was beautiful to see this man's man be able to access his emotions in the company of men. As we parted, I reminded Keith that his job today, just like his job every day, was to stay sane, safe and sober.

I have no idea how all this emotion will play out but I have faith that their marriage will make it and that their life will get better. Then again I am an eternal optimist.

APRIL 30

PRELUDE TO FATHERS AND SONS

The first time I heard the song "Cat's in the Cradle" and really listened to Harry Chapin's words, I cried. The words haunted me for a long time.

I am well aware of the sheer numbers of men who could not, or would not, show up as fathers in their children's lives. It's scary when you look at the stats. The "deadbeat" dads who skip out on child support are the easy ones to spot. The world points a finger at them and no one co-signs their behavior. The internal cost to the children they abandon is staggering; the damage eternally profound. I deal with the wreckage twenty, thirty, or even eighty years later. Most of the men I see have huge issues around their fathers. This is no coincidence.

For the men who grew up with fathers in the home, the damage was more often covert rather than overt—covert abuse is much harder to wrap their arms around. Most NMS men had fathers who provided a decent living, a safe place to live, clothes and food and some comforts in life. What these fathers didn't give their sons was time and attention. They never taught their sons how to be a "Man in a Man's World."—not communicating or modeling emotional openness, emotional care and emotional concern.

My men for the most part had one of three types of dads. The first type was physically absent where the child's feelings of abandonment were, and continue to be, real and pervasive. The second type of father was physically in the home but emotionally unavailable. That dad modeled a very small emotional bandwidth consisting of only two basic emotions: quiet or rage— the quiet was deafening while the rage was scary. This was sometimes accompanied by alcohol and or domestic violence. Lastly, and most often, the dads were home in name only, forever stuck in their workaholism, trying to avoid conflict and feelings of being controlled by a powerful, angry and dominant spouse at all cost. The external world viewed these dads as nice guys who worked hard for their families. In reality they were internally weak men raising boys to be just like them.

Their boys grew up to be men feeling unworthy, inadequate, alone and afraid. They retreated into the world of addiction to compensate, which only added to those feelings; lost inside themselves they are really losing their lives. First they became sex addicts and then turned into "Love Cripples" as the multi-generational cycle continued, leading to, as the AA Big Book says, "Institutions, Asylums or Death." Their best hope was and is recovery.

The first verse of Harry's song pointedly reads:

My child arrived just the other day
He came to the world in the usual way
But there were planes to catch and bills to pay
He learned to walk while I was away
And he was talkin' 'fore I knew it, and as he grew
He'd say "I'm gonna be like you dad
You know I'm gonna be like you"

Fathers and Sons

I'm a firm believer that nothing happens in God's world by mistake and that my job, as an aware man, is to continuously ask myself at each turn of my life one eternal question: "What am I learning?" The answer is always different. Yesterday I had a growth opportunity; yesterday God gave me a chance to be a good shepherd and create a safe harbor to help bring a man together with his father. I do not get this kind of opportunity very often. It was precious to me. I treated this opportunity as if it was sacred and, at the end of the day, it was. And, boy did I learn!

Two years ago when Harry, the previously mentioned high school basketball coach walked into my office, he needed help to deal with his adult porn use and compulsive masturbation. After just a brief time together we both had a good understanding that of all the options where he could look for help, it was no coincidence that he was sitting in my office. I do not believe in coincidence; for me it's just God's way of being anonymous.

Harry's behavior was on the low end of what Dr. Carnes calls Level One. He has no history of acting-out with anyone, ever. In fact he was a virgin when he got married, yet his chronic relationship to adult porn and masturbation goes back to when he was in the eighth grade and is now problematic inside his marriage. It needed to go away and he had willingness.

Harry presented in a boyish, clean-cut, all-American guy kind of a way. Harry's image was penny loafers, crew neck sweaters, cuffed Dockers and an impish smile. Any mom would welcome him into her home, if her daughter brought him, with open arms. Harry grew up in church and graduated from a Catholic college. What more could anyone ask for? He was the picture of virtue and apple pie. All that was missing was the thick black horn-rimmed glasses of Clark Kent and an "S" on his chest. All wrapped up into one great guy. Oh yeah, except for his shadow side!

Harry grew up completely surrounded by males. He played high school and college basketball, lived in athletic dorms, and as a youngster would go to his dad's practices and basketball summer camps. In spite of all these external experiences, Harry had a severe intimacy disorder. As incongruent as it might seem, he had no real male friends. He could "Chalk Talk" about X's and O's all day long but he had absolutely no ability to identify a feeling. I used to kid Harry that he could not find a feeling even if he tripped over one. The guy had no clue whatsoever. The more we visited, the more I saw the extreme level of untreated trauma Harry had suffered—first as a boy, then as a young adult, and even now as a married man in his early thirties. Life was hard for him; harder than it needed to be.

As always, my first point of attack is to stop the behavior. That is the only real gold standard for efficacy. Once I got Harry to buy into the "Game Plan," we set the play in motion, and he jumped in. I dropped him in Gavin's Monday night group with Stan, Kelly, Kevin and old man Shane just to name a few. Even though Harry's life and relationship were flailing all around him, he was able to put together nine months of continuous sobriety. In spite of this apparent success it was hard to keep Harry connected. Little things like returning support phone calls or sharing fears and concerns were very difficult for him. The more of his story I learned the more evident the trauma became, so as I said in the earlier chapter, off to the Meadows he went for a week in the desert.

It was difficult for Harry to go. His wife, like so many of the wives, didn't want to see how damaged her husband was. She had fear around spending the $2,500 on a coach's salary and of Harry being away for the better part of a week. In her heart, Harry's wife also had the distorted belief that Harry might come back healed and that he wouldn't want her any more. It's amazing how many women feel that way, yet their false pride would never let them put language to it.

Harry returned home more aware of the role his childhood played in his life but also in despair over his relapse while at the Meadows. It was time to get back on the horse. When dealing with an addiction there is no room for a pity party. If you can't measure sobriety, it doesn't exist.

Historically Harry goes dark, for the most part, during the basketball season. He lives on an emotional roller coaster driven by the pressures of the game and the capriciousness of teenage boys. I would remind Harry after a tough loss that he personally didn't miss one foul shot! His entire sense of worth was wrapped up in the "game." All during this time Harry's father was facing his own travails during his own basketball season and Harry's emotions always got sublimated to second place whenever they spoke. Dad's coaching was always more important and the feelings of yesterday's abandonment continues in Harry's present.

On the home front, the more Harry did recovery, the more conflict there was in his marriage. In short, Harry was a "Yes Ma'am" kind of a husband. His mom had trained him well in the art of compliance and his wife continued with the tradition. It wasn't a hard sell. As always, conditional love has its price. As Harry's recovery was starting to take root he was finding that little muscle deep inside of him where he could every once in a while say the word "No," even when he said it in a whimper as she raged. Harry was renegotiating their non-verbal, non-written contract and Harry's wife wasn't getting her usual veto vote. She was getting angry and she was getting scared. Today Harry jokes that before he went into recovery he never had a fight with his wife. In this situation, Harry's sobriety would come and go as much as his resolve. The men around him tried hard to keep Harry engaged but he would go silent for stretches at a time.

We also identified that Harry had a problematic relationship with alcohol and I wanted him to stop drinking. Most of his drinking was done with his wife's family. In that system, the "Don't talk, don't trust and don't feel" model was cast in cement. Harry's mother-in-law is a practicing alcoholic and his sister-in-law went to treatment for two years, leaving a small child behind. All the while, no one ever talked about it. Harry's wife's biggest fear was that if Harry all of a sudden stopped drinking it would create a problem for her inside her extended family. The internal and external pressure was too great for Harry and he continued to struggle with sobriety.

Another already mentioned noteworthy part of Harry's story was his deceased Mom. She was murdered when Harry was in his last year in college. Harry was already partnered with his soon-to-be wife and was student teaching at the time. As Harry talked about losing his Mom it wasn't until I pushed that he revealed that she had been murdered. What a tragedy. Within days of her murder Harry went right back to work! And his sex addiction spiked.

In one of our first conversations, the more I pressed Harry the more I could see that this young man had been beaten down to the point where he did not even allow himself the privilege of a dream—the dream of becoming a college basketball coach. That was so sad to me. The contract with his wife was simple. Harry would be a high school coach forever, live geographically close to her family, raise their two kids and never, ever dream. I got out my can opener and started to pry open his dream can. The more Harry started to dream the more ripples there were in his marriage.

It became clear to me that Harry's unresolved trauma needed a higher level of care and, even though he was only a Level One guy behaviorally, I had tremendous concerns that his disease would escalate beyond just porn and masturbation. As Harry's dream started to take root, I also realized that this shadow side of him needed to be addressed before he got on the merry-go-round life style of a college coach. College coaches lead a lifestyle of hotels, airports, nightlife, media attention, co-eds and the constant pressure to win. A year ago Harry became convinced that he needed to go to KeyStone to "Flush this Crap" out of him. He was going to go in the summer when school was out. It was a hard fight with his wife but Harry made it happen.

One of the main points of focus in Harry's KeyStone treatment was his relationship with his father. It was suggested by KeyStone, and I agreed, that it would be best for Harry to institute a "no-contact" with his dad. Our hope was that, with some space and more emotional growth work, Harry could get a real clear sense of where he starts and where he ends when it comes to his dad. That was in August. This week, after eight months of a self-imposed "no-contact," Harry was willing to talk to his dad again, but only in the safety of my office. I applauded his courage.

We had scheduled my standard two hour session, and Harry and his father showed up with less than an hour to go. As the two men walked into my office, I could see on Harry's face a scared little boy fighting within to act grown up and be brave. I met them at the door and, while shaking his father's hand, I thanked them both for coming. I didn't have time for small talk; we had already lost an hour.

I asked Harry if he was nervous and he said yes. I thanked Harry for being honest. I immediately directed my conversation at Dad by framing for him some of the backdrop for the meeting. I asked Harry's dad what he knew about Harry's stay at KeyStone; he didn't know much. He even thought that Harry's problems might be centered on gambling. I was somewhat taken aback by Harry's father's comment since gambling had never come up. He went on to say that when Harry was in college, he had concerns around Harry's potential for problematic gambling. I asked Harry about it and he said that a gambling addiction was starting to take root but his girlfriend, who is now his wife, didn't like it and that was that. If only stopping the sex addict was that easy.

I was very careful to not shame Harry's father. I know how easy it is for a parent to get defensive about their role in creating their addict child. I told him a little truism I use when talking about this subject. Really good parents can raise really troubled kids and really terrible parents can raise really good kids. Harry's father was somewhat relieved by my effort. It was hard for me to get a read on how defensive he was or how he was seeing me in relation to his son, but I knew for sure Harry's father was not dismissing me.

Harry got to tell his father the story of his addiction. He told his father that the addiction got fostered when he was a boy after his parent's divorce—during the time he lived with his father and his sibling lived with mom in another town. Dad was deep inside of his own coaching career and Harry was a "Latchkey Kid" long before it was a popular term. I kept on pushing Harry to talk about his feelings and not just the facts. Several times I asked Dad if any of this was making sense to him; he always answered yes.

Then I brought up Mom. Harry's biggest issue with his dad around his mom's murder was that he felt that he was never allowed to talk about "it" with his father, not then and not since. It was hard to watch Harry confront his dad, the internal struggle to push through all the years of private internal conversations that he never had the ability to initiate in real time—right here and right now! I could see on Harry's father's face that he felt trapped by the dialogue and then I saw it—I'm not really sure how I saw it but I believed I did.

In a soft voice, I looked at Harry's father and said: "I can only imagine how difficult it must have been for you to honor your new wife, who always saw your ex as a threat, and still grieve the loss of the love of your life, both at the same time!" I was aware that Harry's father had never wanted the divorce and had gone into a depression because of it. Harry remembered clearly as a fourteen year-old watching his dad "crater" before his eyes.

After my statement, Dad exhaled as if the wind had come out of his sails. His head sank and he responded by looking directly at Harry and admitting that he wasn't there for his son or any of the kids at the time Mom was murdered or since. Harry's father said he would be open to talking about Harry's mother and the trauma. It was a huge first step at repairing this relationship.

We were running out of time. I told Harry that I was proud of him. I could see how my words impacted him, hearing me say that in front of his father. I had told Harry that before. I always said that it was not my intention to be Harry's surrogate dad, but to just be a man in his life who would not abandon him or only show him conditional love. I meant it before and I mean it now.

Right before the two men left I made a request of Harry's father. I stated that Harry had always felt that the only safe conversations he was allowed to have with his dad were about basketball. My request was that his father try to change that dynamic. I also acknowledged that trying to change a lifelong pattern like that would be difficult; basketball was always a safe place to retreat. Harry's dad said he would try.

As they were leaving, I gave Harry a hug as we always do. As I held out my hand to his father, Harry's father wanted a hug. Our hug did not go unnoticed by Harry.

After they left I literally had two minutes before Owen came in. Harry and Owen talked for a second in my waiting room like two ships passing in the night. As Owen took his seat, he asked who that was with Harry. I told Owen it was Harry's dad. Owen's reply was "Wow, that must have been intense!" I nodded as we began our session.

Hitting the Pause Button to Reflect

We are four months in with eight months to go in this year's experiment. This has been a typical stretch in the annals of NMS. Four men left our program and four new men joined. We have four men currently living out of their homes and four other men at home, but not in their marital bed. We have two alumni expecting the birth of their first babies with wives they did not have before NMS. We have witnessed six disclosures, four cost letters, three empathy letters and one forgiveness letter with the rest of the process still to come. We have one marriage ending because of lack of sobriety—one of the men who has left NMS—and one marriage that might end because the wife is refusing recovery. Three men are on the verge of dating. Two men, Norm and Keith, just celebrated a year of sobriety and are ready to sponsor for the first time, and Dean has started a "Back to Basics" AA type newcomers meeting for the greater SLAA community. Hell, all this and it's only the end of April! Stay tuned. We really are a composite of *All My Children*, *General Hospital* and *One Life To Live*. I couldn't make this stuff up even if I tried.

~

April is about courage—the need for the courage to change cannot be understated. The courage to confront past relationships, behaviors, hurts, resentments and fears does not come without cost. Sometimes quickly or sometimes slowly, courage will appear as an outgrowth of honesty, hope and faith and that courage creates the potential for a new-found freedom.

May

~

Integrity

MAY 7

RIPPED FROM THE HEADLINES!

There is no such thing as a boring week in NMS. Each week creates a ton of real life drama and trauma. By the sheer fact of who I interact with, the population oozes with chaos. It is inherent to my program and is not avoidable. I am sure that as long as we cater to, what we call in AA "such unfortunates," that truth will continue. So what exactly did my week look like?

On Monday I met with a couple for the first time. I had met the man two weeks before and, as always, I had to start the recovery birthing process. My job is to push past his intellect, denial and belief that he can think his way out of this dilemma to change his ways based on his own self will. This man's thought process was in concert with every man who ever walked into my office. It usually takes a while for the inevitability of this illness to sink in and break though. Once it does, the fun really begins as I have to convince each man to get his spouse on board. Any man's ultimate success or failure will be greatly affected by the participation level of his wife. The late Dr. Al Cooper of Stanford University made it his practice to not treat men whose spouses refused to participate. Even though we do not do that at NMS, I can see the wisdom of the philosophy.

With both husband and wife in the room, I used empathy, fear, her anger, her defensiveness and every skill I know to encourage her to at least "be willing to be willing." All I wanted of the wife was for her to be willing to talk with another woman in our NMS program—someone this wife already knew from their religious affiliation long before her husband showed up at my door. I pushed the wife for a commitment. I think I was marginally successful. Time will tell, the jury is still out but this is not the story I want to tell this week.

In my Monday night group, Norm talked about getting back into his marital bed for the first time in nineteen months. Norm had been out of the bed for nine months—starting before his disclosure. Leaving the marital bed was Norm's decision and that decision hadn't sat well with his wife. Norm's wife didn't like losing her power over being the arbiter of their sex life. At month nine, Norm decided to move out of the home—again it was without his wife's consent. As the SLAA Basic Text says on page 73, Norm's "was not willingness that came from strength, but from the certainty of the dire consequences of continuing in our addiction." Leaving the marital bed was the hardest thing Norm had ever done, but he did it. With two children under six, Norm's decision to leave did not come lightly, but he and his wife were battling daily and could not play nice in the sandbox of life for more than a few hours. That kind of toxic interaction is very damaging to children and needed to stop.

After five months out of the house, Norm moved back home but, not back into the bed while he tried to create some healthy boundaries with his wife. Now at nineteen months into recovery, it was time for the next hurdle. The introduction of healthy sexuality into a marriage that never previously knew what that meant. What a task, what a story, but that's not what I'm going to write about this week either.

On Tuesday morning, I witnessed a young, thirty year-old woman find her voice and speak her truth for the first time in her life. Amber read her cost letter to her partner of eight years. The letter was powerful, clear, concise and brutally honest. I had cautioned Amber to not protect her partner. I feared her "niceness" would lead her to rescue him from the brunt of her true feelings about his abhorrent behavior. Amber heeded my advice and wrung the sponge dry with her pain, hurt, anger and betrayal pouring out. She never cursed or berated him. She just told her truth. Amber's partner was numb after three minutes and he went into a shell of despair. Wow what a story! But I'm not going to write about that one either.

On Wednesday, Tonia came in and "confessed" to breaking her bottom-line by having sex with her partner Dante. It was clear to me that Dante had groomed Tonia to be sexual once again. He pandered to her neediness, her fear about her cancer and her fear of abandonment to get her to consent. It's deep! The level of dysfunction in this relationship is so subtle and opaque that I could write a book just about them.

On Thursday I met with Owen's twin brother, Nigel. When Owen began to unravel and was forced to leave his home for his own well-being, he was forced to open himself to his brother. After hearing Owen's story,, Nigel was able,, for the first time in their relationship history,, to get honest with Owen about his own sexual compulsivity. The dam of silence had been broken between the brothers. The two brothers started to share openly for the first time ever. Owen brought Nigel to a SLAA meeting and then referred him to me. Owen is more than fine with Nigel joining his

Wednesday night men's group and Nigel agreed. With ten new men, that group is forever closed to new members. Now there's a story for sure, but I am choosing not to write about them now either.

Like I said, there is never a dull moment in my work, yet this week I'll pass on all the trials and tribulations of our recovery family and take a page from the TV show "Law and Order." This week my editorial comment is "Ripped from the Headlines."

Editorial Comment

Before sitting down to write this morning, I started the day with my Starbucks coffee and the *Seattle Times*. As always, trying to put the external world to bed before I enter my interior world. There in bold print was a huge story that caught my eye: "Rick's strip club's last dance." I was aware of the long-standing legal issues surrounding the owner of Rick's. I had read other articles in my years here in Seattle about him and all of his strip clubs. These clubs were often described as a "Scourge on our community." Times staff reporter Erik Lacitis did a fine job getting as much inside scoop as possible. Convincing people to open up on the record when the topic is dealing with the underbelly of society is a difficult task.

Some quick facts from the article bring home the microcosm of a much larger overriding issue, but the dialogue needs to start somewhere. As reported in the paper, the FBI stated that up to 15,000 customers per month visited Rick's. That comes out to 180,000 a year! The article goes on to say that Rick's grossed over $10 million a year. There was a $10 cover and a $5 nonalcoholic drink minimum, plus the "dancers" had to pay the club $130 per night as a "rent" fee. You do the math. Factor in that Rick's was open 365 days a year and we're talking beaucoup bucks. The owner also owned three other clubs in the greater Seattle area. These are thought to be worth $4.5 million in property alone. Rick's also came with its own condom dispenser. I leave the implication of that to your imagination. Today they are all closing down. The long arm of the law has finally got their man.

One of the patrons interviewed in the article, when asked why he comes into a strip club, said that "Sometimes it's nice to get some attention, have a girl flirt with you, even though you know the role she plays." As I always say, it really is an Intimacy Disorder. The internal feeling of being lonely all the time drives men to seek false comfort even if they have a loving wife and family at home.

Most of the men that have been in NMS have been in strip clubs—and I don't mean for a bachelor party or as a college kid. I had one former client who blew up a seventeen-year marriage while giving away his entire 401(k) to a stripper he was addictively enamored with. I cannot begin to quantify the total manifestation of the damage and toll this club, and other clubs like it, have taken on its patrons' lives. There is no such thing as casual sex, no such thing as a casual disease, no such thing as a casual baby, no such thing as feeling casually objectified and no such thing as casual heartbreak. It's a high price for a low life. In the end, just like alcohol or drugs, strip clubs are just a delivery system for another anti-social behavior.

As Rick's twenty-two year run comes to an end, there is a new strip club opening up after years of legal wrangling and just within an Ichiro's throw of Safeco Field. Safeco Field is home to the Seattle Mariners and their two million fans—including children—walk by it annually, and the cycle continues. Maybe it will not take twenty more years for the façade of legitimacy to be exposed with this new club. Strip clubs take and create hostages; it comes with the territory.

Flooded with strong opinions I put down my morning paper and check my email. There in large letters from AOL's Daily Finance section was a long story entitled: "Despite Crackdown, craigslist's Sex Ads Are Thriving." This story literally jumped in my cup. Staff writer Abigail Field wrote an excellent column about the money, law and loopholes that allow craigslist to be pimps. That's my comment, not hers. Then Connecticut Attorney General Richard Blumenthal issued a subpoena on Monday stating, "We are asking craigslist for specific answers about steps to screen and stop sex for money offers and whether the company is actually profiting from prostitution ads that it promised the State and public that it would try to block."

Back in 2008 craigslist made a deal with state's Attorneys General stating that adult ads should not be free and that payments must be made with credit cards—trying to shame patrons with the threat of a paper trail. Craigslist also pledged to turn over the revenue from adult services ads to charity. Since then, craigslist raised its fee from $10 to $15 per ad, renamed their site "erotic services" and no longer felt obligated to live by the original agreement—giving no adult services ad revenue to charity. It is estimated that last year alone, adult services ads brought in over $36 billion, which is one third of craigslist's annual revenue, and so far it's all legal.

Way to go Richard Blumenthal! My prayer is that he doesn't follow the path of former anti-smut district attorney and former Governor of New York, Elliott Spitzer and become another "Client #6." I hope Blumenthal's public value system is in sync with his personal value system! I get nervous when I read of crusaders publicly proclaiming morality because this brings to my mind the old adage "Thou doth protest too much." Attorney General Blumenthal ran for Senator Dodd's vacant Senate seat and won, so maybe he's just driven by a sense of right, wrong and ambition. I'll keep the Senator in my thoughts and prayers as he goes after the bad guys.

Not everyone who gets a DUI is an alcoholic—for most it was just an "Error in Judgment" that will never happen again. Not everyone who goes into a "gentleman's club" is a sex addict. The difference is that bars are used for many purposes, but you typically only enter a strip club with one intention. What I know is that all my men have acted out compulsively in some sexual manner, whether in strip clubs or craigslist. There are many different delivery systems for this illness. As opposed to crack cocaine for instance, sex and love addiction is often legally protected and culturally camouflaged, yet the personal devastation to men, wives, children and the women in the sex industry is laden with incomprehensible demoralization. There is a powerful quote in the SLAA Basic Text on page 70 that sums it up best for me: "The guilt of prior deeds and passions or missed opportunities gave way to the deepest, most pervasive guilt of all: that of having left life unlived…"

Our mission statement is simple: We are trying to repair the world one family at a time. If nothing else, I believe this to be a noble and just cause.

MAY 14

HOCUS FOCUS: KEEPING YOUR EYE ON THE DISEASE

I'm by nature not a game player. I do not play cards or computer games. I never do crossword puzzles. On occasion, if cornered, I'll play Scrabble or Trivial Pursuit. I used to play chess when I was younger but it just saps me of my energy so it's gone by the wayside. Sudoku sounds good in theory but after two minutes I'm done with it. Even fantasy sports which given my background would appear to be a slam dunk doesn't even make my radar. I just don't do games but there is one newspaper "do" that I never miss and that's Hocus Focus, a syndicated visual game published in local newspapers created by Henry Boltinoff.

It's a visual observation game designed to make you seek out and find anomalies. I love it. My eye scans in nano bytes the two side by side cartoon panels looking for what's wrong with the picture, looking for what doesn't belong. I find it relaxing while being a challenge. The entire event takes three to five minutes. It's almost instant gratification! I try my best not to cheat. The answers are upside down under the pictures. What a great mix for me.

In the first ten minutes of my very first counseling class I learned basically everything I ever really needed to know. The first truth was that the person sitting in front of me IS my client, meaning it's not his wife, mom, boss or lover! The second truth I learned was to keep my eye on the disease. That's it. Make a note. It's very simple yet very hard to do. This is a disease that tells you that you don't have a disease. It's definitely not like cancer—cancer doesn't lie. When the second opinion Doc says you have cancer, you have cancer. No denial there.

This week was another installment in the Dante and Tonia show. When last we met our recovering couple they were in a very porous "no-contact" mainly due to child care for a toddler. After three months Tonia got diagnosed with a very aggressive form of breast cancer. The reality of being home alone with a small child coupled with the fact that she has no family other than Dante in this country led us all to a sober conclusion that cancer trumps the "no-contact".

Dante has been back in the house two months and it's been leaky and toxic to say the least. Trying to get an active love addict who is appropriately needy and physically ill from daily hormone therapy to stay contained emotionally is next to impossible. Then, put that love addict in daily proximity with her sex addict affair partner who has himself not successfully come out of the other side of his withdrawal is a prescription for disaster. It is like watching a train wreck in slow motion.

We tried to set up some ground rules. First and foremost was NO sex. They were both clear that if Tonia had not be diagnosed with cancer there is no way Dante would be back in the house now; they were a whole reconciliation process away from being sexual. Second rule was that they each had to continue doing their own recoveries. That looked like meetings, sponsor, weekly NMS group and fellowship. Both boundaries are proving to be a huge challenge, but in all fairness to them, trying to fix this is like trying to fix an airplane still flying at 30,000 feet and still going 600 miles per hour. It is very hard.

The symbiotic addictive nature of their relationship is so difficult to see. Each of their own pathologies creates a gravitational force field that leads them to collision yet to the naked eye of the casual observer everything is beautiful. As far as anyone knows they are just a normal family!

Every Thursday night Tonia goes to a SLAA meeting followed by fellowship with her recovery women. She did that before Dante moved back in and she continues to do it with him home. The only difference is that now Dante watches the clock to see what time she returns. He makes up stories in his head about who she is with and what she is doing. He gives her the third degree upon her return and then punishes her emotionally if she doesn't allow herself to be browbeaten. The first few times this happened Tonia had no awareness of what was transpiring, she just would get caught up in his game and then a huge fight would always erupt. You could set your clock by the predictability of this scenario, and if it didn't happen on Thursday night it would certainly happen on Saturday when she left again to do her own recovery. Dante has absolutely zero ability to be alone.

At the end of "the game," he would turn his back to Tonia (that's the punishing piece) as all of her abandonment issues would come flooding back to the surface and then she would do what he has groomed her to do for some many years. She would do a right about-face and chase him. As always the end result was sex, then they would both feel like they collectively failed and go into despair. Now that's insane!

In group or in session I would hear Dante talk about his resentments. He is treatment wise and verbally savvy, but in the end it was just his addict talking.

Two weeks later it was the same dance to a different song. This time Dante told her after the fact that he had resentment towards her for not allowing him to go to the KeyStone reunion, to which three of our men had gone this past week. The truth is that five months ago when Dante was in KeyStone and Tonia was there, she came up with a list of fourteen "Deal-Breakers." Since then, they have never been questioned or mentioned again. One of the fourteen was that Dante could not travel for work unless it was mandated by work. His history was to act out every time he would go out of town.

As Dante started to spin internally he made up in his head that Tonia was stopping him from going based on his interpretation of a four month old boundary that had never been revisited. As always he conveniently built a resentment. He didn't talk about not going to KeyStone in the days leading up to the reunion with anyone: not me, not Tonia, not his sponsor, not the men who were going and not anyone in his group. He had a private conversation and came up with a private conclusion.

Dante was reeking with righteous indignation. Whatever empathy he felt during his empathy letter just two short weeks before, that stated the facts of the harm he had done to Tonia, had long since evaporated. This time at least they did not have sex but the same game played out just the same. In the end he went to sleep in the other room to punish her, then she got frantic in the middle of the night and texted him twice and of course he purposely did not respond. It's the true picture of the sadist and the masochist. She did show some growth by not going into his room, but she did stay up all night crying. The subtle nature of this illness is so insidious and difficult to see.

Processing the events with her I tried my best to get her to see what Dr. Charlotte Kasl so aptly writes about on page 1 of her book *Women, Sex and Addiction* where she wrote that "sex is not nurture, sex is not proof of being loved, sex is not proof of being attractive, sex does not solve problems and sex is not a guarantee against abandonment even if you're great in bed!" It takes years to change this paradigm.

Working with Dante I tried to get him to see that his contrived "resentments" were created by his addict. He needed to ask himself, whenever he felt a resentment, two basic questions: Where is your addict? And what's the payoff for the resentment? In the end it's always about sex and power for him.

Then I went on to tell Dante that if he still felt resentful he might want to try to find some empathy for this woman, the mother of his child who still loves him in spite of all the harm he has caused her by betraying her over and over again. Whatever is driving Dante's resentment if its legitimate will pale in comparison to the harm he has caused Tonia for more than a decade of deceit. Compassion is the best cure and God is the answer.

The mercurial nature of the illness makes it so difficult to define. It appears so stealth-like in nature yet the pain is profoundly deadly. Walking into my office directly after Dante and Tonia left was a new woman who just found out that her husband of thirty years has had an affair for the past eleven years. Ouch! It seems like people are always "dying" to get into my office—literally.

MAY 21

REST FOR THE WEARY

My job is intense and I wouldn't want it any other way. My work is my passion but my passion can be a burden and that burden has a price. In the course of an average day I ask people (mostly men) questions they have never been asked before in their lives. It ain't pretty; in fact oftentimes it's downright ugly, but the questions need to be asked and the light needs to be shined. Like I said, it's a dirty job.

Levels of sexual deviancy covers a broad spectrum of behaviors. I jokingly say that the sex addicts I see can rationalize any behavior between being caught with a live boy or a dead girl. It's not cute, just the truth. This disease can create social pariahs and a ton of heartbreak. With each life story, disclosure and cost letter I hear I get emotionally drained as I become a voluntary receptacle for each person's shame and pain. As a result I make it my practice to get away as often as I can. It's my way of doing self-care. My longest stretch of solid work is always from New Years until mid-May. Thank God it's mid-May. This week I got to go play in the sun with my very understanding wife in beautiful Santa Fe, New Mexico, and boy, did I need it.

Right before I go anywhere I change the message on my cellphone. I inform folks that I will be out of the office until my return date and I also tell them that if they need some quick counseling they can call my colleague Hilarie.

Not so fast for my free get away. Then my passion takes over as I continue on in my message saying that I will be checking my messages and that I will get back to people in a timely fashion. There's the hook, there's where the passion takes me—cell phones on vacation—but at least I get to pick and choose.

It's almost like the addiction gods know when I'm out of town.

Invariably I will get a frantic phone call from a new man whose wheels have come off and is freaking out. It never fails to happen. This trip was no exception.

On Thursday I got "The Call." I just couldn't let it go, the burden was too great. All I know is all I know. I received a panic call from Brent. He is a thirty year-old man whose fiancé of four years caught him looking at porn again. I had a sense that there was more to his acting out story than he gave up but I didn't want to probe long distance. I asked the same questions I always ask trying to determine the level of the real situation—not the perceived situation. They seldom are the same.

Have you been thrown out of your house? Has she given you back your ring? And are you out of the bed? No, he replied to the first two and yes to the third. I told him that the truth is she's not going anywhere. We could all breathe, at least for now. I asked him what part of town he was in and he told me. I looked at the time and saw that he had twenty-five minutes to get to the Thursday night SLAA meeting. I asked him if he had willingness to go. He was in enough pain so he said yes. I told him to get going and call me after the meeting and then we hung up.

Soon after talking to Brent I received a S.O.S. call from Owen, who wanted to talk about his very un-treated wife. After our little chat I asked him if he was on his way to the Thursday night meeting and he said he was already there. I told him to look for a newcomer named Brent. Not knowing what he looked like, all I said was his age and that he probably would have that first time deer-caught-in-the-headlights look. Owen knew the look and would know what to do from there.

An hour and some change later Brent called me back and left a message. He did show up, Owen did reach out to him and also introduced him to Kelly, who spent time talking with him. Brent went on to say how hard it was for him and that he didn't know he would have to do a "program." He sounded scared. I called him back and left another message for him telling him that there is a Saturday night meeting at the same time and place and that it would be good if he went back. I told him I would call him when I returned the following week.

I got home from my R & R in time for my Tuesday night group. I called Brent back on Wednesday morning just as my recording had said, again leaving a message. I have yet to get a call back. Maybe his crisis has passed, maybe he found a softer, gentler and kinder way to fix his problem. Maybe he told his wife for the umpteenth time that he will never do it again and she bought his tears again. Time will tell. The one thing I know is that he, just like any addict, cannot successfully outrun this illness; it never sleeps.

I feel great that my "guys" did reach out to him. They did what I have modeled for them to do and that is to reach out to the newcomer. The ball is now in Brent's court as I am back in the fray of NMS, just as if I had never left.

MAY 28

ALL IN A DAY'S WORK

Let's get real. How hard can this be? It's definitely not rocket science but it does take some insight into how this illness manifests itself in the lives of the people who suffer from its relentless rage and pain. On Thursday of this week I had four sessions; I saw three couples and one new woman. By the close of shop that day I was emotionally drained. The first couple I counseled is my story of the week.

My day started with Owen and his wife, Mary. This was my third time seeing them together. He has been with me since January and has taken to the twelve steps and NMS like taking a plunge into the deep end of the recovery pool. He has written his life story and a disclosure letter. He has gotten a sponsor and, for the most part, hasn't made any meaningful decisions on his own in months. It was suggested that he do the SLAA Back to Basics Program and he did. He even brought his twin brother into the fold. When I met Owen, God was not in his logical and linear vocabulary and now he has found a God of his own understanding. In short, Owen has taken to this recovery process like a duck to water. It's been a pleasure to watch him grow as a man of integrity.

On the other hand, I have experienced his wife as manipulative, controlling, and scared but most of all not stable. Her hurt and devastation over Owen's infidelities has decimated her. Her old wounds, that I make up go back prior to meeting Owen, have created a woman not amenable to any real input or recovery. Today she is the designated "Sick One", only she doesn't know it. For her, it's still all about Owen.

Imagine for a moment someone taking a container of milk and pouring it onto the floor. The milk would go "splat" into an indistinguishable configuration of randomness; a dozen pours and a dozen different Rorschach tests. That's the way I have experienced her, metaphorically. She has no personal container. I realized early on in our dialogue that I could never get in front of her in any conversation; kind of like trying to herd cats! Owen has experienced this phenomenon throughout their entire relationship but had neither the language nor the emotional sobriety to name it or claim it. Today he can. She struggles with being contained, which she experiences as being controlled. It is an interesting dynamic to observe.

Two months ago they collectively rushed to get disclosure done against my advice and my innermost voice. She really had not demonstrated any real start in her own personal recovery other than starting to attend one of Hilarie's women's groups. Before the disclosure she was well aware of the mechanics of how our process works, yet her immediate response after receiving disclosure was to shut down the process by stating that she wasn't going to write her cost letter. She followed that announcement by forbidding Owen to see his kids, claiming that he might be a "molester" even though none of his reported behavior would even remotely indicate that. She was very good at emotional blackmail.

She was just a hurt wife trying to punish her cheating husband. The accusation that he "might be a pedophile" was devastating to Owen, as was not being able to see or talk to his children for weeks. He was ready to get a lawyer and to attempt to get a legal parenting plan in place even though he does not want to get a divorce. This entire scenario was so avoidable. I have seldom if ever witnessed a woman's legitimate scorn ending up going off on such an ugly and superfluous tangent.

After a lot of posturing on both their parts, she agreed to write a cost letter. She went to see Hilarie and read it to her. Hilarie thought that she had done a good job so we proceeded to set an appointment. In the meantime, her unwillingness to let Owen see his children became the topic of the day. In the middle of this, she demanded that he take a lie detector test. I believe it was just to humiliate him. Owen had willingness to do anything she demanded, but I wanted him to understand that this latest hurdle could be the first of many ploys to come. Before disclosure Owen had only been allowed to see his kids four hours a week on a Saturday. The kids have been a pawn for her in this equation since long before disclosure.

The reality is that if Owen did file for separation the State would give him access to his kids every other weekend and one night on the off weeks. I suggested that he tell her that he would be willing to take the Poly only if, when he passes the test, a traditional parenting plan becomes the parenting plan. She didn't like that idea. The conversation was extremely contentious. She was like that carton of spilled milk all over the floor in every direction. She went from demanding a Poly to telling Owen he could have the kids every other week, all week after only an hour and fifteen minutes of our session. She had displayed a full 180-degree pendulum swing in a blink. As an observer, her degree of vacillation was truly amazing to watch. For me it was also symptomatic of other issues.

Owen, to his credit, did not take advantage of her bounce. It ended up that he would start with the original four hours and put a parenting plan in place that would not be determined by her whims. That situation is far from resolved and I will not even venture a guess as to the outcome.

The best news is that in two weeks she is going to the Meadows to attend a workshop for wives of sex addicts. It's a start. She certainly does qualify. My only concern is that by her choosing that workshop it will only reinforce her notion that her only problem in life is him. I am hoping that the Meadows can shine the light back on her enough to get her to start doing her own work.

It's been three days and I haven't received any S.O.S. calls from Owen yet. Maybe it's a good sign. Owen has clarity that the only way he is willing to move back into the house is as a full partner. He will not live in the guest house or the spare bedroom. He also knows that the way they represent to each other has to fundamentally change. He's not sure if that can happen. I'm not either. We will just let this unfold on God's time.

～

So here we are at the end of May. That's five months down and seven to go. NMS is so fluid in nature that every day and every week creates new changes and a new course, while our focus stays the same. Stop the behavior, live a God centered life and be the very best you that you can be.

Yesterday I had the honor of going to Group Health Hospital in Seattle to see my Alumni, Craig and his wife, in the maternity ward celebrating the birth of their first child. She's a precious little girl who will be well taken care of in a healthy family system with parents who will love her forever. As Craig and I hugged each other tight he said "Thank you."

I continue to see miracles all around me on a daily basis. As the great twentieth century Jewish scholar Abraham Joshua Heschel, said, "Life without commitment is not worth living." I'll accept the burden with the passion of my commitment.

Addicts have no integrity. Active addicts are liars, cheats and thieves. The feelings of having been betrayed and violated pre-dominate the lives of those who love the addict the most. A very true riddle heard in the halls of AA is: How can you tell when an alcoholic is lying? The answer is, sadly, when his mouth is moving! May is about restoring integrity where there has been none. The measure of a man is in his word. Getting the missing component of integrity back takes time. Living with adherence to moral and ethical principles has to be earned, one day at a time.

June

~

Willingness

JUNE 4

BRICK BY BRICK: KEITH AND ELAINE

I like Keith and his wife of twenty years, Elaine. There is something about them that's endearing. I wish I could say that about all my clients but that's just not the case. I'm sure that what I see that I like is their ability to be confronted with the truth. Individually they each have some grit to them, and collectively they do not take their ball and go home when it gets too hot in the kitchen. That strand in them frees me to not have to manage their sensitivity and allows me to be candid. This seems to work for the three of us and I'm grateful for it.

Each of them has been, in their past, what I call "self-seekers" for many years. Keith began twenty years ago by starting to see a PhD to stop his compulsive sexual behavior. That relationship lasted seven years. Keith ended that counseling experience when his need for wellness outgrew the clinician. The therapist told Keith that an occasional "Blowjob when out of town on business was no big deal." Keith knew it was time to leave. He started to see that the last thing he needed was to have his lower nature co-signed by a mental health professional. He was a seeker.

From there Keith found Sexaholics Anonymous (SA) and tried his first attempt at the 12-Step model. That was in 1997 and the rooms were just too toxic back then. He ended up acting-out with someone in the program. Shortly thereafter he stopped going. Also in 1997 Keith was introduced to the Man Kind Project (MKP), sometimes referred to as the New Warriors. It's an international men's movement designed to empower men and to help them find their healthy King, Warrior, Lover and Magician as first described by Carl Jung and later expanded by Robert Bly. Keith's persona is larger than life. His struggle, beyond sexual compulsivity, is to find a way to be "Right-sized." As Keith says now with affection, "MKP makes you more of what you already are." His success in MKP only added to his grandiosity and lack of humility. In fairness, MKP is not designed to stop addictive behaviors. It did not stop Keith's. In his MKP group he was encouraged to get honest, so he did and announced that he thought he might be a sex addict. The next week two men quit the group in response to his admission.

Two years ago Keith and Elaine were forced by her medical condition to move to the Pacific Northwest. He found a MKP group here while his acting-out behavior continued. A year ago through some NMS alumni in MKP, Keith was directed to me, and here he landed feeling grateful, safe and willing. Due to the extreme nature of his acting-out behaviors I believed from the start that he was a "KeyStone" candidate but time, money and commitment made that not happen. Keith did take a week and go to the Meadows for their Survivors five-day retreat. I guess he was in enough emotional pain to finally "get it," because it appears that he has. It sure has been a blessing for me to watch.

Elaine knew a ton about Keith's behavior but was a co-conspirator in the creation of this very dysfunctional system. She had joined the women's branch of MKP called "The Woman Within" and had sat in circles with women for years, but the sex and love addiction piece of her shadow side remained well hidden. When Keith joined NMS she really didn't want to "do more work," but she watched him and slowly realized that she needed to take a look at the piece of herself she had been running from for years in spite of being a seeker. The stage was nicely set for the two of them to really start to grow.

Over the past three months Keith has read Elaine his disclosure letter, she has written and read a cost letter, and Keith was able to effectively find some compassion and empathy for the pain of what being married to him had cost her. Through it all they never separated but did stop being sexual. They both realized that the love addiction piece in each of them was at the epicenter of it all.

About six months ago Elaine finally was able to honestly embrace her part in the equation and verbally acknowledge her own love addiction. Her love addiction, just like every other woman connected to an NMS man, pre-dates the last relationship. She has gotten a sponsor, started going to meetings and doing her own step-work. This work is arduous and painful but she has willingness.

This week we started doing real repair work on their marriage. Their old marriage is dead and thank God for that; it needed to die. It needed to go away, but neither one of them seems to have any real tools in their collective tool belts other than hammers! Hammers are great for nails but not much good for anything else. We need to try to build a real house, built on a real foundation that can withstand storms and the test of time. They each need a lot more tools in their tool belts. There is a wonderful quote in the AA Big Book on page 82 that sums it up best: "We feel a man is unthinking when he says that sobriety is enough. He is like the farmer who came out of his cyclone cellar to find his home ruined. To his wife, he remarked, 'Don't see anything the matter here, Ma. Ain't it grand the wind stopped blowin'?'" It is time for Keith and Elaine to peel away all the layers in their relationship onion and to rebuild their relationship "home."

My assignment to Elaine was to make a list of "Deal-Breakers." Her love addiction has allowed her, time after time, to give huge pieces of herself away when it came to tolerating Keith's behavior. That is not about Keith—it is about Elaine. Her fear of abandonment and of being alone has kept her a prisoner while placing herself at physical risk as a result of Keith's high-risk sexual behaviors. She has to find a way to love herself enough to never again be willing to ever make that brutal bargain. She continues to struggle with that concept.

I made it perfectly clear that Keith's sobriety is not contingent on Elaine's ability to throw him out. His commitment to sobriety has to be an "inside job," as it says in the AA Big Book on page 60: "...probably no human power could have relieved our alcoholism." This is an inside job for Keith, as it is for everyone else, yet he does need to know and believe in his heart of hearts that this time Elaine will leave him if he puts her in harm's way again. It's a delicate balance.

Elaine still needs more time to set in stone those "Deal-Breakers" but she has willingness to work towards them. Love addiction is a bitch for sure.

We started to build their recovery home. We started with the foundational floor well below ground level. That is a mandatory structural necessity that consists of individual strengths that are not connected to being part of a couple. It is only when each participant is strong in their own sense of self that the partnership can even stand a chance. This first repair session was challenging and exposed their individual weaknesses to each other, but they both had the intestinal fortitude to not run away. We have to rebuild this house one brick at a time. At the end I thanked Elaine for trusting me. I hold that trust dearly. Keith is Keith, he can "Take a Lickin' and Keep on Tickin'." I love him for that. For them the prognosis is good and I am cautiously optimistic. I love this work when it works!

JUNE 11

THE GLOVES COME OFF—NEW GROUP #2

I first wrote about my new group back in January and I have talked about some of the men and their trials and tribulations concerning their partnerships. That phenomenon is very typical in the process of a new group's development.

The group was formed just a few months ago with five men. I had a sixth in the wings just waiting to complete an inpatient stay at KeyStone. Over the course of the past ten months the group went through a typical amount of flex, flux and transition. Finally in May the group topped out at ten men and there it will come to rest until the first man blinks. It took fourteen different men to come through the program to eventually make a group of ten. The blink of departure comes with the territory. Like I said at the beginning of the book, NMS is labor intensive.

In the beginning of each group there are two compelling forces that contribute to why a man would do this work. The first is the force that comes from the threat of losing a partner because of hurtful sexual behavior. Second, and for the most part very far behind in the "why" category, is a man's internal desire to stop the acting-out behavior. Some men come into NMS so scared and frightened that they believe that they have been "scared straight." Interesting concept totally based on faulty thinking. You just can't fear this addiction away.

The initial "dance" with a partner is often times started before NMS came into the picture. That dance looks like a series of disclosures that usually take place in the kitchen with a very angry wife trying to make sense of why her life is falling apart. Each disclosure is incremental based on how much info the spouse knows and how much the addict feels they have to give up. It's an ugly process that NMS has to address.

The initial reaction between the spouse and addict to the discovery of his behavior oftentimes dictates the outcome of the recovery process itself long before I meet them. Any hope of reconciliation is always conditionally based on the addict's ability to stop the behavior and get honest. It has to be that way. The woman's safety comes first.

For the most part, during the first year of any NMS group's existence, this issue of the existence of the partnership is the force that itself most often drove the men to do the necessary work.

At some point in the group process, conflict arises that either is directed at me or between two group members. This finally gets the group to defocus on their spouses and look rightly towards how they each do their recovery and develop intimacy within the group. This week the dam broke and lots of energy emerged from within the group. This week's installment of the "new group" had virtually nothing to do with anyone's partner. The gloves came off and I loved it—and to some degree I created it.

I got to see how all the men played out their internal conflicts. Who was the hero, and who tried to rescue others? Who was the lost child and just wanted to crawl under a rock to avoid any conflict even if it had nothing to do with him? Who was the scapegoat? Who dug his heels in, in his quest to be right, and who had the best essence of recovery? It was amazing to watch, but re-configuration was necessary for the development of the group.

In order to describe the group we have to be able to discern how each member is "doing recovery." I have spoken about Dante, who spent thirty days in KeyStone and even though his time since then has been riddled with acting-out, in each instance he has had the willingness to see his part and change. He is dedicated to his recovery and you can hear his commitment in his speech. His partner Tonia did her own week at Survivors and is committed to her own personal recovery. So far they are the best example of a recovering couple. They are now living together but remain on a sexual fast.

Larry and Will each spent a week at Survivors and that experience has opened them to the process. Even though Larry is not sleeping in bed with his wife and the marriage is contentious at times, his personal commitment to recovery has not wavered. He lives two-plus hours away yet he works hard to stay connected. He has done a disclosure letter and we are now waiting for his wife to present her cost letter. She knew 95% of his behavior before he came in to NMS. Larry has just celebrated a year of personal sobriety and his wife spent a week at Cottonwood with Rokelle Lerner.

Will has been here the longest, coming in May a little over a year ago and has been out of his house the longest. Their split happened before he came to NMS. His wife Vanna didn't show up here in NMS until January and her five-plus months of recovery has been amazing. She jumped into the deep end of the recovery pool. She did a week in Cottonwood plus has already finished a Fourth and Fifth Step with her sponsor. She is so "Getting It." Will is presenting his empathy letter this week. I am hopeful for these three couples

Then comes Owen, whom I wrote about in the May 28 chapter. He has been here only since January. When he came to NMS he was still living at home but the home was a war zone. His wife's anger made the home unsafe. He has been out of the house about four months now. Owen was originally a skeptic of the 12-Step method because he did not "Do God." Since his entrance in NMS he has found his God and has embraced this process wholeheartedly. Up until the past two weeks his wife has been counterproductive in any kind of recovery process. Since then she herself has now done two weeks at the Meadows. The initial week was for spouses of sex addicts—which made it about Owen. The second week was Survivors which was totally about her. We are waiting to see if there is any kind of real lasting change post-Meadows. Owen has over five months of sobriety and can't wait to go to the Meadows to do his own work.

After Owen there is Roy. He certainly has his own cadence to recovery. I have taken a different approach with him, kind of letting him be. He is very bright and head strong so I let Dante, Larry, Will and Owen work on him. Using the power of the group is a good tool with men like Roy. They confront him when he exhibits distorted thinking. It seems to be working ever so slowly. His wife knows about 98% of his behavior and is not jumping up and down for disclosure. They have a strange dynamic between them. Basically they both work overtime to act and live "as-if" it's all good, in spite of Roy's penchant for crack whores.

Roy hasn't acted out since before I met him and he is convinced he will never act out again, all based on his own self will. He has never been asked to leave the house and except for a short lived, self-imposed sexual fast, he and his wife are playing in the sandbox of life very well. Roy has not completed any written assignments. He finally committed this week to have his life story done by July 15. He still has no date for a disclosure letter and his wife is fine with that. Roy stays connected on the phone with the group guys, gives great feedback, yet seldom goes to meetings. He chose a non-NMS man with shaky recovery to sponsor him. In the conflict of the group I can always count on him to try to make peace. He is the care-taker.

Those five men are the strength of my new group. I have four men who came within sixty days of each other. Bernie came first about three months ago at the insistence of his wife. He still hasn't gotten a sponsor. He is starting to do the phone pretty well and went to treatment for drinking eight years ago at the demand of his wife, yet Bernie never got a home group or sponsor nor worked any of the steps. He is starting to have some awareness that this piece of who he is isn't going away. His wife still wants no part of NMS. I have yet to meet her. I finally directed Bernie towards one of my older members to see if a sponsorship match is possible. He has some strength in the group when solicited. Left to his own devices Bernie would sooner be a spectator.

In short order, Masu, Aaron and Nigel all came in within a week of each other. Masu is Asian-American, in his late fifties, and his wife caught him in the middle of a long-term affair. Her immediate answer was to become hyper-sexual, meaning that she believed his affair would stop if she just served herself up sexually to him almost on demand. When I met her she had zero ability to show anger. Since then she has finally been able to kick Masu out of the bedroom for the first time in a thirty-plus year marriage riddled with indiscretions and alcoholic rage. He has taken to this recovery thing well, feeling immediate relief in coming into the program. Masu is still passive in group, though. I partnered him up with a NMS sponsor and he seems to be loving the connection with NMS and recovery. Masu's wife is upset because he is feeling joy in recovery. She would prefer that he stay in her constant state of misery.

Aaron is an Orthodox Jew in his early thirties whose internal guilt led him to confess his behavior to his wife. He runs away from conflict at all costs and has used porn and masturbation since he was a teen to mask his feelings of powerlessness, first from a raging distant father and now from a strong wife and small kids. She in turn, is resentful of the fact that Aaron's behavior is impacting her perfect life. I met her once in session and she has started to see Hilarie. Aaron had a sponsor in name only and this week that sponsor fired him. His black and white thinking really wants me to tell him what to do, but he has to find a balance between his life and all of its demands and his recovery. It will be interesting to watch this unfold. Aaron is struggling to make phone calls and get connected. He is riddled with shame.

The last man to arrive in the circle was Owen's twin brother, Nigel. He's a porn and masturbation guy whose behavior has butted up against his version of Christianity for years. It was Owen's honesty that got Nigel to self-examine enough to seek counsel. Nigel can emote but is hesitant to share his feelings in group yet. His wife chooses to "Not Know" the details of her husband's behavior. I have not met her yet, and I have been unsuccessful so far to get Nigel to put enough pressure on her to go see Hilarie. Nigel met with another NMS guy to see about sponsorship so I have some hope for him in that arena.

These three guys are still ducking for cover in the heat of the group, yet there is potential there for all three. I have to remember to be patient with them.

The tenth man on the list is Wayne, who hit my door in late December and started group the first of the year. It is Wayne today who is the straw that stirs the drink.

I am an affirmed zealot when it comes to how recovery is supposed to look. I take my cue from the Big Book of Alcoholics Anonymous and life. For me it is a simple program that is very difficult to do and I have found that the key to this malaise is a person's ability to be teachable. The watch word of AA is to be Honest, Open and Willing, that's the "HOW" of how this works.

Chapter 5, beginning on page 58 of the Big Book, is called "How It Works" which describes what it takes to put this disease into remission and live a God-centered life. The first sentence in the first paragraph sums it up for me: "Rarely have we seen a person fail who has thoroughly followed our path." Webster's Dictionary defines the word "thoroughly" as "omitting nothing: complete," and I believe in that definition. On page 60 the AA Big Book goes on to say "…that any life run on self-will can hardly be a success" and then on page 62 we read "So our troubles, we think, are basically of our own making. They arise out of ourselves, and the alcoholic is an extreme example of self-will run riot, though he usually doesn't think so."

For me that is at the essence of Wayne. It was evident to me that his need to "Do Recovery" was focused on keeping his partner. Wayne's was a relatively unique situation as compared to a lot of NMS men—he was about to be married when he came in my door instead of trying to save an existing marriage. His need to do recovery his way had also crystallized as time passed. Since his disclosure Wayne has been out of the home and in a "no-contact." His partner, Amber, was devastated when she found out about the extent of his sexual acting-out. What compounded the situation even more was that they were to get married this week, ending Wayne's eight years of procrastination. After his disclosure the wedding was postponed.

Wayne and Amber came in as a couple every thirty days to do a check-in. At the ninety-day mark we started doing disclosure, cost and empathy letters. He was counting days and had very little patience for the process. At the fifty-day mark he announced that if nothing had changed by day 150 he would start doing "healthy masturbation." It was getting clear to me that Wayne was "Writing his own Prescription." Many men often times do; it seldom works.

After the empathy letter was read and processed I asked them individually if they each had a desire to reconcile this partnership and they both said yes. I then gave them an assignment to break this almost six months of "no-contact." I suggested that they talk on the phone twice a week for thirty minutes each call just to start to get to know each other minus addictive distractions. They both agreed. We had a plan.

Then word got back to me through the men and women in NMS that their thirty-minute phone call lasted forty-seven minutes. When I confronted Wayne about that fact in group he became flippant and didn't see the importance of having strong boundaries or how that was connected to integrity in any way. Wayne's true self was coming out. It was also clear that Amber equally co-signed the length of the call. Wayne commented in the heat of the moment that he was just "Finally feeling good again and didn't want to end the call." I told him it sounded to me that he put his morphine drip back in his arm. The famous jail house poet Etheridge Knight wrote in his chilling poem entitled *Feeling Fucked Up*: "All I want is my woman back so my soul can sing," and to me and the other men in the room it sounded like Wayne was in the bubble.

He's a skittish kind of a man. Thirty-five, highly educated, hates his job and is very much an under earner. Amber has been supporting them for most of their relationship. Wayne's manner of speech is difficult to follow. He has a cadence that tends to ramble especially when he's emotional. In the middle of this intense group dialogue he appeared to be right on the edge of bolting out of the room. I wanted him to "Man Up" and not run so I said to him directly, "What are you going to do now, take your ball and go home?!"

My words reverberated around the group. Some wanted to find a rock to hide under even though the energy had nothing to do with them, while another tried to rescue Wayne. Two wanted to get to harmony as quickly as possible and two others got what I said and all of its implications instantaneously.

As I always say, NMS is not for the faint of heart, and yes Wayne was safe. I just didn't want to pander to that little broken boy in him. It is such an easy place for him to retreat to.

Since that group night I have spoken with many of the men. The group appears to be functioning well. Many have fear that Wayne will leave now that Amber has decided to leave her group. It seems that they are both co-conspirators. I am clear that you cannot deny anyone their desperation, and misery is optional.

For Wayne, the undercurrent of his time here can best be described by a line in the SLAA Basic Text: "How long do I have to refrain from acting-out until I can begin to act out again?" I believe his experience has been tantamount to one long hold your breath. For Amber, I believe it's always been about Barbie and Ken, the white gown and a baby before the ticking clock expires. I get a sense that this is like watching a train wreck in slow motion, but I respect their right to be wrong.

Page 59 of the AA Big Book says, "Half measures avail us nothing. We stood at the turning point." I believe that quote with all of my being.

JUNE 18

THE PROMISES

At the bottom of page 83 and the top of page 84 of the AA Big Book is written (in verse form and not numbered) what has come to be known as the Twelve Promises of AA. To the casual observer it might appear to be quite coincidental that in this paragraph there are twelve individual statements about what someone can expect as a result of "doing this simple program" beyond that of just staying sober. The principles set down in the Big Book are designed to go way beyond the pale of mere sobriety. It is certainly my goal to get the men and women of NMS to use all of these principles in all areas of their lives.

In the beginning of any recovery program the focus is always on stopping a behavior "one day at a time." A specific behavior and a very angry partner are the initial points of attack in the strategy planning. The longer anyone does this recovery work the more they begin to see that the specific behavior is but a symptom and that we must get down to causes and conditions for any long lasting change to take place. As I always say, this process is like having a root canal done without Novocain.

Somewhere during the first year to eighteen months, our men start to get it or they just go away. All I'm asking them to do is to change four little pieces of how and who they are. They have to be willing to change People, Places, Things and Situations. That's all. Oh! That's their whole life!

As their denial starts to evaporate they start to see that I'm asking them to change everything!. It's at that point in the journey that some balk, believing they can't go through with it and settling for sobriety as the high point of their emotional growth bar. Those men usually limp along in NMS for a while before developing an exit strategy, all the while believing that sobriety is enough. For the brave men who stay, they become conscious enough to know what they do not know. They stay and continue on in their personal development. That entire process within NMS lasts about four years, even though it is never stated as the end game.

Over the years we've had nine graduating classes. I believe the over forty alumni of NMS have gotten as much out of me as they were going to get. It is at this four-year juncture that it becomes time for me to kiss them goodbye—not in a forever sense but in our weekly group work and our one-on-one sessions. For me it is truly the sadness of a happy time.

Of the forty-four NMS alumni, I have had contact with thirty-five of them during the past two years. They attend our Holiday Party in December, our NMS Summer Softball/BBQ Picnic in August and our Mariners Baseball Game in July. I see many of them at SLAA meetings during the course of the year. It brings me real joy to catch up on their lives learning about all the new blessings of a reborn life.

One of the four alumni that I haven't seen for two years has moved out of the country. The second has dedicated himself to his church and except for his participation in the annual SLAA Men's Retreat he has decided to put his time and energy into other places. His dedication to God is a real life example of someone being restored to sanity through a faith in a Higher Power. The third man is still sober, I believe, but his workaholic nature has seemed to engulf him. The fourth, our dear recovery brother Ivan, passed away at age sixty-five on September 11, 2008. This adds another sad data point to an already sad date.

Our groups always graduate, befittingly, in June. With each group I do an exit exercise that takes the entire last two months to do. The goal of my last assignment is to get each man to stop and reflect on their journey and on all the men who came and went with them along the way. It is a chance for them to honor their process.

This year's graduating group is a composite of two groups that I merged two years ago, and during that time has since lost men along the final leg of the journey. The title of my assignment is "How 22 Became 5."

Each of the men get an assigned day to talk in group, using the language of the heart, about every other man who has passed through their lives and share three things about each of them. The first is: describe the essence of each man and what they saw in him. Second: your observations of his struggle combined with how you felt about his premature departure. And finally: what did you learn from each man? This first phase forces them each to reminisce and put words with feelings. It is amazing to hear them retell history though recovery lenses, feel compassion and share their fears.

The final group day is all about us. Each man gets to talk about each remaining man face-to-face. They have to recall some of the trials and tribulations each have lived through during the four years. They have to share what they believe is the essence of each man and where their growth work continues to be.

The truth is that each man is each other's witness to their life, process, recovery and redemption. Theirs is a cemented relationship built on both a shared common peril and a shared common solution. My prayer is that the cement of NMS that binds them today will last a life time.

This group is unique to itself as were all the proceeding groups, but in one aspect I believe this particular group's uniqueness really epitomizes what the founding father of AA had in mind when he started this whole thing decades ago. Bill Wilson fought long and hard to have AA be a spiritual program rather than a religious one. His own experience led him to believe in inclusion rather than in exclusion. There were many back then at the formation of AA who only wanted God defined as Jesus. Bill knew better. I told my group that Bill W would be smiling at them if he was here now. This NMS group consisted of two Orthodox Jews, a devout Evangelical Christian, a devout Mormon and a New Age former agnostic who now invokes God in his daily conversations.

I get a chuckle whenever I hear one of the Gentile men use a Yiddish word in the course of their sharing, while a Jewish man would ask the question, "What would Jesus say?" while trying to make a meaningful point. Their love for each other and the respect they all have for each other's spiritual path has been amazing to watch. I am blessed to have been a witness to it.

Gavin was the first man in. He was in a double-digit year, childless marriage to his high school sweetheart. He comes from blue-blood old money stock and was highly educated, very humble and aware of his good fortune. Gavin's wife had enough of his porn use and the dishonesty. He came in focused on "Getting an 'A' in recovery." He was with me three months before we had enough men to start a new group. I suggested that Gavin try to connect with NMS guys already here, and boy did he. Gavin is great on the phone and he is one of the most connected NMS men we have ever had. He has taken to recovery and has tremendous insight into himself and others. Gavin started running a new group for me two years ago. He has a passion, a talent and devotion for this work.

Ben was referred to me by another Orthodox Jew I had already taken into this new group. Their world is so cloistered and land locked. Of the six Orthodox Jewish men I have had in NMS over the years, four embraced the openness and two did not. Ben was also in a long-term year marriage to his high school sweetheart. They had a large family. Ben's wife, Beth, had her own issues and presented "as-if" she were above it all. She is the only wife that has ever sat in my office proclaiming that it didn't bother her at all that her husband looked at naked pictures of twenty year-old females. When Beth told me her opinion on porn I pushed back on her hard. We got off to a very rocky start. I just didn't buy that an early forty-something Orthodox Jewish woman, mother of many children, stretch marks and all could really be okay with her husband looking at porn. Ben has embraced 12-Step recovery and has opened his world to non-Jews and the gifts they bring to him. Ben and Beth as a couple have brought recovery to their children as well.

The third man in was Ellis. He was one of three NMS men with a Jehovah's Witness background in this initial group. Ellis was married for the second time to a woman who had children of her own, while Ellis had a couple from his first marriage. He joked when I asked about the large number of children and referred to his family as the Jehovah's Witness Brady Bunch. Ellis was working two jobs and living a life of quiet desperation when we met.

Ellis is just one of two men who came into NMS married and wanting to save it., but during recovery decided to end it instead. Ellis, after two years of trying to fit a square peg into a round hole, surrendered out of a need for his own mental health and walked away from his marriage without fear and while sexually sober. His personal growth has shocked me more than any other man. He ended his marriage with integrity, not by imploding it through acting-out as several other men who wanted out of a marriage had sadly done. I'm very proud of him for that.

These three men were from an original Wednesday group of ten. They settled in at eight men for a long time. The group whittled down to six when the group combined with a dwindling Tuesday group. These three guys have been through the wars together.

The remaining two, Toby and Evan, came from what I have called the most aloof group I have ever had. They went through twelve to settle in at ten and limped to four by the time we merged. The Intimacy Disorder was profound with those men. These two were at least trying.

Toby came to NMS from Ben's religious community. Their wives are longtime friends. Toby, like all the men in this group, is very smart, linear and logical. When I first met with him he was talking to me in code about his acting-out. The best he could say was that he looked at inappropriate web sites. The first time I met with Toby and his wife, it was during the conversation that I asked him how he felt. He deferred to her, stating that she always tells him how and what he is feeling. They were both very serious about that fact and both were very okay with that dimension in their marriage. Boy what a starting point!

Evan came to NMS after a failed attempt with Christian counseling and a sexual recovery program called "Prodigals." He was in so much shame that he was willing to step outside of his comfort zone to heal.

After about six months with NMS Evan told me in session that he loved my "ministry." It was the first time I had ever heard that word in conjunction with what NMS is about. Knowing the source, I was honored by his comment. Evan is the only man to become an Alumni whose wife was a disincentive for doing the program. She didn't value his time or work with us. She never came to any events, and, sad to say, when Evan played the oboe at our holiday party two years ago, and wowed everyone with his talent; his wife was a no show.

The bond between Evan and Toby was in place when they merged with the three guys from the other group. Toby knew Ben but their recoveries were separate. I had some concerns if they could get rigorously honest with each other. To my amazement they could, but come to think of it, all five men amazed me for their entire time in NMS.

The final group session with these five men was intense. Their individual testimonies all contained lots of feelings and love flowing in every direction. Their ability to put it all on the table was astounding to me. None of us wanted the evening to end.

The six of us had been in the foxhole of war and life together, I as the trusted sergeant leading the troops or maybe just a good shepherd. What a journey. What a gift.

Before we parted they presented me with a gift. It was a wall clock for the group room with a wonderful inscription on the top. The running joke was that we were the Wednesday/Thursday Group because we never minded the time. Every minute for me was well spent.

How did twenty-two men become five? The answer is with God's help and a lot of sheer determination. The Twelve Promises did and continue to come true for these men.

From pages 83 and 84 of the Big Book of Alcoholics Anonymous:

The Twelve Promises of Alcoholics Anonymous

If we are painstaking about this phase of our development, we will be amazed before we are half way through.
1) We are going to know a new freedom and a new happiness.
2) We will not regret the past nor wish to shut the door on it.
3) We will comprehend the word serenity and we will know peace.
4) No matter how far down the scale we have gone, we will see how our experience can benefit others.
5) That feeling of uselessness and self-pity will disappear.
6) We will lose interest in selfish things and gain interest in our fellows.
7) Self-seeking will slip away.
8) Our whole attitude and outlook upon life will change.
9) Fear of people and of economic insecurity will leave us.
10) We will intuitively know how to handle situations which used to baffle us.

11) We will suddenly realize that God is doing for us what we could not do for ourselves.

12) Are these extravagant promises? We think not. They are being fulfilled among us—sometimes quickly, sometimes slowly. They will always materialize if we work for them.

JUNE 25

IF I WERE A RICH MAN

"Dear God, you made many, many poor people. I realize, of course, it's no shame to be poor. But it's no great honor either! So, what would have been so terrible if I had a small fortune?" Those are the opening lines from the song "If I Were a Rich Man" from the Broadway classic musical *Fiddler on the Roof.* The hugely successful show was based on a novel written by famed turn of the century Yiddish author named Sholem Aleichem entitled, "Tevye and His Daughters." Set in a small rural town in Tsarist Russia in 1905, the story is about a hardworking milkman named Tevye who makes a meager living. It's about his family and the prospect of marriage for his three coming of age daughters. The truth of the show and of life is that wealth doesn't always equate to money.

This week's installment didn't happen in an NMS Group or in a one on one session in my office. This piece is not about betrayal, deceit, heartache or pain. This piece is about the priceless gift of recovery. The last line in the 12th Step, written on page 60 of the AA Big Book reads, "to practice these principles in all of our affairs." This week's segment is about joy. The last of the Twelve Promises on page 84 of the AA Big reads as follows: "We suddenly realize that God is doing for us what we could not do for ourselves." This snapshot of NMS is about being rich beyond money. This vignette is about redemption and recovery.

Last night I went to my first Orthodox Jewish wedding. It was on a Thursday night, not a big wedding night in American culture but the night of choice in that culture. Words are inadequate to describe the sights and sounds of the experience. A piece of me felt like I was back in a time warp in the late 1800's Poland—it kind of reminded me of *Fiddler.* The men all wore black suits with white shirts and big black hats. The women were separated by a partition; all wore modest dress with legs and arms covered.

It was very different to say the least from my other wedding experiences.

At one point during the sit down dinner reception the bride was lifted up on a chair and presented to the groom on the men's side of the room. The Hassidic music was fast and lively as the men danced around the couple to a fever pitch of excitement. It was fascinating to witness their unencumbered enthusiasm and revelry. The young couple had met only months before in a very formal dating process that is very unfamiliar in our society. Marriage without even as much as a kiss! Like I said, descriptive words fall short.

I was there as a guest of the bride's parents, Ben and Beth, whom wrote about in my last chapter. During our four years I have come to know all of their children, her parents and brother, and other important people in their lives. When I met them, the wheels of their life had begun to fall off. Today their family is healing and as they say: "Praise God."

Ben's behavior was "just adult porn and masturbation." I use quotes because in the full range of the sexual behaviors that NMS men indulge in, Ben's behavior appears very tame. Yet it had been just as destructive to his life and marriage as men who acted in more egregious ways. His wife of over twenty two years turned a blind eye to his behavior because she was deep inside of her own set of addictions. They had created a mutual non-aggression pact with each other built on the concept of *quid pro quo*. It was so elaborate that they presented to their families and religious community as the quintessential Orthodox couple, yet right beneath the surface all hell was breaking loose. While they were acting "as-if" everything was beautiful, they were drowning in the deep end of the pool of life.

When I first met Beth I asked her, given their economic plight, why they had so many children and she replied that she was doing her part to replenish the six million Jews who were murdered in the Holocaust. That's a nice sentiment, but truth be told having babies kept her addiction in quasi check. The babies finally stopped coming when Ben said no more! It was hard for him to find his voice and the courage to say "No" to her.

Both Ben and Beth were not born into Orthodoxy. They were both born into suburban middle class families. Ben's family was a bit more traditional but nothing like his life is now. Beth had a rebellious streak in her coupled with a severe learning disability. She was done with traditional high school by age fifteen when she met Ben and held on for dear life. They made separate sojourns' to Israel where they both found their religious zeal. They each jumped into their new religion with both feet.

Beth today does have a clear understanding that her entrance into Orthodoxy in her late teens and early twenties probably saved her life. The strict social rules saved her from the blunt force of her full blown addiction which her faith calls the "Evil Impulse." Her addiction for the most part was stealth-like in nature until she hit a hard bottom. It was three years ago when she came undone.

Beth was snorting her son's Ritalin on a mirror during Passover. Ben had been in recovery for almost a year by then and the strain between them was escalating. Ben was coming out of his own internal stupor and he was in need of renegotiating their existing marital contract. Beth was not a happy camper and I was not one of her favorite people to say the least. A piece of her knew that I saw through the veneer and she pushed back.

Beth had quit one of her addictions over two years before I met her with some minor help from a 12-Step program that she no longer attends. She never got a sponsor or worked a recovery program. After a brief run through their Big Book she pronounced herself cured and walked away. When I met her she believed she was in no need of anyone's help. Her addiction was morphing.

Ben was emotionally numb to life when I met him. His emotional bandwidth was almost non-existent. His intellect got in his way. Sometimes after a conversation with Ben I felt like I needed to go take a nap, he was so exhausting to try to follow. His stream of consciousness was as fractured as trying to predict the trajectory of a ball in a pin ball machine being played by a blind guy. Together, Ben and Beth were a mess.

Without going into tremendous detail, Beth's real recovery journey started when she ran away from home. That is a powerful cry for help from a forty-something Orthodox Jewish woman and mother. Ben was beside himself trying to find her. In the middle of it all, when I called Beth's cell phone she answered. It took two days of dialogue, but I was finally able to talk her into going home. By the time Beth crawled back home on her emotional belly, we had located an inpatient treatment program for her just north of Dallas, Texas. It's a long term facility. Ben got her there. Their religious community helped defer the huge cost of treatment. Beth stayed for more inpatient treatment days than any of my men! And Ben became a single dad. Since then they have worked hard on their own recoveries and collectively to save their marriage. Their intensive work has paid off with dividends.

Fast forward to now. Beth has gone back to school to become a counselor. She volunteered at a local support hotline. She has finished her first nine steps, has a kick-ass sponsor and sponsors women in need of help. She is now finishing up her time in my NMS women's group. She attends at least five AA/SLAA meetings a week and her recovery has been inspirational to watch. Beth is showing up for her husband and the children in ways that she never could have imagined before recovery. When she talks about her relationship with her Higher Power she says that she's "Plump with God"!

Ben sponsors and is sponsored. He is willing to take phone calls from anyone and he helps in any way he can. He too is showing up for his kids and wife in a myriad of new ways. Ben has kept the same job for the past four years, something that had not happened in his employment history for a long time. His work history has always been spotty. He is still under-employed but he is working on that issue. Ben works in an industry within his Orthodox Community, a little better than Tevye the milk man.

Last night, among the two hundred-plus black hatted wedding guests, were three women from Beth's NMS group and their NMS husbands. Also in attendance were Beth's sponsor and a man with his wife with whom Beth had been in treatment. Beth also invited her latest sponsee, Vanna, who is also my client. Vanna is still estranged from her husband Will, so she brought her sixteen year-old daughter, who was open enough to the experience to get up and dance in the circle with the women.

Ben invited the four men who just last week became NMS alumni from his old Tuesday night group: Gavin, Ellis, Evan, and Toby.

I stood back at one point watching the joy and uniqueness of the moment. I watched all of these NMS men and women interacting, people who normally would have never mixed, all having an experience of a lifetime. I saw the gift that being known brings to each one of them. I saw five marriages repaired when not too long ago divorce was an imminent possibility for each of them. I saw proud parents of a beautiful bride.

I saw a recovering couple bring their very distinct worlds together without fear or concern about who would ask who all these strangers were, how Ben and Beth knew them or why they were there. I watched addicts interact in an odd social setting in a very healthy way. I saw NMS working in real life and in real time. I saw redemption and grace.

With reverence in the moment I too knew I was a rich man. What a great gift I had been given.

~

Willingness comes slowly and painfully. The deck is stacked, leaning towards failure. Yet in spite of it all, when there is willingness within an addict to walk towards the light of recovery, all things are possible. June is about willingness to move out of the shadows and into the light. Developing willingness in the face of the challenges of early recovery is difficult. Accepting by choice and without reluctance the need to follow this simple program is the cornerstone of a new life.

HALF WAY HOME

This brings us to the half-way point of our NMS year-long journey, six months gone with six months to go. The program is moving right along. This week Wayne from the new Wednesday group did take his ball and go home. I guess my intuition was correct. I hate being right. When I'm right someone is usually bleeding. His departure brings me no solace. The group is now down to nine. We all processed his abrupt departure. They reported that they feel mostly fear for him with a touch of personal sadness. Like so many men in the past who have suddenly departed NMS, he didn't have the inner strength to come in for a face-to-face. He just left me a message. Reaffirms once again for me just how the Intimacy Disorder rears its ugly head.

The next day I got a call from a new man. One door closes and another opens up. I can't wait to see what the next six months has to offer up. In my business there is never a dull moment. Eyes wide open, learn, learn, and learn!!

July

~

Humility

JULY 2

MOVIE NIGHT

"We have been speaking to you of serious, sometimes tragic things. We have been dealing with alcohol in its worst aspect. But we aren't a glum lot. If newcomers could see no joy or fun in our existence, they wouldn't want it. We absolutely insist on enjoying life." That wisdom comes from the AA Big Book on page 132. I am starting this week's entry with that famous AA quote to illustrate a basic tenet of NMS: we have to able to laugh, feel and do normal events and reduce the voluminous amounts of internalized shame in order to really heal.

In October 2003 I decided to host a Movie Night in the NMS group room as a way of getting men with severe Intimacy Disorders to socialize, feast, think, feel and share together. I asked each man to bring something to eat for a potluck and I chose a film that was Hollywood-made with a recovery theme. I purposely never tell anyone the name of the film knowing full well that judgments would be made and guys would opt out of showing up. I wasn't about to let the name of the movie be a disqualifying factor in whether they showed up or not.

Choosing the right film would be critical to the success of the event. I needed a movie that we as a recovering community could relate to and that I might be able to use as a teaching tool. For our inaugural Movie Night I wanted funny, pointed and a little outlandish. I was also very aware that I needed to be cautious concerning nudity, sexuality and anything that might be "triggering" to the men. There are many great and powerful movies that I have passed on over the years because of our sex addiction "X" factor. That first movie hit my bull's eye dead center. The first movie I showed was a feature film created from a long running Saturday Night Live skit called *Stuart Saves His Family*, written, directed and starring the now Senator from Minnesota, Al Franken.

Movie Night starts at 6:30pm with an hour of food and fellowship. It is a time for new NMS men to meet others in the NMS program. I have had, on a few occasions, men who I had just met for the first time earlier in the day show up to Movie Night looking dazed and confused.

This is a time for one on one talk in a low-key setting. At about 7:20 we all grab our plates and get a seat. The first night we had fifteen men show up. I thanked everyone for coming and then we went around the room and we did introductions. Each man said his first name, which men's NMS group he was in, how long he had been in NMS, who his sponsor is and who he sponsors if he was at that point in his own recovery journey. For the newcomer, it's a chance to see how everyone is connected and how real the relationships are. These are men who are learning how to be intimate with men. For most of them this is the first time in their lives that they can feel this safe and be this honest.

After the movie I went around the room and called on each man, one by one, to share about their impressions of the movie. I made precise teaching points as the dialogue continued on. I tried to get certain men to share how the movie hit a specific point in their own lives. Franken's movie was about a socially awkward, multiply-addicted, recovering man who had to go home to deal with an adult family crisis. His dad was a chronic drunk, his mom was weak, co-dependent and self-effacing. The sister was a neurotic with an eating disorder. His older brother was functionally useless as a result of years of smoking pot all day. What a perfect prescription for hilarity in the middle of this absurdly addictive family setting. Everyone laughed and cried. Everyone loved the camaraderie, the food and everyone wanted me to do it again. This week's event was Movie Night #34!

We had a wide range of men show up for this Movie Night to honor our recent graduates. I presented Evan, Gavin, Ellis, and Toby with a framed picture for our last group. Ben wasn't able to make it since he was still attending events connect to his daughter's wedding. They each got to say something meaningful about their NMS journey.

To honor this year's class, many of last year's graduating group came back: Bruce, Dirk, Carl and Darryl. It was great to have so many of our old members at Movie Night again. For some of our new NMS men it was their first time to have met old timers.

For this Movie Night I did something different. I had been tossing around which movie to show. I had two that I found that I thought might be a good fit. I decided to bring them both and have the men vote. My criteria was going to be which movie was the least known or seen. As it turned out both were for the most part obscure, so either movie would have been brand new to the men. I chose a movie called *Adam*.

Adam is a movie that by definition would not appear to have anything at all to do with sex and or love addiction, but in fact I saw a connection.

Now it was my job to see if I could connect the dots for the men of NMS. I believe that the more recovery you have the more nuances you can see in the world in terms of seeing commonalities within us all.

Adam is about a late-twenties/early-thirties man living in New York City who suffers from Asperger's Syndrome. This disorder was first identified in 1944. Up until very recently this syndrome was considered to be on the Autism Spectrum. "Aspy" people lack nonverbal communication skills and often times have difficulty expressing empathy or are limited at best in that arena. It has been my observation that a fair amount of the men I see have several of these common characteristics. I was curious to see if the NMS men would be able to identify with the protagonist in any way.

Adam is in a relationship with a "Normie" woman who comes from a dysfunctional family. She is a rescuer by nature and works overtime to make the relationship work. In the end, she finally gets the reality that he will never be able to meet her emotional needs and that she deserves more. In the end she voted not to settle, so there was no Hollywood ending for this movie. The men were greatly impacted.

The movie brought out a full range of emotions. There was a lot of laughter and a lot of tears. Most of the men were able to take a scene from the movie and personalize it into their own life experience. In one scene Adam gets very angry and, in what would be construed as domestic violence, throws and smashes stuff around the house. As his girlfriend recoils, she tells him that she was afraid he would hurt her. He is dumbfounded by her response, never being able to draw the connection between his behavior and her fear. That is so in line with many of our men—the sheer inability to pick up on social and sexual cues. So, for a movie that supposedly had nothing to do with us, it sure hit the bull's eye.

Over the years I have shown a wide variety of movies from the 1962 Black and White classic *Days of Wine and Roses* to Sandra Bullock in *28 Days*. Our culture is rich with images of addiction and dysfunction.

As we began to clean up and put the room back together the men were in fine spirits, laughing and feeling connected. As AA teaches, "We are not a glum lot." The next Movie Night is in two months. If it ain't broke don't fix it! And besides, it really is fun.

JULY 11

BUY ME SOME PEANUTS AND CRACKERJACKS

"We are people who would normally not mix. But there exists among us a fellowship, a friendliness, and an understanding which is indescribably wonderful." So it reads on page 17 of the AA Big Book. One piece of our mission statement is to continuously try to build community. Every summer for the past six years the men, women, children and friends of the NMS program go to a Seattle Mariners baseball game. I must admit that my initial reason for doing it six years ago was to get to see the Yankees play when they come to town, but since then the event has taken on new meaning for us all. Today's installment is written on a Sunday night instead of a Friday. Today fifty-nine of us went to the ball game.

Once again our model is definitively "Coloring Outside the Lines." The NMS posse consisted of ten active members, eleven alumni and one SLAA man who is a friend to the program. We also had thirteen children between five and eighteen, one child over eighteen, one newborn and a teen friend of one of our men's kids. There were ten wives/spouses and two moms connected to three of the men. Included in the wives/spouses category were five women who are currently in one of the NMS women's groups and three who had been in the past. We had nineteen new first timers and thirty-nine who have come to our game before. The age range was six weeks to the mid-sixties, and the most amazing thing for me is that everyone, for the most part, knows everyone and, except for the children, everyone knows why everyone is there. Midway through the sixth inning on the Mariners' huge message board in center field appeared in living color: "The Mariners welcome NMS to our game today"—and we all cheered. The outcome was indescribably wonderful.

Thrown into the middle of the mix was my wife, my adult step-daughter and her partner. Everyone understood the implied level of healthy dialogue.

Boundaries were respected and everyone had a great time, save, as far as I can tell, one of the new wives who really didn't want to be there but was arm-twisted by her husband.

Earlier in the week, at group on Wednesday, this man shared about a "Lying by Omission." In the addiction world that's called a "Dope-Fiend Move." His wife has not wanted to have anything to do with recovery or this process. He has been with me for five months and I have never met her. She has so far resisted calling Hilarie and we only know her through his distorted lenses. He gave it up to us that when he got his ballgame tickets a month ago he told her that he got four tickets for a game for the family, but failed to tell her that the tickets were through NMS and that his recovery group buddies would be there. He finally told her this week. At the game, I could see by her "If looks could kill you'd be dead" response when her husband introduced us that she was definitely not a happy camper. She couldn't even say hello, nor could she look me in the eye.

It once again so clearly demonstrated how insidious this illness is. His fear of her anger drove him to withhold information. Her unabashed "dis-ease" with being there reinforced his need to shield her from information. That kind of "Catch-22" is a prescription for disaster inside a marriage. Their two small daughters seemed to be having a good time sitting between their parents. It will be interesting to hear in group next week how he cleans this up. What I do know is that if this emotional logjam does not break, there is no real way that he can sustain his relationship with NMS or even with recovery. Time will tell and besides, the picnic is coming up on August 22.

Craig and his wife came to the game with their newborn. Darryl came with his mom for the third year in a row, as his wife stayed home close to delivering their first child. Ben and Beth brought their remaining children as they all settle in to life without their oldest daughter. Sophie came without her soon to be ex-husband Matt while her child was spending the day with him. Last year Sophie came with her child and life looked much different for them both.

We had six generations of sponsor/sponsees there. Trent, who was my very first Alum, sponsors someone who in turn sponsors Quinn, who sponsors Craig, who sponsors Darryl, who sponsors Dante. As I witnessed that "bloodline" of mental health, it really demonstrated the power of recovery and the strength of the NMS program. Those bonds are strong. Except for Dante, who has only been here for a year, all of the other men are also in MKP. They have become a true fraternity of brothers.

All in all, it was a great day. The Seattle summer weather was pristine. Everyone who was slated to come did come. The Yankees won and Ichiro got a hit. I took a ton of pictures that will be shown at our holiday party in December and a good time was had by all. We are certainly mixing well now. Ah the roar of the crowd and the smell in the air; a little kid's dream to last a lifetime.

JULY 16

A NEWBIE

"My life was now rigorously segregated into closed compartments. All of my efforts went to keeping them closed..." Page 8 of the SLAA Basic Text says it all. This addiction, like any other addiction, is only sustainable by keeping secrets. Can you imagine an active addict operating in openness? That dialogue might sound like this:

"Hey hon, I'm going down to the strip club for a couple of hours, I'll be home late"

"Okay dear," she replies smiling and adds, "Now don't be putting too many twenties in some pretty stripper's G-string!"

"Okay sweetie I won't!"

"Okay have a good time, love ya!!!"

What do you think? Can you really see that conversation happening? Get real. This week I got to see a new man for the first time. His closed compartments got a little light shown on them. The heat in the kitchen of his life got turned up, so there he was, warts and all.

I received a call last week from the internationally known therapist and author Dr. Claudia Black. We had met last year. I attended a workshop that she gave and I introduced myself to her after she was finished. To my surprise, she had heard of my NMS program. As recently as last month Dr. Black had spent some time with Hilarie at a professional conference, so I guess NMS was fresh on her mind when a "Wife in Need" came into her world, not as her client but just through divine intervention. I was honored to get the referral.

Dr. Black's book *Deceived* is one of the most compelling and inclusive books I have ever read on this subject. It's a must read for anyone, especially a wife who is touched by this illness. Dr. Black gave me a little heads up about this man through the eyes of his wife. I knew there was more to the story, as there always is. Addicts lie and live in closed compartments.

I didn't want to see them both at the same time. I never do. Why bastardize our relationship right from its inception? The truth is that I'm going to ask him questions no one has ever asked him before, and we can 100% guarantee that he will lie to me if his wife is in the room. Having her come is a giant set-up. He came alone.

Ian is in his mid-thirties and in a longtime marriage. He is a blue collar, practicing alcoholic who is drowning in the addictive currents of his life. In the last six weeks, Ian lost his job of four years in an alcohol related event that got him arrested and his wife saw him dancing with his latest bimbo. The wheels fell off, but not enough to stop his wife from still being sexual with him. The insanity of her sexuality is beyond words and oh so predictable. Catch your man cheating equals be more sexual. Now that's love addiction at its worst.

Ian is a likeable guy. He is very much a man's man; football, well built, work's out, dirt bikes and loves the outdoors. I started the conversation by telling him my truth about where men are usually in their life when they walk into my office for the first time. Men never come in just when they get married, buy their first house or get a promotion at work. My work is crisis generated. He laughed nervously and agreed that there was indeed a crisis.

I shared with him also that most men do vomit up a certain amount of information to their partners at the time of "Getting Caught," or shortly thereafter, as his betrayed wife figuratively chases him around the house with the proverbial rolling pin. That concept is known as serial disclosure. That leaves couples with a ton of self-induced trauma, kind of like throwing her under a bus over and over again.

My theory is that if a man tells his wife 90% of the whole story or if he tells her only 10%, what the two numbers have in common is that the men stop at the point that they believe would cause their partners to leave them. Ian's story was right in that bell curve. She only knew about 10% and the big stuff she didn't know was about the four women Ian had had intercourse with. Whoops.

The other pertinent data point that she did know about was Ian's addictive relationship to alcohol. He had an MIP (Minor In Possession) as a teen and a DUI in 1995, whereupon he promptly moved out of state to avoid prosecution. Ian didn't return to the area until the statute of limitations had expired. He went on to tell me that he stopped drinking on September 11, 2001. Ian simply put a plug in the jug. He didn't start drinking again until 2008, and his re-acquaintance with alcohol was done in full view of his wife. She co-signed it. A few years back she also taught him (if you can believe this) how to access porn on the computer, claiming that now he could leave her alone and not hound her daily for sex. How about that fact for an example of distorted thinking by a spouse! At the end of the day she's a co-conspirator, and yes he did betray her, and yes, she is going to be traumatized when she finds out. "What a tangled web we weave...," Sir Walter Scott penned back in 1808 and it's still true today.

They met, had sex and a month later started living together. Did I mention that she was still married at the time and had two kids ages four and one? Oh yeah, and she had only been separated from her husband for two weeks. Before they got married, Ian did tell her that he had cheated on every girlfriend he had ever had. Let the buyer beware. It appears that they both had broken "pickers."

So, as the fairy tale goes, Prince Charming does rescue and marry Cinderella, but then the Prince cheats on her and it breaks her heart. When confronted with the betrayal he calmly states: "I was raised to be Charming, not faithful!"

What a mess. Ian emphatically, on a stack of bibles, stated that he loves his wife and doesn't want to lose his family, yet his behavior says otherwise. It's the insanity of addiction.

Money is tight for them, Ian lives two-plus hours away from me including the ferry ride, and he is awaiting a union job that demands him to be on call so he cannot leave the area. Coming up with an action plan that will work for him is going to be hard. Dr. Carnes says that when it comes to multiple addictions, you deal with the addiction that's going to kill you first. My vote is for the alcoholism. Lucky for Ian, I knew of a treatment center in his town that does assessments for free and has an Intensive Outpatient Program (IOP), but it still costs some money and takes some kind of commitment. I'm hoping that maybe the IOP will be able to flush some stuff out of him and get him to go to AA. That's my hope. Without AA he's probably dead in the water. I suggested that his wife go to Hilarie.

We set a new appointment for two weeks out. Ian is supposed to go for the IOP assessment and try to work out a payment plan for alcohol treatment. In the meantime, Ian has to read *Out Of The Shadows* and find an AA meeting close to home. I doubt that he will do either.

If we lived in a perfect world, I would have hand delivered Ian to KeyStone Center ECU in Pennsylvania tomorrow for a thirty-day stay, but that's not going to happen so I have to improvise. Ian does have a certain amount of awareness that he doesn't really know who he is, and that fact does upset him. He does have a little awareness that his family of origin was a nightmare, that he needs to deal with that, and he does have some real fear that his wife is done with all of the games. All that just might be enough to keep him in the game. I hope I do get another shot at him.

Ian came to see me for some guidance and to stop the bleeding. I threw him the only life preserver I know to throw. There is a good possibility that Ian will not like the color of my life preserver and throw it back at me. We are all autonomous in the end. The prognosis for him to have a life that is happy, joyous and free is highly guarded to say the least. It says on page 32 of the SLAA Basic Text "Whenever and wherever I am vulnerable, I will be tested." This is some test, but I still believe in miracles even if he is a newbie.

JULY 23

SHOWING UP

Dag Hammarskjold, the famed U.N. Secretary-General from 1953-1961, once said "Life only demands from you the strength you possess. Only one feat is possible—not to have run away." That quote runs through the epicenter of my program and my own personal life philosophy. I tell my men that my ultimate goal for them is to learn how to be a man in the world. To put down the armor that dictates that their shadow side runs their life. I try my best to make people not run away. It's the largest obstacle an addict has to face. Their own distorted thinking feeds their own distorted fear. I fight that fight every day. This past Sunday my wife and I went to the home of Darryl, one of my alumni, to see his new baby. Seeing him with his new family only re-enforces to me that this program, this model, can work and that miracles can happen.

Darryl crawled into my office six years ago. He had just been thrown out of his home and his life was in disarray. There are a couple of interesting things about Darryl that makes his journey a little different than most.

Darryl worked in the next cubicle to my very first alum, Trent. As Trent's life was unraveling in January 2002, Darryl was very aware of what was going on in his co-workers life. Trent would share about his behaviors, his then-wife's response and his early entry into recovery. Darryl was aware that Trent was seeing me, went to 12-Step meetings and joined a men's group. Yet with all of this private and personal information about his co-workers behavior, Darryl never once thought to share with Trent that he was facing the same exact issues. If you ever wanted to see an illustration of how paralyzing the shame of sex addiction is, this would be it. Darryl's mantra was to keep his secrets at all cost, even from a friend with the same behavior. Now that's a prime example of toxic shame.

Fast forward two years and now Darryl was experiencing the exact life challenges that Trent had. The good fact for Darryl was that he knew exactly who to go to in order to find a solution. Trent sent him to me.

The other interesting point about Darryl's story is that his then-wife had not found out about his sexual addiction. She never did find his porn nor did she discover any of his other acting-out behaviors. The reason she had for throwing him out was because he just wasn't emotionally available to her on any real consistent basis. She could feel it, but she just wasn't armed with any evidence. She trusted her intuition and forced a break. He was devastated by the separation when I met him.

The long and short of Darryl's story was that his wife really didn't want to reconcile the marriage. She did come to my office a few times, but really, she was done. As part of Darryl's work, he had to disclose his behavior to her. She was not very surprised. Taking stock of her own life and considering that they didn't have any children, she voted to run. Can't really blame her, and I never can. But the truth is that she was divorcing a stranger. She didn't know him because he didn't know himself.

It's at that "Marriage is Done" point that addict men need to either choose recovery for themselves or walk away from the rigors of recovery back into their old untreated, and now single, life. Most choose to leave, not in enough pain even with the impending divorce. Darryl chose to stay in recovery. Over the course of his stay in NMS, Darryl stopped acting-out, learned to live a sober life as a healthy single man, and then started to date, all with the eyes of ten men on him. By year three he had met a wonderful woman who was healthy, open, and honest. As part of his recovery, Darryl had to share with her his entire history in detail. He did and she didn't run. She could see what a good man he had become. Their honest and open relationship is built on playing life's cards face up.

Upon finishing NMS, Darryl joined MKP with the other NMS alumni from his group, continuing on with his men's work and having some accountability partners. In November 2008 my wife and I got the chance to dance at his wedding. There were eleven NMS men there. One of those men was his best man. Trent was there with his new life partner, as well as Darryl's sponsor and his sponsee. It was a blessing and a joy to witness.

The last Saturday of June, just three weeks ago, Darryl shared his story at an open SLAA speakers meeting in front of 100 people. His almost full term, very pregnant wife was sitting right there listening to her husband, soon to be the father of her child, tell his story warts and all. Last week Darryl brought his mom on our trip to the baseball game. If addicts are only as sick as their secrets, then Darryl is really healthy because those addictive secret compartments are long gone.

So there I was on Sunday, holding his seven day old son, knowing that this baby does have a father who will show up for him beyond the paycheck. His new wife was living proof that one woman's trash can be another woman's treasure, and Darryl is proof that people can and do recover if they have the capacity to be rigorously honest.

On page 33 of the SLAA Basic Text it reads "...I now felt I had reached a point in withdrawal where I had been granted the Grace of choice in my sexual and romantic life. This new state of affairs was born of the long struggle between addictive temptation and personal autonomy." Darryl is the third NMS alumnus to marry. He is the second previously single man to have a child. Altogether, six NMS men have re-partnered and two others are currently dating.

There *is* life after sex addiction. Men really can recover, and I believe most importantly that this world does not have to be seen through the lenses of scarcity but can be experienced through the God-given sense of abundance. Anything is possible in God's world if only you can just show up.

JULY 30

THE DESIRED SHORE OF FAITH

People walk into my office in all degrees of disarray. Some walk in with a pin prick while most others walk in profusely bleeding. My standard line is that people do not recover at the speed of light; people recover at the speed of pain. The trajectory of each person's time with me is different. I like to believe that what each and every person sees in me is consistency. I believe that addicts live in a world of variables and that when they start the process of recovery they need consistency. I try to model that to the best of my ability. I also believe with all my heart that if they follow this simple prescription their life will, and does, get better. This week's installment illustrates some points along that continuum.

I like to make my work relatable to our national past time of baseball. I believe baseball is the most difficult sport of all the sports to play and I believe that getting someone sexually and emotionally sober is the hardest of all addictions to be put into remission.

What makes me say that? It's easy. If a professional baseball player gets a hit three out of every ten times at bat, he will end up in the Hall of Fame. If an NBA player makes only three out of ten shots they will tell him to go home! The same is true for a football quarterback or a tennis player. It is an interesting concept for sure. Not only does a baseball player have to hit a ball moving upwards of ninety MPH coming at him with a wide range of spins on it, but then he has to hit it with a round bat to where nine defensive men are not. Now that task is very hard. No wonder three out of ten gets you in the Hall of Fame.

In recovery each man has his own ball—wife, career, children, active addiction and time—and I give them their bat—tools of recovery, men's group, sponsor, assignments and time. The pieces I cannot give them are God, willingness, and time. Those they get to find for themselves. Some do it better than others.

We have a pretty good efficacy rate here at NMS as recovery programs go, but it's baseball type numbers. Attrition over the course of our four year program is consistent. The old adage of "When the going gets tough the tough get going" certainly applies here. I have always had a clear understanding that I cannot do or want recovery any more for my clients than they are willing to do or want it for themselves. They have to personally want it more for them than I want it for them, and I want it for them a lot! My passion isn't always a burden for me, in fact sometimes it's a gift. This week, four different people on their own journeys took time to say thank you to me. Their gratitude cannot internally be measured; their outward words are priceless.

On Monday night in our group, Sam was struggling to stay sane, safe and sober. He had been out of his house, away from Zoe and his kids, for over ten months. He was getting hopeless. His living arrangements would need to change again. He had been staying with our recovery brother Trent for the past six months, but now Trent was going to sell his place in order to cohabitate with his partner. For Trent, who is one of the leaders in our community, this move will be the first time in over eight years that he will be living with a woman. I am so happy for him, but this safe haven time for Sam is up; he has to move.

Sam's general mood was somber. Living out of his home was wearing on him with no apparent end in sight. The reconciliation process was going very slowly. We finished all the letter writing but Sam's wife was in no way, shape, or form ready to forgive him for his very egregious and hurtful behavior. She could barely stand to look at him sitting in my office. Her anger, rage and pain combined with her traveling work schedule contributed to us not meeting with the much needed regularity necessary to overcome the situation. She was, however, still attending the NMS women's group and still seeing Hilarie twice a month. I was constantly propping Sam up emotionally, pointing out to him that she was still in the game and that his marriage wasn't over yet. I always believed that her strong religious beliefs would keep her from running away. In Monday's group, the idea of Sam moving back into the home was not even on the radar.

Wednesday I received a message from Sam telling me of his miracle. He was overwhelmed with emotions. The previous evening he met with his wife and their religious leader. Unbeknownst to Sam, his wife had been receiving counsel to move beyond this frozen situation. Their religious leader asked her what was her payoff for not letting him back in the house. She didn't know how to reply. He told her that she needed to be in his presence to see if any real change had taken place. His words aligned with ours. The next day Sam was back in the home, still not back in the bedroom, but at least back in the house. This is the first time since he left for treatment in KeyStone, the first time since his wife knew his entire story of betrayal, that they were living under the same roof. Woo-hoo!

It just so happened that the following day we had an appointment set to meet. There are no coincidences. I believe it's just God's way of being anonymous. Here we were in my office less than twenty-four hours after Sam had moved back into the house. We took this opportunity to set up some boundaries to keep them both safe in this transitional period back into married life. Later that night I got to hear Sam share at a SLAA meeting about how grateful he was. After the meeting he said thank you to me. I told him it was God's doing not mine.

Also at the Thursday night meeting was Ben, who I hadn't seen since his NMS group ended in June. Ben was at this particular SLAA meeting for the first time in eighteen months, as his life schedule had opened making it possible for him to come back. He once was the chairperson at this meeting some years ago. It was the place where he attended his very first SLAA meeting. He was glad to be back in his recovery "home."

At the end of the meeting, as customary, sobriety coins were handed out. Two of my NMS folks stood up to take six month coins. It was good to see the joy on their faces. Then at the end Ben stood up to take his four year sobriety coin and to give a customary brief speech. His gratitude was everywhere. At the meetings end we hugged and he said "Thank you for giving me back my life" and I replied: "God saved your life not me."

Last night my wife and I went to see a WNBA Seattle Storm game. We are big fans. Sitting in a local Starbucks before the game, I saw I had received two phone messages so I stepped outside to check them. The first one was from Dean, who happens to be Ben's sponsee and Sam's group mate. Dean called to tell me that he had just handed in his last paper and had just completed his two year MBA program. He was full of emotion. He told me that two years ago when he hastily started this program, he didn't have one man in his life he could talk to about his struggles. Now he has many. He went on to say that he does not believe that he could have successfully completed his MBA program, considering that his interior world was falling apart as a result of his addiction, if it had not been for NMS and the work we did. He was just calling to say "Thank you." Hearing both his success and his gratitude moved me.

The last call was from a woman named Tasia. Tasia is English shorthand for a long Serbian name that, here in the States, we just can't pronounce. Tasia has been seeing me for about three months. Tonia and Vanna met her in a SLAA women's meeting and sent her my way. Her life is a mess, her life bus looks like one big rolling detox center. I placed her in our recovering women's group and she has been seeing me every other week without much sobriety success. She hits the addiction trifecta: she is an active alcoholic, an active sex and love addict, and she has trauma issues dating back to her childhood from growing up in an alcoholic home in the middle of a war zone. The most important fact about Tasia is that she has some internal fortitude and can stand the heat I put on her. So far it appears that she will not take her ball and go home; she keeps coming back.

This past Tuesday, Tasia came to see me. I had already heard about her latest debacle. After all, it is "No More Secrets." She was actually relieved that I had a heads-up about her latest binge, because she knew she had to get honest and that she couldn't minimize her actions.

Over the weekend, she drank again while in the company of a twenty year-old young man. Tasia is well over thirty; she took him hostage. She always takes people hostage. In the middle of our session I told her that she needed to go into inpatient treatment for her alcoholism and that she needed to go now, ASAP now. As Dr. Carnes says, you deal with the one that's going to kill you first.

I stopped the session and made a phone call to Residence XII women's alcohol and drug treatment center here in Kirkland, Washington. I cut through their red tape to get her an assessment appointment on Friday afternoon. I then arranged for Vanna to take her so she wouldn't be able to bail out. Before she left my office, I told her that I would come visit her while she was in treatment. She was overwhelmed that someone would care for her that much. She's a million miles from home, a stranger in a strange land without any family. I will not, and this NMS community will not, abandon her. That's my pledge and that's my truth.

The phone call I received was to tell me that Residence XII has a bed for her, and that her insurance will pay for it all. Help and hope is on the way. She will get her chance and a choice. At the end of the message she said, "Thank you" even though she doesn't have a clue how hard it will be.

It was another week in NMS, not unlike any other week. Ben celebrated four years of a new life as Sam gets a second chance at a second life while trying to rebuild a twenty-year marriage mired in deceit and betrayal. Dean gets to relish and bask in his academic success as he reflects on how he got here, and Tasia has taken a huge step to plant a seed that just might grow into a new life if she can give it water, air, sunlight, fertilizer, God and time. All this happened one day at a time, just as it always does.

There is a great AA Big Book quote on page 53 that is seldom referenced: "Some of us had already walked far over the Bridge of Reason towards the desired shore of faith. The outlines and the promise of the New Land had brought luster to tired eyes and fresh courage to flagging spirits. Friendly hands had stretched out in welcome."

These small miracles keep me afloat as I remember what my very first instructor said to the class on my first day in Counseling 101: "Never, ever take your eye off the disease." The SLAA Basic Text puts it another way on page 115 "...a simple intimacy had come into being for us: we had met ourselves, and found ourselves worthy."

~

Untreated addicts are ego-maniacs with inferiority complexes. When interacting with the world they seek only to be understood. In recovery they begin to seek to understand. From humiliation to humility is a journey into the realm of enlightenment, self-awareness and virtue. The concept of humility addresses intrinsic self-worth. This is an integral ingredient to healing.

August
~
Love

AUGUST 13

HERE TODAY, GONE TOMORROW

I came back to work this week well rested after a week off for summer fun, but as always the warm and fuzzies usually do not last too long in my work world. This week's installment once again reaffirms my belief in the insidious nature of this very mercurial "ism." I call it an "ism" because of how hard it is to define and the fact that this piece of the human experience can so often go un-noticed. Getting a handle on this "ism" is difficult at best. The best way to describe this is with an old time riddle from the halls of Alcoholics Anonymous. The riddle goes like this: "What do you have left when you take the alcohol out of the alcoholic?" And the answer is, "You're left with the 'ick.'" At the end of the day, that's the work—eliminating the "symptom" (stopping the behavior) is the start of the work, you have to get down to lifelong causes and conditions. That heavy lifting is where the rubber meets the road.

One of my clients for the past two years just became a sponsor for the first time, and since this is his "virgin" experience he needed all the direction he could get. His new sponsee is a thirty-eight year-old computer guy named Barry who showed up in SLAA about a month ago. My NMS guy pushed him to come see me. After two failed attempts at keeping his appointment with me, he finally showed up on Tuesday.

I could sense his apprehension, yet he presented as cool and at ease. His recent life story was complicated, so I took notes just to make sure I got the timeline of it all. Back on January 19 while Barry was in the middle of a five month affair with a co-worker, he was told by her that she was pregnant with his baby. That's where the story starts. In his infinite wisdom, based on a private, inner conversation, Barry decided to tell his wife of seven years. As the wheels of his bus fell off on top of her, he was swearing that it was his wife that he loved and that he would end the relationship with the co-worker while honoring his financial obligations to this unborn child. Here's where the story really gets interesting.

His wife's response to this horrific news was to do nothing. She didn't get an attorney, didn't kick him out of the house, and didn't even kick him out of the bed. What she did do was to drag Barry to a couple's counselor to try to fix their marriage. When I pressed, he disclosed that after a brief period of time they resumed being sexual while the couple's counselor suggested that they do some individual counseling at the same time. Wanting to save his marriage more than anything else, Barry proceeded on to get a counselor with whom, of course, he was less than honest.

On February 10, just three weeks later, that co-worker contacted Barry and told him that she had lost the baby. Relieved and overjoyed over the reality of not having to pay eighteen years of child support and any additional strain this child would have placed on his current marriage over time, he called his wife to share the good news. There was "Joy in Mudville."

Now a normal guy with all of his gratitude would have proceeded on, trying to make daily amends to his wife for all the hardship he had just put her through, and this chapter in their life together would have been placed in the "Error in Judgment" category. The only problem is this guy's not normal, and the "ism" again shows its ugly head. So with baited breath you may ask, what happened next? Well, Barry goes back to the co-worker, of course!.

Within a week of hearing that the baby is gone, he is back having unprotected sex with his co-worker. All while Barry's wife, believing that the crisis has past, goes back to feeling safe. And no, he didn't share this with his counselor.

In fact, when I probed for more details, Barry shared that there were some days when he would be sexual with both of them in the same day. So what exactly would you call this "ism"? The SLAA Basic Text on page 11 describes this obsession as, "Each of us seemed a candle into which the other's moth would fly." Any way you slice it, his actions define insanity. Yet all the while, he proclaims that he loves his wife and wants this marriage to last!

The affair continues and life goes on until the absurdity of absurdities happened; The co-worker gets pregnant again! That announcement came on April 26. Barry again proceeds to tell his already once thrown under the bus wife. This time she asks him to leave the house and he does.

This time, with even more conviction than the first time in January, Barry tells his wife again that he is done with the co-worker. This time in counseling he gets honest about his behavior to the best of his memory, which is quite selective historically. It is at that point that Barry shows up at a SLAA meeting.

During the course of our session, it was apparent to me that Barry wasn't sure if this was an addiction. He feels much more comfortable believing that the co-worker seduced him back into the bed. So now he's the victim. Barry really didn't like it when I pushed him on that point. Another point of contention was my assertion that his wife wasn't all that healthy. That struck an uncomfortable chord in Barry.

Since his wife threw him out of the house on April 26, they have talked on the phone at least five times a day every day, so the "Thrown Out of the House" routine is just that, a routine. Then, when I factor in that over the past three months Barry has spent nights back at the house, back in her bed and back being sexual with her, for me it's a no-brainer. She's not all that healthy; scared, but definitely not healthy.

I asked Barry some questions about the counselor who he is still seeing. He told me that he felt he was receiving good counsel and that he believed that his counselor was skilled in the arena of sex and love addiction. As we proceeded this assertion became questionable to me.

So here Barry is eight months into counseling, three-plus months into SLAA, and yet he has never heard of Dr. Patrick Carnes nor has he read or heard of *Out Of The Shadows*. That is frightening to me. For me, it's just short of criminal but I held my tongue. It wasn't my intention to rag on his counselor.

I spent the last fifteen minutes of the session telling Barry about NMS and telling him what we could offer him. He shared with me that his sponsor had asked him to call other men in program and that in fact he has talked to several NMS men. Barry shared that his wife was looking for a support group. I told him about Hilarie and gave him her card to give to his wife. He also wanted to come to our annual picnic on August 22.

The last thing I told Barry was that this experience would be labor intensive and that a real solution with real recovery can happen but it takes time. He was good to go as we set another appointment and shook hands. Then on Tuesday Barry called and told me I was fired. I pray he finds the help he needs.

Picture if you can a huge pulley system with sex addiction on one end connected to love addiction on the other. When a sex addict initially meets his mate, the two facets of his addiction appear to be in sync and very normal. The blush of first love is followed by the rush of new sexuality. Everything appears in balance. As the relationship progresses and a higher and more sustainable degree of intimacy is demanded, usually by the female, the man's inability to emotionally show up consistently creates some degree of underlying stress or frustration. At worst it creates some real conflicts and resentments. It is at that moment that the tricky balance between sex and love begin to change. The pulley silently moves the sex addiction to the forefront as the love addiction recoils. With each next acting-out experience, the sex addiction becomes more pronounced and the love addict disappears. Then, as the event of the sexual acting-out becomes known, in an instant the pulley pushes the love addiction to the forefront and the sex addiction recoils into a state of temporary remission. The first words spoken by a man after getting caught are always, "Please don't leave me," directly followed by a solemn oath of, "I promise not to do it again." That's the dance, that's the "ism."

In less than twenty-four hours, I'm sure in complete concert with his wife, the fear of the uncertainty of what a relationship done cards face-up would look like led Barry to call and tell me he was cancelling our next appointment and that he really wasn't sure that he was a sex addict. All that info was left on a voice message. I found out later that day that Barry also ended his relationship with his new NMS sponsor.

Denial's a bitch. Once again we can see that this is a disease that tells you that you don't have a disease. It is so sad. This is so fixable, and yes it is so scary. As I always say, you cannot be a victim of a situation you create. God bless Barry.

That night, he did show up at the SLAA meeting. The topic I chose was "How do you know if you're a sex and love addict?" The conversation was honest and forthright. Barry never said a word. Maybe he fired the program that day too. Who knows?

AUGUST 20

BY EVERY FORM OF SELF-DECEPTION

At the Thursday night SLAA meeting, one of my men who had been in turmoil for a long time got honest in front of his community. The first words out of his mouth were "I fucked up." He called his behavior a relapse. As he continued sharing, all those listening could feel the depth of this shame and his sadness. His share sucked the air out of the room. His share was about a piece of this program not often heard or expressed: "Healthy sexuality in recovery as a single man." Now there's a topic.

I met Kelly over two years ago. He was in the middle of what is called a collaborative divorce. It is a therapeutic/legal model designed to end marriages as a win-win for both parties. The counselor doing that work was located in my building, and believed that Kelly was an untreated alcoholic and sex addict and referred him to me. As the collaborative divorce process continued on, it became more and more contentious, eventually evaporating into a very messy and ugly divorce. It was during that time that Kelly first came to see me.

I liked Kelly right from the start. Maybe it was his ability to be brutally honest, or maybe it was that he was from back east, but either way we clicked. He didn't hide his feelings or his past. Kelly, beyond a shadow of a doubt, qualified for our club and there was not a lot of push back from him when I laid that label at his doorstep. Kelly had done a wide variety of behaviors that could have ended up with him getting divorced, fired, arrested or dead. At that time it was the divorce that was getting to him.

It was my opinion that Kelly needed a higher level of care and that KeyStone would be a great place for him to go. Since he was in the middle of this legal maneuvering, and half of his money was his wife's money, he needed to get her on board with the idea. He was able to get her to come see me.

First I tried to see if there was any hope of reconciling on her part since they did have a very young child. She was crystal clear that she was not only done with the marriage, but she had already re-partnered. It appears that she never did let the bed get cold.

She was, however, very open to Kelly going to treatment. Her feelings were clear. He was going to always be the father of her child and if this treatment could help him to be a better father she was all for it. She was very matter of fact during our visit. I never did see her again.

KeyStone was great for Kelly. They were very pleased with the effort and progress he made. He was able to deal with a lot of the anger and rage from his childhood. He learned to see himself in a more sympathetic way chipping away at those core beliefs that keep men sick. He came back to us determined to stay sober from all of his bottom-lines and to try to be a man of integrity. For the next year and a half Kelly stayed the course, until being single hit him between the eyes.

Just because Kelly went to treatment didn't mean that life got great. The divorce ended messy and he had a ton of resentments directed towards his ex-wife. During the parenting evaluation, Kelly's ex-wife screamed about an incident of domestic violence that had happened over ten years before. Kelly never did deny the incident, but he did develop a huge resentment over how it landed on him.

Here's what happened. In a fit of anger, while they were both drunk, she began to flail at him. At six feet seven inches, Kelly stood there and took it for a while; eventually he pushed her away and she fell. No police were ever called, and there was no evidence of the incident at all. Yet as the divorce proceeded, the court determined that Kelly could only have limited contact with his child until his completion of a voluntary domestic violence program. Kelly's participation in a domestic violence program was not court-ordered. He felt compelled to enter the program to gain more time with his kid. But it came with a pound of flesh.

Kelly took a huge economic hit. His ex-wife had a high-end degree but was a stay-at-home mom. The court gave her spousal support for a year. Again the anger simmered just below the surface. Also during this time, Kelly's fifteen-year job was coming to an end. This was a composite of a combination of the difficult fiscal times we live in and a career at a dead-end point. Kelly went into panic about his career future for the better part of a year. He finally got a new job at the same company.

For his first year in recovery, while the divorce was proceeding, Kelly rented a room in a house near work. He was living a life of poverty consciousness for sure. After the divorce, their house finally sold and his ex-wife moved in with her new boyfriend at the other end of the city. Kelly rented a home nearby so he could have easy access to his child, but the move isolated him from his recovery community and created more stress in his life. Throughout all this Kelly remained sober, but the pot was marinating and the meter was running. That is the backdrop of Kelly's story.

Kelly successfully shut off all drinking and sexuality for a very long time. As the dust was starting to settle issue by issue, it was time to think about Stage Two recovery. Kelly had done a lot of good self-care. He lost over forty pounds and was in great shape. He started to go on day hikes with a local hiking club. He started a new SLAA morning meeting that was now solid with twelve men, one considered to be a strong meeting in the SLAA community. Kelly also started to sponsor. His step-work stalled because he was bouncing between having an AA and an SLAA sponsor, but he appeared solid and life was getting better.

We talked about Kelly need to date. He was uncertain about where he was in the process. The domestic violence program was an internal deterrent for him, since he believed that no healthy woman would date a man in an active domestic violence program. The domestic violence program was run by two women whom he saw as controlling and a bit anal. The other men in the program were all court ordered, so it was an offender based program. There appeared to be no clear exit strategy for Kelly from the program. He was truly at the mercy of the people who ran the program.

We started to talk about the concept of healthy masturbation. The attempt to take the shame out of what historically had been a very shameful behavior proved very difficult for Kelly. He never could establish a healthy pattern, so he decided to shut the spigot off again. This time it was very difficult, even more problematic than it was when he first entered recovery.

He started to talk about wanting a "Fuck Buddy" or as nowadays referred to as a "Friend with Benefits" but without even the friend piece. His thinking was starting to get very distorted. He had no interest in coming up with a dating plan since he didn't want to re-partner. He was caught in his own mental quicksand.

Now back to his painful share in this week's SLAA meeting. As I mentioned earlier, he created an online dating profile and then threw it out into the universe and waited for the fish to bite; they did. Three weeks ago, he reported that he went out on a coffee date with a woman he met online. He could see some toxicity in her so he decided he would not see her again. We were all pretty proud of him. I am a firm believer that my men have to learn how to say "No" to a woman before they can successfully say "Yes."

So what went wrong? Unbeknownst to anyone in his support group, that woman called him back and asked him out. This time he said yes. Then on the date she asked him back to her place and he said yes. Then once there she initiated sex and he said yes. He described the experience as out-of-body. Kelly stated that he knew that it wasn't right and that he should stop but he was powerless in the moment. The experience left him depleted and internally demoralized. Without the "hammer" of a wife, his own value system deserted him, and for this he was sad. It says in the AA Big Book on page 31, "By every form of self-deception and experimentation, they will try to prove themselves exceptions to the rule, therefore nonalcoholic." Kelly tried to do this with sex and the results were nil.

After the meeting we talked outside. I played devil's advocate. I told him that if I polled 100 forty year-old men, and told them about a man who had been divorced for over a year, who had not been sexual with anyone for well over two years, who then met a woman on a dating site and on their second date they had sex at her initiation, I believed that a vast majority of those random men would think it was not that big a deal. That is my truth. That would be no different than a man having a glass of wine with dinner. No big deal.

The problem is that Kelly is a sex addict and an alcoholic, and that for addicts it is easy for the disease to hide inside the picture of "normal." Kelly's episode was not going to get him divorced, fired or arrested. We really can't say not dead since he didn't know what her sexual history was. Now that's a scary thought. Oh yeah, by the way, they did not have safe sex. In Kelly's mind it was alright because he got snipped—never wanting any children again. Whoops! HIV never made his radar.

A basic challenge for Kelly is his "hearing." When I say "date" he hears "partner." The problem with "partner" for Kelly is that he hears "equals" —meaning giving away half of his money, losing a house that he doesn't own now, being cheated on, and facing another contentious divorce. All I said was to date!

So where does Kelly go from here? How did he let this happen and what does it all mean? Those are some pretty important questions that will need to be answered. I am sure that Kelly has no clear direction and cannot state an intention when it comes to dating. That internal ambivalence in and of itself will become even more problematic for an addict as time goes by. I believe that Kelly has a ton of anger at women that needs to be worked through before he can move on with a normal life. The anger is at his ex-wife, and the two women who run the domestic violence program, not to mention Mom. If his rage becomes eroticized again, his life threatening behaviors will return and that scares me for him.

Kelly is a great guy and a great dad. If he stays on the recovery path he can have a great life with a healthy woman. Like it says in the AA Promises on page 83 of the AA Big Book, "We are going to know a new freedom and a new happiness." I believe this for Kelly with all my heart. It goes on to say on page 84, "They will always materialize if we work for them." I tried to get him to see that one dalliance is an error in judgment; after that, it's a lifestyle.

AUGUST 27

WE ARE FAMILY

At the end of some "S" meetings, before the traditional Serenity Prayer, the group will collectively say: "We lift our eyes from shame to Grace." It is a powerful affirmation for people who do behavior that is deemed immoral at best and illegal at worst. The internal self-loathing that comes from decades of licentious behavior often times leaves an indelible mark on the psyche of a man, even when to the outside world he presents as moral, high functioning and healthy.

Fighting that internal and external stigma takes a lot of work. I often times tell my guys when they come into my office smothered in shame that they did a "bad thing" but they are not "bad people." My truth is that I do not take bad people and make them good. I do not have that gift or power, but I can be a good shepherd and help people who are ill get well.

One of the best components of NMS, and one that would raise the most eyebrows, is our annual NMS Summer Softball/BBQ Picnic. With all the openness and honesty at our command we come together for an afternoon of fun with family and friends. As contrived as this community is, and I acknowledge that initially it is contrived, over the course of time people without knowing it create relationships that might well last a lifetime. As opposed to our birth families, this NMS family is chosen. As Sister Sledge sang in the last verse of their 1979 hit song, "We Are Family," "Just let me state for the record, we're giving love in a family dose." It's the best antidote for toxic shame.

This year's installment of our NMS Picnic, held under the threat of rain, brought out eighty-two people plus three dogs. Ages ranged from sixty-five years to six weeks. We had sixteen couples, seven of them being first timers. Seven of the couples came with children. Along with the sixteen couples we also had fifteen men who came without a significant other. Of them, only two of the men were first-timers. Five of the men who came without a partner brought their children. It is so great to see men being dads. Six of the men came when their spouses refused to attend, fighting their temptation to acquiesce to seek harmony. They thought it was important to their personal recoveries to fight that fight.

We had a total of eight women come without a partner, and five of them were there for the first time. One of the eight women brought her adult daughter and one woman came while on an eight hour day pass from her drug and alcohol inpatient treatment center—our event is alcohol free. She was transported to the picnic by her sponsor and driven back to the treatment center by a woman from her NMS group. Now that's sisterhood working.

Four of the women who came with their spouse did not know anyone there at all. Three of the four I had not even met before. With these new couples you could see how the men struggled with an internal need to cater to their wives fears and their own need to socialize with the men in their group. The caretaking was interesting to observe, and it is all very predictable with enmeshed couples.

There was even a brand-new couple there. I have only seen the guy three times and he had yet to go to a meeting or meet any men. They brought their three kids plus their dog and only stayed about an hour, sticking to each other like white on rice. There was one man who came about thirty minutes before we ended. His fear and trepidation were easy to see. I have only seen him twice and he had not yet met anyone in the program. I got a chance to introduce him to four software guys like himself, plus the chairman of the Monday morning SLAA meeting that he swore he was going to attend the next day. It is always easy to spot the newbies— they're the ones who look like their faces are frozen.

Midway through our picnic it was time for our annual group photo, shot by one of our alumni who is a semi-professional photographer. This time there was a nearby bleacher that could accommodate us all. By photo taking time we had lost a few from the "hi-and-bye" crowd. Several of the kids were playing in our huge park and trying to get them herded would have taken a miracle. We had one wife and one NMS man who didn't want to be part of the picture.

The sun was finally out. We all sat up straight smiling and the photo was taken. I had a four year-old girl on my lap, the daughter of one of my new men whose wife chose to not partake in the picture taking. With my wife next to me and Hilarie nearby, my relationships were memorialized for posterity. There are fifty-five smiling faces in this year's photo. It is currently being framed and hopefully it will be hanging up on my office wall with all the other photos within a few weeks.

I would be less than candid if I did not get honest about all the conflict that comes between the couples where the wife has a different point of view, or has dug in her heels stating unwillingness to participate in any of our NMS events. Sad as that fact is, it is a truth. The internal fear of self-examination pushes people to recoil. I would be remiss if I didn't list some of our noted MIA's from this year's picnic.

The chance of rain kept old man Shane away and we missed his wit and humor. Dean was in Disneyland with his daughter for their summer vacation and his sponsee, Owen, was at the Meadows doing recovery at Survivors week.

Other no-shows from our active groups were Norm and Kirby. Norm chose not to fight his wife for power. They took their kids and went to a county fair three hours away. He might have come alone but there was no way she would have come, nor would she allow him to bring their small kids. Norm can acknowledge his sadness over his lack of equity in the marriage but she's not changing. Harry was in the same boat as Norm when it comes to his wife, but he chose to come alone. Norm is already starting to fret about our holiday party scheduled for December 9 which is still over four months away.

Kirby, on the other hand, has a new job with lots of travel and a wife who feels the marriage is fine and everything is right with the world. That's the same wife who stuck her head in the sand sixteen years ago when Kirby got arrested for exhibitionism and successfully completed an offenders program. They do that old AA Big Book quote from page 82 really well: "Don't see anything the matter here, Ma. Ain't it grand the wind stopped blowin'?" They did go through the repair process, but neither can admit to any new frailties. That scares me. This is a disease that tells us that we do not have it. Kirby is in "Orbit then Exit" mode. I fear that shortly he will walk off into the sunset believing he is cured.

The other active MIA was Roy, but I'm clear he will never attend anything we do at NMS except his own group and an occasional movie night if it happens to fall on his group night. He seldom goes to a meeting, he has a non-NMS sponsor who himself is sponsor-less, and he hasn't had time to write his life story in nine months. He gets a free pass from his wife on a daily basis, even though he does behavior that will get him dead, arrested and fired. Sad to say I believe he's the next to blink. In the end, all you can do is lead the horse to water. Whether he drinks or not is up to him.

One notable woman was absent, but she was in our thoughts and prayers. Tonia was forced by American immigration laws to fly back to her native country to get a visa to come back here for three more years. It was scary for her partner Dante and their toddler, not to mention the huge economic burden it placed on them as a young family. Our recovery community raised $700 anonymously for Tonia before she left. As I handed the money to her she broke down emotionally. She was overwhelmed that people whom she has known for less than a year would do this for her. This week we received word that the embassy stamped Tonia's visa and she is coming home on Saturday. I can't wait until next year to see her at our picnic with her family.

There is a great quote from the AA Big Book on page 128 that fits our picnic experience: "Joy at our release from a lifetime of frustration knew no bounds." Each of these positive social interactions helps us to change those toxic core beliefs from our childhoods. Those old beliefs of, I'm basically a worthless person, no one would love me if they knew me and I'm never going to get my needs met by anyone else, could finally start to evaporate. This happens one sane moment at a time. I'm sure my detractors will be aghast at an event like the NMS Summer Softball/BBQ Picnic, but in spite of the protest I can see how this model is working in the family lives of the men and women in NMS. As the former number one hit song proclaims: "We are family, Get up ev'rybody and sing."

~

August is love. Having made amends for addictive behaviors and being somewhere in the healing process, we came together in community to feel an unbridled love for one another that has been so elusive to us in our past lives. Love is truly the antidote for fear. Fun in the sun coupled with laughter and hugs left the NMS family with a huge abundance of love. I love August.

September

~

Discipline

SEPTEMBER 3

TOMBSTONES IN HIS EYES

Look at a junkie, a street inebriant or a crack addict and what's the one common thing you see? They have tombstones in their eyes! Their souls are lost along with any real shred of their humanity. Their vacant eyes remind us of the walking dead. It is so sad that when we do come in contact with a person like that we, as a culture, usually look away. It's almost like they become invisible to us out of our own necessity to feel okay. This week that man walked into my office.

Jerry is in his late thirties. He has been married for seven years and they thankfully do not have any children. They moved to the Seattle area three months ago from southern California for his high paying tech job. Then last weekend his wife left town to visit some friends and Jerry's addict came out to play. When she arrived home she happened to look at his computer history and to her amazement his "Low Bottom" sexual addiction literally jumped into her cup.

The concept of low bottom comes out of treatment for alcoholism and chemical dependency. The clearest picture of a low bottom drunk is the guy living under the freeway with a "Will work for food" sign. In the sex addiction world it be acting out in a compulsive way that can bring on death or arrest. That's way beyond looking at "adult" pornography—the key word there is "adult."

The concept of "Jumping in Your Cup" is a reality check, in that most people can go their entire life without coming face-to-face with heroin, crack cocaine or methamphetamine. Those drugs are available if one seeks them. For sex addicts, though, all it takes is a warm sunny day at the beach, or walking around a college campus in the springtime. The "Eye-Candy" is everywhere in this visual "looks-ism" society. This particular "drug" can literally jump in your cup from anywhere and at any time without being sought out. There is no defense against the first visual "hit."

Jerry's wife, Sally, didn't have a clue about any of his behavior. Even though Jerry's behavior was no more illegal than that of any one who hires another adult human being for sexual gratification, his particular manifestation of that behavior landed him on the edge of that continuum. Any woman would have been unprepared emotionally for the gravity of the shock, regardless of her background.

Devastated and feeling lost in space, Sally didn't know where to turn. New to this state, the only person she knew in Washington was Jerry's mom. Crying, confused and weeping she made the call and of course was welcomed over. That's how the story starts.

Two years ago, Hilarie and I were guest presenters at a Washington State health care provider association's convention held annually at a Seattle area hotel. Hilarie talked about Internet addiction and my presentation was on NMS. Jerry's mom was sitting in the room getting continuing education credits that day, never thinking for a second that the topic would ever become personal. When her daughter-in-law made that fateful call, it got personal real fast. She referred Jerry to me and I got him in ASAP.

Very seldom do I see a new potential client for the first time and talk about the possibility of going into an inpatient treatment center immediately. I usually like to get to know them better and initially I just try to get them in the fold first. I knew five minutes in that Jerry was different.

Jerry's behavior hit all of my four marker indicators. He did behavior that was going to get him divorced, fired, arrested or dead and did it all without any real regret. Jerry's regret was only about not erasing his computer history. He was also, at best, ambivalent about whether he even wanted to stay married. He didn't retreat to the usual stance of, "All I want to do is save my marriage." In plain English, Jerry just didn't give a shit about anything—not his own wellness, not his marriage or whether he even lived or died.

He answered my precise probing sexual questions honestly with a very matter of fact candor. As I looked into his eyes I saw tombstones. I know that look. After you have experienced that look, it doesn't take much to connect those dots. He reminded me sadly of Marcel.

Marcel hung himself alone in a rented room one morning in early March, only days before he was to leave to go to KeyStone. His bereaved wife, to whom I had never spoken before, told me that the last eight calls he made in his distorted state of mind, within two hours of his death, were all to escorts. This is a fatal illness.

Jerry likes to have paid-for sex with high-risk people. Jerry's thing was made doable by craigslist, with just a click of the mouse and a phone call. He has a long history of sexually acting-out, starting with porn at nine. As he grew his addiction grew also, often times masturbating to abrasion trying to achieve four orgasms a day. He had a ton of early childhood trauma and lots of abandonment issues. Within the past eight years he made two sex junkets to Thailand, once during his marriage. His tolerance for sexual stimulation was increasingly forcing him to keep upping the ante, trying to find a new high. The God-size hole in his heart just kept getting bigger, with no real way to fill it.

In *Out Of The Shadows*, Dr. Carnes writes about the Four Core Beliefs and how they drive the addict. The progressive nature of this illness was easy to see in Jerry's story. He is driven by self-loathing, self-deprecation and self-condemnation. Any emotional discomfort, shame, anger or unresolved conflict triggers the need to act out.

Prior to the acting-out episode, Jerry began to go into what Dr. Carnes calls pre-occupation mode. As soon as he knew that his wife was leaving on her weekend away he was planning his own weekend away, all the while moving away from whatever feelings he might really be experiencing connected to his life.

The pattern looks like this: as the dissociation took root, Jerry went into an altered state of consciousness where reality got blocked, going into what addicts call "The Bubble." Once Jerry, or any addict, enters the "ritualization" stage, the chances of stopping diminishes greatly without some outside intervention or event. The sexual compulsivity usually ends with an orgasm(s) and is connected to extreme degradation. Once Jerry came out of "The Bubble" he went into a state of despair, coupled with a profound sense of loneliness, hopelessness, depression, isolation and suicidal ideation. Jerry felt betrayed by his own lack of integrity, his own lack of right and wrong. Historically, his one sure way to cure the feelings of despair is to start the cycle all over again, but this time he got caught. Now the only out for Jerry was alcohol, with which he also had a long history of abuse.

I managed to get Jerry to a SLAA meeting within three hours of our first appointment. At the meeting, I introduced him to four men who had gone to KeyStone. I asked him to call me every day and I had set up an appointment for him to come back in four days. My men were great. They took his number and started to reach out. Jerry confessed to me that he didn't believe any of it, and that they were all just lying about stopping whatever behavior got them into the room. His addictive thinking was well formed. For people who lie, deceive and manipulate their way through life it is virtually impossible to believe that anyone is truly healthy or moral. This attitude of his has diminished a little over the last week, but not much.

The next day I got a call from Jerry's mom. I called Jerry and asked him if he knew that his mom was going to call me and he said yes and that he has been talking to her a lot. Without going into any real details about Jerry's behavior, she did ask me about KeyStone. She was all for it. I asked her if the money was going to be a concern and she said absolutely not. The next day I also got a call from Jerry's dad, with whom he has a very distant relationship. We had the same kind of call as with his mom.

Sally got to see Hilarie very quickly and revealed that as much as Jerry is addicted to sex, Sally is addicted to Jerry. Now how about that for a fast start! She has also agreed to join one of Hilarie's women's groups.

As I sit here and write, I really haven't got a clue as to where this story might end. Jerry might just choose recovery and give life and NMS a chance as much as he could just say "Ah fuck it" and check out literally and/or figuratively. I told Jerry the last time we talked that his painful life is optional, and that I am well aware that I cannot deny anyone their desperation if they choose it. I called him yesterday just to check in on him but he hasn't returned my phone call yet.

I believe that without inpatient treatment Jerry will not be able to stop his behavior or his drinking. I also believe that without KeyStone he will not have a prolonged safe place to touch the shame, guilt and self-loathing necessary to get to the root of his behavior and his life. I believe that the only hope Jerry has is to go away for a while. Jerry needs a time out from life. I pray he chooses life. It's just my opinion and I could be wrong. Through it all, all I see is the torment in Jerry's eyes.

SEPTEMBER 10

THE END OF SUMMER

The summer is always hard for the men of NMS. People come and go more. Close proximity to family looks better on paper than it does in real life. General connectivity lessens and sobriety often becomes more problematic. As a general rule, I let my advanced groups choose how often they want to come to group during the summer. The newer groups do not get a vote. Recovery is too difficult to achieve, and early on their recovery is less than transportable. As we exit the summer with eight months gone and four more to go it feels like a good time to catch our breath and reflect as it says in the AA Big Book on page 64, "It is an effort to discover the truth about stock-in-trade."

My Monday group is now starting its third year and is once again in transition. We have been at seven men for well over a year and a half. As the dust settles on all their collective personality traits, there is movement afoot. Five of the men are solid, at least in their commitment to each other and to the group. Two of the men are orbiting us at best, and I feel they might drift away before the end of the year.

Dean is the recovery anchor of the group. His last year has presented him with sobriety challenges that for over fourteen months he didn't face. His most licentious behaviors are long gone but he still is challenged with low level behaviors such as masturbation. Dean has had tremendous successes this year both in and out of recovery. He completed his MBA while taking a new position within his Fortune 500 Company. He is in a painstaking reconciliation process with his long-time partner who is doing her personal growth work in another program, but to date not done any recovery work. I spend a lot of time coaching Dean on how to show up in her couple's counselor's office. His work is paying off and I feel they will be living together again, possibly before the end of the year.

Dean also had the opportunity this year to drive out of state to do some relationship repair work with his mom. He also took his daughter on their first real vacation; they went to Disneyland. As cliché as it might sound, Dean is anything but a "Disneyland Dad." This year Dean told his story at the monthly SLAA speaker's meeting and started to be a sponsor. He is moving along in his step-work and has done a great job of finding a "Higher Power," considering there was no God in his life when I met him. Dean is a gift for me to work with, and I tell him that all the time.

Norm is another key member of the group. His sexual recovery is well over a year. He is working the steps with his sponsor and has recently started to be a sponsor. He was the chairperson for the Thursday night SLAA meeting for six months and is a mainstay in the SLAA recovery community.

Norm describes his recovery these days in terms of his love addiction. I often hear him say that his "Love addiction is kicking his ass." He was out of his house for five plus months that ended just before Christmas. His return was based mainly on financial concerns. Too quickly, as often is the case, he and his wife re-started their power driven sex lives. Within a month the old sludge of resentments was coming back up again.

His wife never embraced her own personal recovery and, while attending Hilarie's women's group for a short time, never was willing enough to do much introspective work. This was a major source of concern for Norm, as it is for many of the NMS men. As a couple they did some counseling work with Hilarie, yet months later his wife claimed that he has never said he was sorry. She took her ball and found another therapeutic setting. She is in a new group but many of their issues remain the same. Norm has been working with me on his codependency and his very active love addiction. He is really working to stop his internal need to avoid conflict and please others. This is now at the epicenter of his addiction.

Keith was the last man in my Monday night group. His work in MKP has served him well. He has over a year of sexual sobriety for the first time since he was a teen. He has a crazy work life, but he works hard at arranging his schedule to be in group on Monday nights and also to be available to the men. His wife, Elaine, has joined an NMS women's group and now self-identifies as a love addict. Her own entrance into the recovery world has gone a long way into helping them as a couple. They have been on a sexual fast for some time, yet they appear to be getting along splendidly for the most part. There is more repair work that has to be done, but they both have the willingness to work on it.

Sam is finally back home after being out for ten months. His wife has made it clear that his return is as "roommates only," but initially he was glad for that. Sam was advised by many men who had gone before him to increase his participation in his own personal recovery, to up his meetings and step up his connection to the men. It is my impression that Sam did just the opposite. He has all the willingness to do couple's work but hasn't come to see me alone for three months.

It also has become increasingly clear that it is going to be very hard for Sam to be present in a relationship minus any addictive distractions. Since his return to the home he has re-engaged his other addictive distractions like board games and cards. In and of itself, board games and cards do not appear to be that big a deal. But Sam has hundreds of board games and can play for up to double digit hours. It appears he just can't stay in close proximity with his family without having a back door escape route. His sexual sobriety appears strong, but I have a sense that his sobriety is driven by self will more than recovery itself. It will be interesting to see how this story plays out.

Eddie is the youngest man in NMS at twenty-eight. He is also the younger brother of one of our alumni, Caleb. Eddie introduces himself as a sex addict/love avoidant at meetings and it's a spot on label. When I met him he had never been in a "real relationship." All his relational interactions with women were cloaked around church and God and they all had a very adolescent air to them. Eddie was also a virgin.

His sexual addiction to porn and compulsive masturbation kept him in a forever shame cycle. He could never get more than six months of sobriety. I also came to see that one of Eddie's payoff's for acting-out was that it constantly placed him back at square one, putting the concept and reality of "healthy dating" always at arm's length. After his last slip I told him to go find a partner and he did.

Eddie is going back to college to finish what he started at eighteen. He is supporting himself and trying to pursue his passion and talent for the arts. He is showing up for his new partnership trying to find the balance not to drown and not to run. Some of the men are fearful for Eddie. He is in the middle of a huge transition period and it looks like he is about to move in with his "true love" after only five months, but I'm fine with it. Eddie needs this "real-life" experience. If he ends up doing a face plant over any or all of this he will still be alright. I believe for the first time in his life, Eddie is acting in an age appropriate way and I support him in his adulthood. I support Eddie in his quest to be a real man in a man's world.

The two orbiting men are Kirby and Earl. Kirby has recently found a job after seventeen months of what is being called downsize-driven unemployment. During that time they lost their house of twenty years and have gone into bankruptcy. Also during this time, Kirby started his recovery.

Kirby's sexual acting-out first surfaced in his marriage seventeen years ago, and he whitewashed it with the help of his wife. They are both equal partners in the "Everything is fine here club." They each have a barrel with an unending supply of shellac.

They pushed through disclosure, cost, empathy and forgiveness letters. Kirby never left the house or the bed, not even for a day. Once those T's were crossed and those I's were dotted, they moved on quickly toward nuptial bliss. Now that his new job is pushing him for time and attention Kirby's recovery is way on the back burner. No group, no real calling, no meetings and no problems. Kirby also happens to be the only Monday night man who did not go to the Meadows for Survivor's week, nor has he done any substantial step-work. Not surprising.

My fear is that Kirby's Teflon skin is back and he, with the encouragement of his wife, will boogie on down the road. Kirby's the guy who did a very funny standup comedy routine at our holiday party last year. I pray there aren't tears behind the laughter.

Lastly for the Monday group is Earl, who has been with NMS for over six years in three different groups. The truth is it's just Earl being Earl. He stopped taking his bi-polar meds months ago and is back to reporting his life with huge brush strokes. Earl is back living in his closed box. His love addict is alive and well, along with his distorted thinking. I'm done pushing back on him. He came to only two groups in the last three months, claiming work as the issue.

Earl came in to see me about a month ago and asked me to let him leave group, but he wanted me to list him as an alumnus. I told him I could not do that in good conscience. On the way out of the building, he ran into Hilarie and he asked her if she would override me since she has a PhD! That's Earl. He is forever trying to do an end run around authority.

Earl came to our picnic with his tween going on twenty year-old son, but he didn't want to get in our team picture. I didn't push the issue. His distance from the other men is getting wider every day. It's sad, but as I have said many times before, some people can only get so well.

Gavin's Monday night group is still at seven and has been that way for two years. Everyone has gone to some type of inpatient treatment and six of the seven have been to KeyStone. With that said, they are still in flux when it comes to recovery.

Luke is our resident minister and he's rock solid. NMS has and is working for him. For Luke it was a high bottom. Shane, who I have written about, is still periodically acting-out with hookers at the age of ninety-two. His elderly brother passed away two weeks ago and that seems to have had a profound impact on Shane. He claims he is done acting-out, but in truth I have heard that before. I love Shane's involvement in NMS, even though I would have hoped for a more sobering outcome, but the story continues and hope springs eternal.

Keenan is our only Native American, who acts out every three to six months mainly because he lives in a sexless marriage with a rage filled wife who has chosen to not do any recovery work. She appears to be only marginally miffed when Keenan does act out and we force him to tell her. There are never any real hard consequences for his behavior. He does live for their pre-teen daughter, who gets to sleep in the same bedroom as her mom every night while dad sleeps in the other room. Keenan is passive by nature and avoids confrontation at all cost. The story has remained the same since he went to KeyStone, minus the suicidal ideations.

Harry also lives with an untreated wife who would rather him not be in recovery, even if that meant that he still looked at porn. His masturbation and porn habit will never be a "Deal-Breaker" for her. In fact, I do not believe she will ever have a "Deal-Breaker." Harry's love addict, combined with his people pleasing and conflict avoidant nature, keeps him on the edge of disaster all the time. Harry and Keenan both are in the same spot. Fighting this type of epic fight can kill a sex and love addict. I do not see a soft and kind way out for either man.

Stan and Kevin are both hanging in with marriages that keep them less than satisfied. Their wives have done a ton of personal work, yet harmony comes in small bits and pieces at best. Kevin's wife Teresa is never happy for a long period of time. She is forever dissatisfied with Kevin's inability to express emotions. In short, she wants him to be what he's not. Kevin, for his part, is stuck in a small emotional band-width life with a large band-width wife. Their marriage reminds me of oil and water, but through it all he does appear to be sexually sober.

Stan and Marianne are almost polar opposites. She is cautious and conservative and he is a larger-than-life guy. He talks without much of a filter yet is not quick to action. She gets scared by his words and, like Teresa, remains in a low marinating constant fear about his potential for acting-out again. At our picnic Stan and Marianne sat apart for the photo. Neither one of the four in either couple really wants their marriages to end. Their marriages are a real case of "Can't live with 'em, can't live without 'em." I, for one, would never place a wager on the outcome of either relationship. They are both symbiotically enmeshed enough to be a "Until death do us part" kind of a deal.

Last of the seven men is the only single man in that group, Kelly. I have written about his struggles with finding willingness to create a dating plan, his unresolved anger with women, and his lack of surrender. Throughout it all, he stays in the group. I pray he continues. I have been giving him lots of space this summer to sort stuff out.

The last group is my Wednesday group, that is finishing their first year together. Of the nine men, five have been working together almost from the start. Dante, Will, Larry, Owen and Roy were in place as the year started. Bryan, Aaron, Masu and Nigel came in the past six months. I feel that the group is coalescing. The only guy seemingly not on board is Roy, who is very self-willed and up in his head. Owen, who just returned from a week at the Meadows, is constantly struggling with his marriage. His wife left NMS and gravitated with Matt's wife to another program. The conflict avoidant piece of these two men is huge. Once again the love addict piece is rearing its ugly head. Who wins or loses in this constant marital tug of war remains to be seen. I have a strong sense that Matt, Wayne and Owen will blink before the end of the year.

Dante and Will's wives, on the other hand, are the poster children for women in recovery and it's refreshing to watch recovering couple's heal. I know it is hard for Roy and Owen to watch. Masu and Aaron's wives are set to start in a women's group shortly. Nigel's wife opted out behind the veil of Christianity. He is standing tall in his aloneness.

Charles' wife came to the picnic and is in couple's counseling with a therapist, but has not yet decided which way she is going to go in terms of doing any of her own recovery work. As Charles gets ready to do disclosure she will be forced to decide. The prognosis for her involvement in recovery is highly guarded.

Larry is doing NMS long distance with a wife who is willing to do counseling but not do group. She was willing to go to Cottonwood and spend a week there with Rokelle Lerner. That week proved to be very important for her personal growth and for their marriage. They have gone through the disclosure and the cost letters so far, and we are expecting the empathy letter in the next month. Larry's recovery appears strong. He has never been out of his home and they have been abstinent in separate beds for well over fifteen months. I am hopeful for their marriage even though the progress has been slow.

All in all, I am pleased with the Wednesday group. I am hopeful that they will stay together for a while and keep working and growing in their recoveries while repairing or ending their marriages. I can never tell who will get it and who will not, and I still can't. My job is just to keep holding up the mirror.

Currently with the graduation of the old Tuesday group in June I am down to only three groups. I am hopeful that we will be able to start another group before the end of the year.

This program is fluid in nature and all the men in it are morphing somewhere in some direction all the time. It is always good to stop and reflect about stock-in-trade. My work product is life, addiction-free. My mission is to restore order where there was none. My goal is to give healing a chance. As it says in the SLAA Basic Text on page 159, "We don't know where it will lead us. We just don't know what the upper limits of healthy human functioning are." My passion is to push the envelope and see where it will take us. Stay tuned…

SEPTEMBER 17

FRAGILE FLOWERS NO MORE

Tuesday was a hard day emotionally for me. Entering my room for the last time were six women who have allowed me access to a piece of their own life journey. I have seen them all cry, rage, sob, be in despair and laugh. I have heard stories of woe that brought tears to my eyes. I have watched them find their voices first as women, then as wives, and finally as moms. I have seen the spark of life come back into their lives and today was the last time that they would all sit in my office together. This chapter is ending.

As it says in the Bible: "To everything there is a season, and a time to every purpose under the heaven." Today is the end of this season, the season of finding the truth, digging deep inside, and taking a stand. We came together to reminisce on the distance traveled and to honor each other for their work. Like all seasons this one had to end, and it did, but it did not go quietly into the night.

I gave them all the same ending assignment I give to my men at the conclusion of the group: Take time to put down on paper how you feel about the other group members, what you learned from their individual story and what you wish for them in the future. As always, the results were astounding.

For me this group was different, not just because of gender but also of timing and all the different "hats." I will explain. I met each woman in a different way. Five of the six I met through their spouses. I had done one-on-one coaching with each woman, as well as couples work. Each of their husbands had at one time been in one of my men's groups. One of the women had become my peer in the NMS Program by the virtue of running a women's group for me. Two of the women live on the same block and have known each other for almost twenty years.

The length of time I know each woman ranges from over fifteen years to just under three. The one fact that really separates this experience for me from others is that I have only been running this group since January, at a time when five of the six had been together for over two years and the sixth had been their facilitator. Now there's a story…

Last December, Sophie's life began to unravel again. It was her husband's fourth breech since I had met her. She had entered my life five years ago with an infant child and a husband with a penchant for prostitutes. As I look back on my time with Sophie, what I see is a woman who was willing to go to any lengths to save her marriage and in the process found herself. Now five years later with a child now in kindergarten, her husband's desire to interact with the sex industry was still in place but no longer acceptable to her. As they sat in my office last December and he once again confessed more of his addictive behavior, Sophie announced she was done. She now had the inner strength and conviction to hold on to her own "Deal-Breaker" and walk out of the marriage. During the five-plus years they spent in recovery, the only one of them who changed was Sophie. Her husband had finally disqualified himself from the privilege of being her husband. I still don't think her husband Matt gets it.

One of the many additional fallouts from her husband's actions was that, considering her emotional state, she now needed more support than she could give to others. She is a psychologist by profession, and by her third year in NMS, in which she learned a ton about sex addiction. I asked her to lead a women's group of beginning women whose husbands had done similar behaviors.

At the time it was a no-brainer. Sophie and her husband appeared to be the poster children for couples in recovery—plus she was skilled at running group. She did a great job shepherding these new women into their own personal recoveries. They loved her and she loved them, and since this is NMS, her own life story was one of the tools she used. Sophie was even contemplating a true career shift towards developing her own private practice aligned with NMS.

Then the roof fell in on Sophie's head. The women in her group surrounded her with love and support. They gave up their own group time to listen to her bemoan her own fate. It quickly became apparent that she could no longer be the facilitator of this group. In December they all approached me about taking the group over. My main concern was more logistical than anything else, since I already was maxed out with my time, but in the end, with some minor tweaking, it all worked out. I officially took over Sophie's group in January with Sophie now being just one of six. For me it's been a great experience both personally and professionally.

Of the six women, four of them have been to KeyStone to receive disclosure, which gave the women a bonding life experience not easily matched elsewhere. Of the six women, all have been to some inpatient program for their own wellness. Four of them had spent a week with Rokelle Lerner at Cottonwood in Tucson.

Sophie had been invited to participate in Cottonwood's Inner Path Program as a clinician-in-learning when her life collapsed. She took the allotted space initially intended to teach her how to become a facilitator and instead became one of the clients. One of the other women attended Survivors week at the Meadows to deal with her PTSD, while one spent nearly 100 days inpatient reclaiming her own life at a treatment center outside of Dallas. Two of the couples attended the couples retreat at the Meadows while repairing their relationship. For a group of six women, that's a lot of treatment. All that work made my job easy.

Two of the women had lived with husbands out of the house for a year and a half, at their instigation. Two others had their husbands live in a separate part of the house for well over a year. Sophie had kept her husband out of the house from July to December two years ago after he returned from KeyStone claiming to be "cured." All that alone time helped them each in a myriad of ways.

All this did not come without a cost. These six women have collectively seventeen children between them. Two are grandmothers and three currently have children still living at home. All the kids, whether thirty-five or six, are a byproduct of this addiction. Sex and love addiction does not happen in a vacuum.

Of the six women, five of the marriages are still intact. If I had to guess when I met each of them which one would be getting divorced today, my vote would not have been Sophie; she wouldn't have even been in my top three. Two of the husbands are now NMS alumni, two are still in a NMS group and two have left. Sophie's soon to be ex-husband left three months short of his completion, but given his last relapse it would have been a shallow graduation. Her husband needed a higher level of care than NMS can provide. We don't do polygraphs.

Two of the six are practicing a fundamental religion and another was born Jewish but has traveled to distant places religiously. One was raised Protestant and is now a practicing Catholic. The remaining two are non-generic Protestants who are more Pacific Northwest Woo-Woo (new age) than anything else.

Five of the six are not from Washington State. Three of the six have different careers now. One has built a private practice in health care during this time. One went back to school, got her first job in twenty-eight years, and is on her way to becoming a counselor. The sixth woman found art when she found her voice and is now selling her passion for profit.

I could go on and on about each one of them. Their inner strength and beauty has come through the turmoil of addictive life. They are each in a way a tribute to the will to survive, that indomitable spirit that is WOMAN.

Maybe it comes from childbirth, I'm not really sure, but it is there.

I wouldn't for one second claim that the dust has finally settled on the craziness in their lives. After all they are still married to addicts, even in recovery.

Sophie, even though she has "fired" her addict, still has a lot of challenges ahead and will one day need to trust a man again. This game is far from done.

As in all recovering people, the best we can expect is a one day reprieve. As it says in the AA Big Book on page 120, "If a repetition is to be prevented, place the problem, along with everything else, in God's hands."

As we held hands and said the Serenity Prayer for the final time, I thanked them all for trusting me, no easy feat for women who have been betrayed by men throughout their lives, not just by their husbands.

I feel honored and blessed. They each will have a special place in my memory forever, and I know I have not seen the last of them.

SEPTEMBER 24

SOS

I always turn my phone on right at 9am. During the next hour, I drive to my office, make phone calls (yes with a Bluetooth) and, if I'm lucky, I get to listen to a few minutes of a local sports talk radio station. Yesterday was different. The moment I turned my phone on, it rang.

On the other end was a man's weak voice asking for me. Once I established he had in fact reached me, we started to talk. I could hear him holding back the tears. I told him to take a moment to breathe. After the pause, he said he needed to see someone fast. I asked him when had the "Wheels fallen off" of his life and he said "Last night." He added that he and his wife had been up most of the night fighting and talking. He was a mess. It just so happened that I had an opening in three hours. That's a rarity for me. He hesitated for a second saying that he doesn't have a car. We talked logistics. My office is on the same street as the bus depot. I told him to be here by noon.

When I opened my door at noon I saw him. At first glance I saw a young man around thirty who looked like he had been crying for days. He had the look of an Eastside techie. It's a common look. It's the look of a young male who grew up on the computer with very few real life social skills, very bright, logical, linear, and generically awkward. They usually present in jeans and tee shirt with a few days growth of facial hair. There he was. As he stood up I saw that he was also morbidly obese.

Here's the story in a nutshell. His name is Damon. He is not even thirty yet and weighs over 400 pounds. His parents got divorced when he was in grade school, after several split ups, when his mom finally moved out of state to be in a lesbian relationship. Dad worked and had porn in the house, which Damon found early on. His dad remarried shortly thereafter. By the time Damon was in high school, Dad took a job at the other end of the state and left him with Grandma, where the computer and porn became his best friend. After graduation he got a job in the computer field and did well for a while, until the downturn and the lack of formal education took that life away. In the meantime, two years ago, he met a girl who is several years his junior who had just earlier given birth to a girl whose father split and moved back east without the courtesy of child support. Damon was smitten instantly as his rescuer emerged, believing he could save this girl and her infant. This was his second marriage. Are you getting the picture? This is a mess even without the porn addiction.

As I probed more, Damon disclosed that his wife had caught him with porn during their very fast eight-month courtship. Then she caught him again just a few days after the marriage. I guess he was tired of the "Same ol' thing." To top off the misery, he is currently unemployed and is on medical marijuana for chronic pain. I'd love to hear a traditional counselor come up with a treatment plan for this guy! Oh yeah, did I mention that his wife is bi-polar as reported to me?

We talked for two hours and Damon was as honest as he could be. He has no friends or support system to speak of. He managed to get his grandmother to drive him to my office and give him the money to pay me. Damon is locked into his wife and her family, which doesn't appear to be all that healthy even though supposedly his mother-in-law is in the mental health business (go figure). He told me that he found my number online and that his mother-in-law doesn't believe in sex addiction.

Damon was so raw and scared. He was starting to get an inkling, if only a little, just how huge his problems were. Yet all the while, all he could really focus on was not losing his wife. I described our NMS program to him and he has willingness to try. I asked Damon if he could get to a SLAA meeting tonight to get him going. I had fear for him being so isolated. He said he would try. Sure enough, at 7:00pm Damon walked into the meeting looking, as they typically do, scared, dazed and confused. He sat there quietly listening. After the meeting, during fellowship, I introduced Damon to four new men who he will be joining in the new group I am starting the first week in November. They all exchanged phone numbers. In all honesty, all of them are real squirrely right now, with marriages on the line and their lives turned upside down.

I also suggested that Damon come to the Saturday speaker's meeting and listen to Carl, one of my alumni, tell his story. I made a point to tell him to do whatever he could to bring along his wife. Listening to Carl's story of experience, strength and hope while Carl's partner is sitting in the front row supporting him would be good for Damon and his wife to witness.

I heard from some of the men this week that, in fact, Damon did show and he did bring his wife. He told me that he asked his wife to call and make an appointment to see Hilarie and she was open to it. At the conclusion of our session, I felt him out about the feasibility of going to KeyStone for a month. Given Damon's situation I knew it would be a long shot but I had to bring it up. He has so many life-threatening issues. As expected, there was no chance. I guess that makes me the point guy at trying to shepherd this lost young man into some kind of mental and physical wellness. I'm getting tired just thinking about it. It's going to "Take a Village" to fix this one for sure. At some later date, when the addiction has been arrested and he is stable, he is going to need more intensive psychotherapy.

~

Discipline used as a verb means to bring to a state of order. That sense of order must include the smallest pieces of life, like brushing your teeth or combing your hair. The addict's internal and external life is in need of a total remodel. Discipline must be created to sustain real growth: God, meetings, sponsor, step-work, fellowship, group and coaching are all needed to foster the onset of discipline, without which there is no hope.

October

~

Perseverance

OCTOBER 1

AUTONOMY

I started my week with an emotionally hard session that was not unexpected. This end-game has been developing for over three months and I saw it coming. Sometimes life unfolds in incremental segments that ooze out in excruciatingly slow-motion intervals. This was the culmination of one of those movements. NMS has experienced painful departures before, and I am sure that this history will repeat itself again in the future. It's the nature of the beast; it comes, sad to say, with the territory yet I never truly get used to it.

Owen, who walked into our NMS life in January, is now gone in September. He has taken to recovery well and has stopped a three decade old behavior. He has immersed himself in our fellowship and has moved into a state of having some conception of a Higher Power in his life. He openly expresses the gifts of recovery that he has received and appreciation for NMS, and yet it was time for him to go. Owen falls into a long line men who have gone before him. His wife won the battle.

Owen moved out of his house in February. He was calling me almost daily with another installment of the "I can't take it anymore" story line. All the couples who come in to NMS fight, some worse than others. They fought ugly. At one point about a month ago, his wife blocked Owen's path, jumped on his car and started to pound it with her hand. In the middle of that insanity, Owen kept his cool and called his sponsor who suggested that he call the police, which he immediately did. When they arrived, they talked her down and defused the situation and then left. No one went to jail. I am sure if it had been the other way around, and the man had blocked a woman from leaving, Owen would have been handcuffed and arrested. That was domestic violence. Later that week at her counselor's office, Owen reported the event to her counselor but it was barely processed; she said she was sorry and they moved on.

I had her in my office by herself and with Owen a few times. Her range of emotions was beyond the pale, mostly anger and righteous indignation. Some years ago before she partnered with Owen, he told me she had been a drug addict and had gone to some form of treatment. It was not followed up with any type of traditional recovery. I challenged her about her occasional marijuana use, but she was unwilling to explore or be very forthright about it. All she wanted to do was vilify her husband, keep the power imbalance, and win at all cost. She had started out with Hilarie but that experience was also less than effective. I was pushing Owen to stay strong in the eye of the hurricane.

She was the "Queen of Blackmail"; first it was over money, then over the time Owen was allowed to see his children. She doled out time with his children as a reward and not as a paternal right. Then the blackmail continued over demands that Owen give her disclosure on her time frame. The list goes on. She did join one of our women's groups for a short time, but she was poison to the group. Her *modus operandi* was to try to intimidate all of the fragile women in the group and even the group leader. She was good at it. She is a force to be reckoned with for sure, all the while aborting any real chance of healing herself. Her erratic emotional behavior was reminiscent of others I have seen before as a drug counselor who had once used drugs for extended periods of time. Even after long periods of abstinence, it is often difficult for serenity to return. This is just an opinion; I could be wrong.

She finally left NMS, leaving devastation in her wake much like after a tornado has moved on. The female side of the NMS program is just now starting to function again. She landed in a local area sex offender-based program that in recent years has expanded its business towards addiction recovery. Their program, as I understand it, is victim/perpetrator-based.

It just so happens that Owen's sponsor's partner landed in the same program over a year ago without ever giving NMS a chance. As difficult as different modalities are for reconciliation, they were enough along in their reconciliation journey that when Owen's wife landed there it didn't raise much of a red flag for me. I have spent a lot of time coaching Dean on how to show up in his partner's counselor's office and demand equity and it is working well. But that was Dean—and Dean's partner is not Owen's wife.

Another fly in the ointment is that Owen's twin brother, Nigel, joined his group in May. Before Nigel joined, I spent a lot of time clearing with both men about the pitfalls of brothers being in the same group. Owen, during that time, was in a "no-contact" with his wife trying to put some stillness and safety back in his life. Any potential negative dynamic around her brother-in-law being in his group never got discussed. It never made anyone's radar. As Owen and his wife finally came out of their "no-contact," her need for extreme confidentiality became another focal point of contention and yet another point for blackmail. She refused to do any kind of marital repair work as long as Nigel was still in Owen's group.

If my program was a traditionally based model, I would certainly understand. My official position was that I was going to let the men work it out; everyone is autonomous. Last week Nigel, in a surprise statement in group, offered to remove himself from the equation and join my new group that is starting the first week in November. His words caught Owen and everyone off guard.

Once Nigel made that noble gesture, I knew it was only a matter of time before Owen would pull the plug on his NMS experience. His internal guilt over what he would have perceived as having chased his brother out of his group would have been too much for Owen to handle. Owen really is a nice man.

I also think that Owen, deep in his heart, understands that the question of Nigel being in the group was just the latest smoke screen his wife would use to make him muddle through; after that one was successfully navigated there would be another, and in the end she would demand that he leave the program due to her utter disdain for NMS, me, and most of all the open system approach we use. Our open policy is a threat to her. One of the side effects of chronic drug use is protracted paranoia. It does not necessarily end with the cessation of use.

I respect Owen's autonomy. I respect his desire to keep his nuclear family intact at all cost. I respect his right to be wrong. As so many of the departing men express as they walk out the door, he was grateful to me and our NMS community for showing him recovery. His intention is to stay in close contact with the men in his group, his sponsor, and to continue going to SLAA meetings as he tries to save his marriage. I want to believe that Owen will be the exception to the rule and that he will not put his wife's needs above his own recovery. AA teaches that whatever addicts place ahead of their recovery they will lose. Owen's a good man and I will miss him.

OCTOBER 8

LEARN, LEARN, LEARN

Before I start this week's chapter in the NMS tale, I want to draw your attention to a story that broke recently concerning a professional football player's narrow escape from death. The headline read as follows, "Jacksonville Jaguars Wide Receiver Kassim Osgood Jumps From Second Floor Window After Getting Whipped." How about that for an alluring by-line! As I read and investigated more, I found out that Kassim, age thirty, who is a three-time All-Pro player and making over 2.5 million dollars a year, was also dabbling with a nineteen year-old cheerleader named Mackenzie Rae Putnal. As it also turns out, Ms. Putnal also had an irate twenty year-old ex-boyfriend who took exception to her relationship with the football star and administered a sound beating. By the grace of God, a tragedy was avoided, but not due to any lack of effort on the ex-boyfriend's part. The ex-boyfriend was subsequently arrested.

Nowhere in the article or in all the blogs did I read anything about sex and love addiction. Mr. Kassim, to my knowledge, is not married but his inability to make sound and rational decisions when it came to sex and romantic intrigue does not appear to reside in him. It could have been a sad and tragic ending. Mr. Kassim has a degree in sociology from San Diego State University. Now back to NMS.

Last week Owen left our program and his twin brother, Nigel, was a factor in his decision making, (secondarily I believe, but still a factor). I remember when Owen brought Nigel to me and our subsequent conversation about how he would feel having his brother in NMS and in his group. Owen professed great ease and joy at the prospect. When I ran it by Nigel he also gave it huge thumbs up so we proceeded on. As Owen's life continued to unravel, Owen's wife started to see our open system and Nigel's proximity to "private information" as more and more problematic.

As time went on her stance got more and more firm. Nigel, as I wrote last week, volunteered to remove himself and join our next new group— starting the first week in November. Owen, in his heart of hearts, couldn't handle the guilt he would have felt if he had "Run Nigel out of his group." I also believe that Owen knew that the conflict with his wife would not have ended there and ultimately she would have upped the ante and insisted that he leave NMS. With his departure I believed he preemptively tried to cut her off at the pass. As a result, Nigel's noble gesture goes by the board and he gets to stay.

Nigel has been working hard in his recovery. His forty-year love affair with porn and masturbation pre-dates his wife, his marriage and his kids. Nigel like so many others has tried to manage and control his behavior for years and has broken promise after promise to himself. His strong religious values and beliefs also add to the internal feelings of worthlessness and shame. This is the first relief he has ever experienced. As his immersion into NMS continued to grow, his marriage was proportionally suffering. It was time to turn our attention there.

Nigel's wife came to see Hilarie a few times and they also came as a couple to my August picnic, but in the end she was unwilling to self-examine or self-identify as a love addict/codependent. Like so many of the wives, they are just fine seeing their husbands as the designated "Sick Ones." As she ended her short try at counseling with Hilarie, she stated that she would try to find a religious women's support group. Nigel reported that she did find a group and also a counselor, but there hasn't been much dialogue between them to give him a sense of how she was doing. Nigel's process is moving right along. He finished his life story and read it to his group. He found a sponsor and is attending regular meetings. Next up for him is the disclosure process. I asked Nigel to invite his wife to come in since I have never really talked to her besides "hi-and-bye" at the picnic. Nigel set it up, but she had a request that she be allowed to bring her counselor into the session. I was fine with it.

This was a new experience for me. I have never had a spouse's counselor other than Hilarie in my office for a coaching session. After a brief greeting, I got down to trying to see what her counselor's knowledge base on this topic was and to try to outline our program and objectives. The counselor took careful notes while I proceeded to try to educate them both, but I was more focused on the counselor than on Nigel's wife. The counselor was familiar with Dr. Patrick Carnes, yet I got a feeling it was only cursory. The counselor had never heard of Pia Melody or the Meadows. I wanted them to know that what I was suggesting was not the world according to Jay. I kept asking if they understood or had any questions or feedback.

I talked a lot about the "open system" of NMS. I pointed to all the pictures on my wall of all my past and present clients and how I understood how outside the box it was. I spent a lot of time talking about the value of community and how the process of the disclosure, cost, empathy and hopefully the forgiveness letters protect women first and foremost. All along the way the counselor was affirming the new information I was giving.

I also explained my thoughts and feelings on the need for a sexual fast. They didn't get it, and during this time Nigel had unilaterally created a sexual fast. When I spoke in detail about the difference between consent and informed consent the counselor got it. I also took the opportunity to talk about our upcoming holiday party in December and plug the shame reducing potential effects of attending a high-end, dressed-up all-adult event where everyone in the room knows why everyone else is there. The counselor got that too. I was just trying to get Nigel's wife to be okay when Nigel invites her to come.

In the end, we set a date for delivering the disclosure letter in the first week of November. It is definitely time to get the show on the road. As we ended the session and I again asked for questions, thoughts, feelings and comments—all I got was a huge affirmative. The counselor thanked me for my openness and I, in turn, was grateful for her help along the road to reconciliation. I ended it with a "Call me anytime."

Nigel and I sat there for about ten minutes chatting after they left. He was feeling a ton of relief and I could see the tension leave his face and body. His language seemed to flow more easily. As I always say, today was another AFGO: "Another Fucking Growth Opportunity." Learn, learn, learn.

OCTOBER 15

SURRENDER VS. RESISTANCE

Two words—surrender and resistance—will in the end define how someone does in recovery and, I make up, also the rest of their life. The general conventional wisdom for an addict coming into any recovery program is that they will have to change four things in order to be successful: people, places, things and situations. In reality, that equates to the addict changing their entire life. Very few will.

Merriam-Webster defines surrender as "To give oneself over to something [as an influence]." In 12-Step terms, surrender leads to acceptance. The antonym of surrender is resistance.

A certain percentage of my men get "drop-kicked" into NMS and just want the pain in their marriages to subside. The internal motivation to "Change for Change's Sake" is not initially there. Most of those men, if they continue on in the process, will in fact come to understand the gifts of sexual sobriety for themselves and not just in reference to their marriages and or children. Those men eventually will surrender to recovery because of an attraction to it and not just as a reactionary response to the chaos they had in their lives before they walked into my office. When that epiphany happens it is a joy and a blessing to witness.

There are those, too, who never can see the potential of the freedom from their addiction. Their time in NMS is a game of resistance. Merriam-Webster defines resistance as "active psychological opposition to the bringing of unconscious, usually repressed, material to consciousness." In AA Big Book terms, resistance is described on page 95 as, "If he is not interested in your solution, if he expects you to act only as a banker for his financial difficulties or a nurse for his sprees, you may have to drop him until he changes his mind. This he may do after he gets hurt some more."

The two concepts of surrender and resistance cannot live jointly forever within the same human being. My program is committed to moving men from resistance to surrender. Sometimes we are successful and sometimes we're not. This week the inevitable collision between surrender and resistance took place.

In the January 22 entry entitled, "My New Group," I wrote about a new man named Roy. Since his entrance in NMS over ten months ago, it has been evident to me and the other men in the group that Roy has been writing his own prescription for how he wants his "process" to look. His wife was in the NMS women's group for a few months but resisted any notion that she might be a "Co-Addict" in this equation, yet when her behavior and responses to Roy's behavior were scrutinized it was hard to come up with another conclusion. She liked her life as it was and was going to bend and be shaped as Roy wanted in order to keep that life intact. Eventually she did throw down a "Deal-Breaker," but with no recovery demands. She did not need him to go to meetings, to get a sponsor, or go to the Meadows.

Roy decided that SLAA meetings just weren't needed in his recovery plans and neither was getting a sponsor with any real sobriety. He purposefully chose someone not in NMS for that job, to fulfill that role in name only. This man had been sponsored by one of my alumni but got fired months ago for going five weeks without a meeting or making a phone call. Not much of a role model for sure. Roy also verbalized to me that he would never attend any of our group bye-nights or social functions and, true to his word, he has not.

As Dante and Tonia, Will and Vanna, and Owen and his spouse were all living apart and in constant turmoil, Roy reported that everything was beautiful in his home, in spite of the reality that his wife had caught him with a prostitute just a few months before. As Larry, Masu, Nigel and Bernie reported on their sexual fasts with their partners each week in group, Roy reported that everything between him and his spouse was "Blueberries and Pancakes." We all knew better, but Roy was steadfast.

In March, Roy's wife followed Owen's wife to another program that kept the men as perpetual offenders and didn't push the woman to self-identify as addicts nor to stay on their "Side of the Street." This organization views participation in 12-Step work as purely optional at best for the men and of little or no value for the women. At the time, Roy was more than fine with her decision.

Anytime a new guy shows up, I start them out with some written assignments designed to get them to start to see the origin and chronic nature of their behavior. Roy never finished any of my assignments. I like to move the men along quickly to get them to do a formalized life story and then have them present it in group. Dante was the first to present to his group, having come back from KeyStone with it already finished. Both Will and Larry finished quickly. In the year that our group has been in existence, everyone had finished their life story except for Roy. He agreed to a July 15 deadline to read his life story, but that date came and went. I believe he was pleased to see his wife leave NMS, knowing full well that the flow of information to her about his recovery would end with her departure and it did.

I truly believe that the life story is a must before a man can write any substantive disclosure letter. Again, I believe that if we are going to throw a wife under a bus, we are only going to do it once, and that once has to be 100% thorough. Without a thorough life story, it's a crapshoot at best.

The other program reinforced what we had said about the need for disclosure. Roy's wife was putting soft pressure on him to check out the men's side of her program and I encouraged him to do that. He stated that he went to their four week introduction program and that was that. Roy stated that he had set a date to do his disclosure but was not going to finish his life story before that. I was disappointed with his strategy, but it was certainly in character. His wife was driving the timetable of the show now. And Roy was working overtime to not lose control.

During our group on October 6, Roy said that he was doing disclosure on October 12 and he set an appointment to see me the day before. I asked him in group if he had passed his letter by anyone since there are three men who had been delivered their stories, and Roy replied no. I asked him where he got his template for writing it—since I knew it wasn't from NMS. Roy told me from his wife's program. It was becoming clear to me that his payoff for staying in NMS was only to keep information from his wife. His resistance and history of managing her and us was well documented. After group I was pretty certain that I was done working with Roy. Since he was coming in on Monday I thought it could wait.

He called me Monday at ten, and said he was in traffic but wanted to know if we could start on the phone. I agreed. In our conversation Roy finally disclosed that he had in fact joined the other program for their Monday night group and had been going to it for three weeks. He also shared with me that the other program had made him take a polygraph and that he didn't share that fact with anyone in our group.

Roy told me when I probed that one man in our group had known but not from the start. In the past three weeks, he told two other men in his NMS group. After Roy was finished, I told him that I had decided to terminate him from NMS. He didn't like it and he fought back. I engaged him for a while and told him that his behavior was antithetical to the roots of NMS. He was trying to juggle NMS, me, his wife, the other program and his recovery all at once. His resistance just wasn't working for me anymore. In NMS, we do relationships "Cards Face-up" and he was still stashing cards up his sleeve. Roy was trying to manage us the way he tries to manage his wife. My sense is that Roy was playing both ends against the middle and I decided to take NMS out of his equation.

By Wednesday's group Roy had called a few of the men, complaining about me and how I did him wrong. As we processed Roy's departure, I was amazed that not one man pushed back at me or took me to task at all for my decision. The simple truth is that now we are down to seven—we have thinned the herd and we are left with seven men who have made a decision to give themselves to this very simple program. I once heard it said that for recovering addicts the best definition of surrender is to, "Go on over to the winning side." I like that definition the best.

In the end, Roy is just an "Angles Guy"; smart, self-willed, strategizing and resistant to surrender. He is no different than a crack addict trying to figure out how to come up with twenty bucks for the next rock. I believe,. like all untreated addicts, Roy's addict is lying in wait. Roy's pathological behavior can't be self-willed away regardless of what he believes. Time will tell, but I will probably never know about the next implosion. In the end this program is sustained by attraction not promotion, with surrender being the goal.

Of the over 200 men who have joined a NMS group, Roy is the only man that I have ever terminated. My decision did not come lightly. Roy was playing both ends against the middle and I hate the thought of co-signing that behavior. I believe he had turned us into a utility, like a light switch, turning us on and off as needed. The AA Big Book implores us on page 67, "We avoid retaliation or argument. We wouldn't treat sick people that way." When I did the math he just didn't want our solution. I released him to the universe. I was done fighting that war. That was my surrender.

OCTOBER 23

IT WORKS IF YOU WORK IT!

Today is Saturday. I rarely write on Saturday. I usually write on Friday but this week is different. Today I am writing about another illustration of the potential fatal nature of this illness.

The name of this chapter comes from 12-Step meetings. All 12-Step meetings conclude with the group forming a circle, holding hands, and either reciting The Lord's Prayer or the Serenity Prayer. At the conclusion of the prayer, most groups add a program slogan that says, "Keep coming back, it works if you work it, and you're worth it." This expression comes from AA, but has been adopted by other 12-Step fellowships. This phrase is essential for recovery; simply stated, "Your ass needs to be in the room if you're going to get well." I believe that decades of AA success has more than proven that slogan to be true.

Earlier I wrote about a new man, Jerry, who crawled into my room with "Tombstones in His Eyes." Shortly after Jerry landed, I got his wife to go see Hilarie. Her pain and her love addiction were as easy for Hilarie to see as it was for me. Jerry needed to go to inpatient treatment. We negotiated a "no-contact" between them to give them both a chance to calm down and hopefully stop the bleeding. Jerry went to live with one of my alumni, Quinn, while his wife Sally stayed in their home. The "no-contact" was going well thus far and Sally was just now starting to find her voice.

The couple had recently moved here for Jerry's job and neither of them, prior to Jerry's sexual implosion, had any family or friends in the area. I dropped Jerry into the Thursday and Saturday night SLAA meetings and hooked him up with the men who are going to be in his new group that starts November 2. Stan, from my Monday night group, and who has a lot of the same history as Jerry, stepped up to act as his temporary sponsor. Jerry is still aloof, toxic and emotionally shut down. I'm just holding serve waiting for him to go to KeyStone.

His wife Sally, on the other hand, has jumped into SLAA. She attends three meetings a week and has joined Hilarie's new women's group that started three weeks ago. She has also asked Vanna to be her sponsor and they are developing a strong relationship. Vanna suggested to Sally two weeks ago that she come see me to get an overview of how Jerry is doing, since they are in a "no-contact," and to get a sense of the process. She has come to see me twice, the last time being this Thursday.

Sally was much more emotionally intact on Thursday and had reclaimed some of her emotional ego strength. It was encouraging to see. We have a meeting set up for the two of them to come in for a sixty-day check-in on November 1. I went over that meeting and assured her that she would be safe in my office. During our session she asked me if Jerry was going out of the country for work. I told her I had not heard anything new and that, as of two weeks ago, his plans were all up in the air. I told her I would ask him if he showed up at tonight's SLAA meeting. Our session went well. It ended at 4pm on Thursday.

That night Jerry did attend the SLAA meeting and after the meeting I asked him about his plans. Jerry informed me he was leaving tomorrow for Asia and would return on October 31. Since Vanna was at the meeting, I passed the information on to her. After the meeting, Vanna shared it with Sally, who proceeded to immediately go into a deep dark hole in her heart. That was at 10pm Thursday night. The first domino had fallen.

When I turned on my phone the next morning, I saw that Vanna had sent me a text at 4:30am. I was concerned. I called Vanna right away. She shared with me a story of Sally's despair and suicidal ideation. Sally told Vanna that they keep a gun in the house and how good it would be to make the pain go away. Vanna stayed calm and kept her on the phone most of the night. When Sally de-escalated enough, she was able to give Vanna a wellness pledge. When I called Vanna at 9am she had not heard from Sally yet that morning.

For whatever reason, Sally picked up the phone when I called and we got to talk for about twenty minutes. She didn't say much. It was clear to me that the new info about Jerry's trip to Asia set her up against her own reality. The roof was falling on her head as she felt her own powerlessness over what Jerry would or would not do. Sally's love addict was in full eruption. As much as I tried to get her to see the distortion in her own storytelling, she really couldn't let her version of the story go. Sally's story was "Now that we are apart, Jerry would do whatever she wanted to get her back!" It's the magical and mystical thinking of an addict.

Jerry didn't need to travel to Asia to find an Asian sex industry worker. The last time he had acted out was here in Seattle and it was with Asian sex workers. Between Sally's sobs, I got her to promise to not isolate and to go to a noon SLAA women's meeting in Seattle. As we hung up, I had a lot of fear about her well-being and safety.

Following that, my first call was to Hilarie to let her know that her client was having a meltdown. My second call was to Ida, who always goes to that meeting and as a NMS alumnus would do the right thing—I wanted her to be on the lookout for Sally. I wasn't even sure that they had met yet, but in fact they had. Sally did show up and that was the start of the cavalry, circling the wagons for the next twenty-four hours.

After the meeting, Ida stayed with Sally and called both Vanna and Vanna's sponsor Beth who is also an alumnus of NMS. Now the three women had her. As I talked to all three and Ida had called Hilarie, we all wanted to make the right decisions. Since Sally was still talking about suicide, and since there was a gun in her home, Hilarie suggested that they call 911. Ida made the call. We all kind of held our collective breaths. My house became the command center for this very fragile woman's wellness. We all went into action.

The EMT bus was driving Sally to the emergency room and Vanna was riding in the ambulance with her. Ida was following Beth, who was driving Vanna's car to the hospital. The drama was growing.

Upon arrival, someone realized that one of the other women in the new NMS women's group, Dolores, was a charge nurse at that hospital. One of the women chased Dolores down and, luckily, she happened to be on duty. She tried to get Sally to agree to enter the psych ward for a twenty-four hour evaluation, but Sally wouldn't consent. Now all anyone could do was to wait for the on-call staff member to make time for a mental health evaluation. During the waiting time, Vanna called her own group member and closest recovery buddy, Tonia, for her own support. Within an hour, Tonia was there waiting at the hospital with Vanna and Sally to lend a hand. Tonia is a counselor by trade.

As I had expected, as soon as Sally told the doctor that she was better now, they had to cut her loose. It's one of the drawbacks to the mental health codes in Washington State. Vanna and Tonia made a decision to both spend the night at Sally's to ensure her safety. At least for tonight she might be safe. Vanna and Tonia took on quite an undertaking for a woman whom they both only knew for less than two months. Everyone made it through the night intact.

Today they started by all attending to the Saturday women's meeting in North Seattle. Sally didn't talk, but did cry for most of the meeting. A couple of other women from her NMS Group were there also to give support. It seems that Hilarie had made some calls to those women in her new group and put out an SOS. Two of their husbands who are going to be in my new NMS group in two weeks called me wanting to know if they should try to contact Jerry in Asia. I told them not to call Jerry and assured them that Sally was being well taken care of by the women of No More Secrets. The women had effectively circled the wagons.

By noon today I had talked to Vanna again and she was giving me an up-date on the continuing saga. The women in Sally's group were going to take shifts keeping Sally company and keeping her safe. For women who really do not know each other very well, to do this service work is extraordinary.

Vanna sounded relieved when she told me that she was in Seattle at an exclusive private high school meeting with Teresa, whose daughter was at a basketball game there to hand off the gun to Teresa. I'm not exactly sure how Teresa got in the mix except that she is another alumnus from Ida and Beth's group and that she sponsors Tonia. Teresa was committed to taking the gun home and hiding it in her attic for a while.

Vanna went on to tell me that she was going to spend the night at Beth's house because she could use a shoulder to cry on after this ordeal was over. Altogether, over ten different women stepped up to help Sally in her time of crisis. Once again the premise on which this program was founded and how it is supposed to work showed up in real time and in a big time way.

I recently read a powerful book about sexual addiction: *Desire: Where Sex Meets Addiction*, written by the author of *My Name Is Bill W*, a biography of the founder of AA. In her book, Susan Cheever's writes that "as human beings, our first need is community." It is so true. She goes on to say that "an addict is the community of one." She profoundly adds that "Addiction to sex, romance, to the idea of love, distorts many of our lives, and we don't even know it is happening."

This is the current "love" story of Sally and Jerry, and throughout all of the behavior and insanity I still believe in miracles. I'm not ready to tell Sally to run. This process has just now started. Jerry is scheduled to go to KeyStone in December. We will see. The one thing I am sure of—it's God's plan and everything happens in God's time, not Jay's.

Late this afternoon I received a text from Beth who wrote: "I can imagine there must be such a sense of gratefulness/gratitude/pride...to have built a program of people (in this case women) who can support one another in such a time of pain...have a good Saturday." All I can think of is the end of a meeting when the group joins hands and says out loud: "Keep coming back, It works if you work it, and yes you're worth it."

OCTOBER 29

TAKE WHAT YOU WANT AND LEAVE THE REST

Marriage and Family Counselor Stephanie Coontz, wrote a powerful book about marriage in 2005 entitled *Marriage, A History: How Love Conquered Marriage*. Her book covers a cultural and historic look at how we, as a culture, ended up where we are in attitudes towards marriage, love and sex. Ms. Coontz does not use the language of addiction or recovery but her message is applicable in our arena as well.

She also talks about "enmeshment" within couples. Simply stated, that is when a couple has created a closed system where they are each other's "IT." The SLAA Basic Text talks about this phenomenon, comparing a "Closed System" to an astronaut in outer space having a limited supply of food, air and water and how without opening up that "Closed System" they will eventually die. A couple living that enmeshed, closed life is sure to implode.

Coontz continues that since each of the two people in that system is the other's entire social universe, whenever there is an issue or fight in the couple-ship their entire social universe is threatened. When a fight occurs they usually fight until exhaustion as they retreat, only to re-engage while each papers over the issue out of fear of losing their entire universe. We see this pattern constantly in our couples, mainly visible within the wives. Often, when the wife finds out about some form of sexual acting-out, her answer to that knowledge is to suppress her own anger, hurt and pain by being sexual to ensure that she will not be abandoned. It's an insane strategy.

This past Tuesday, I had the opportunity to do a workshop for the women of NMS. I haven't done one in a year and the turnover since the last workshop was huge. Hilarie had her new women's group, now only a month old, in attendance. Some of those women I was meeting for the first time. Out of the ten women, seven are connected to my men. Two of those men have been in my Wednesday night group for six months (Masu's and Aaron's wives) and the other men connected to those wives are going to be in my new Tuesday night group that starts next week. Of Hilarie's ten women, they have all been at this "recovery" thing for less than six months with several less than two months. Their knowledge of sex and love addiction is limited to say the least, and all their marriages are in some stage of disrepair, whether the women are honest to acknowledge it or not.

Along with Hilarie's new ten, Ida's year-old group of five came. These women—Vanna, Tonia, Elaine, Dianne and Daniela—are committed to their own personal recovery and are working the SLAA 12-Steps, going to meetings and doing individual therapy. Also in attendance besides Ida were two of her peer recovery buddies from my recent alumni group, Beth and Tonia. All total there were seventeen women in the room, all at different points along the recovery road. The audience consists of women who have been in NMS from two weeks to four years. Presenting to that range is a challenge for sure. One of my goals was to address the "Closed System" and the need for community to heal.

I started with introductions since most of the ten new women had never met the other women of NMS. I probed a little just to get a sense of how honest they each could be in that vulnerable setting. I started with the "Old-timers" who I knew would "Put everything on the table" and not sugar-coat their personal journey. Hopefully this gave some of the newer women the courage to go beyond the surface.

In the room, sitting very small in the corner, was Sally who just last weekend was the focus of so many of the women in the room. I took time to acknowledge their efforts to keep her safe. She seemed embarrassed by my reference. I told her I was grateful she didn't leave before the miracle.

It was then that I read an excerpt from Ms. Coontz's book and drew a diagram on the board clearly showing the difference between a closed and open system within a marriage. I then began asking questions to illustrate my point of where each of them found themselves when they first showed up here in NMS. One of the youngest women in NMS, twenty-five year-old Nora, was the focus of much of my attention. Her significant other, Nash, came to me a month ago after he had broken off their wedding only weeks before getting married, after dating for more than two years. He pulled the plug because of some facsimile of guilt concerning his constant cheating, 90% of which she still does not know. As of yet he's not too big in the remorse category.

All the wedding plans were in place, over 200 guests were coming in from around the country, the band was hired, the photographer was on call, the bridesmaids were all accessorized with matching dresses, the entire nine yards—and then he bails. Nora's answer to that life crisis was to continue living with him and continue being sexual with him while she never told anyone in her life, not her mom, sister or maid of honor the truth about what was going on in her relationship. Now that's an illustration of a closed system, and that closed system is fueled by carried shame! Nora knew that he had been unfaithful but not much else. For most of my time talking with her I was biting my tongue, I wanted to tell her to RUN, but she's not my client. I suggested that they do a "no-contact" and stop living together.

Earlier this week, Nash told me that he had just broken off with his girlfriend. I instantly thought he was talking about Nora but quickly realized he wasn't. Nash was talking about a "stash" he had back in southern California. I still don't think he's close to a real bottom.

Continuing the workshop, I did some more "Chalk Talk" around the process of recovery—describing my belief of what it will take for their men to recover. We had a good exchange and the new women had a ton of questions that I, for the most part, deferred to the more seasoned wives to answer. I talked about the disclosure letter and the need for that trauma to be a one time and one time only event. I implored the women to fight their internal need to know everything about their husband's behavior with restraint. Disclosure needs to happen in a safe setting, and the living room is not safe.

I could see the width and breadth of the disease right in front of me on the faces of the new women. The new women had the "Deer in the Headlights" look, while the more recovered women had a greater sense of serenity and a clear knowledge of where they started and stopped—not just in terms of their partners but within themselves as women.

The two hours just flew by. I made them laugh, made them cry, made them think and hopefully made them take a peek inside themselves. I told them that it is easy for them to see their partners as the designated "Sick Ones"; but, in the end, they had chosen those men, and as a result they have had a part in creating, or at least perpetuating, the system.

There is a wise expression in AA that shows itself whenever there is some difference of opinion in a meeting or between to AA members. That expression is, "Take what you want and leave the rest." I challenged the women to look inside their own hearts. "When you point your finger at someone else there are always three fingers pointing back at you." Make a note.

Hopefully as time goes on and the recovery process turns towards reconciliation I will get a chance to work with some of these women more closely. For better or worse, I pray they find their own recoveries first.

~

Steady persistence in this phase of the journey is mandatory if the true gifts of recovery are to be attained. Perseverance is that hard-nosed, "Keeping your eye on the prize" mentality that makes anyone successful in whatever endeavor they do in life. Sustaining that level of perseverance can only be done on a daily basis with a tremendous amount of mindfulness, acceptance and surrender.

November

~

Illumination

NOVEMBER 5

ON YOUR MARK, GET SET, GO!

Tuesday night I started a new group. This is the sixteenth group in the history of NMS. I know the drill. Nine out of the ten men showed up with the tenth being out of state on a preplanned trip. Each man coming into the room came in with a ton of feelings, mostly fear, apprehension, trepidation and hope. Their emotions filled the room. I presented each man with a notebook and a pen. I began by telling them that one of the collateral damages of the addiction is their inability to track other people's lives. I gave some examples of how that looks in real life, like when their wife tells them in the morning that she is planning to take their child to the dentist later in the day and when Dad comes home after work he fails to ask how it went at the dentist. We always would attribute this kind of interaction either to her being a nag, or to our busy work life, or just a poor memory. The buck stops here. Each man was going to get a chance to tell a mini story as each man took notes. We were going to practice tracking each other's lives. Intimacy is the key to healing; for most of the men in the circle, I might as well be speaking Chinese.

I decided to start the process in order of who came into my office first, since I am the common denominator for each man. With each story I would ask questions to reveal who they are beneath the facade of looking good and being right. I would start by asking the basic questions each of them asks others when adults meet in the real world: How old are you? Are you married? Do you have any children? How long have you been married? What do you do for a living? As NMS groups go, this group is a bit unique in demographics. The age range is twenty-eight to fifty-four with five being in their thirties. Two are in their forties; one is over fifty and two under thirty. By our standards that's a young group. Another unique fact is that of the ten only four are dads and that's unusual for NMS. Two of the men have never married and have never lived with a woman; both of them present as heterosexual anorexics in spite of their porn use and compulsive masturbation. A third man is also unmarried but he broke his wedding off three weeks before the event.

We have two married men who do not have children and one married man whose wife has a toddler from a prior relationship, but that child only lives with them minimally, making him the only quasi step-father in the group. Another unique factoid of this group is that we have five men who did not finish college, and for NMS that is a very high number. One of the men also has two children under three years of age. There are two doctors in the group and six tech guys, a college grad who does blue collar work, and one man who is currently unemployed and on medical marijuana. This group is quite an eclectic bunch.

Two of the men have lived in the Seattle area for less than four months and one of them still works out of state and commutes every four days. Another of the men is living that same scenario, except it's his wife who works in another state and she is doing counseling there.

Seven of the men have a prior history of substance abuse, and I do believe that four of them currently exhibit problematic drinking or pot smoking behavior. One of the men is currently very obese, while another man was that heavy less than three years ago before having worked a 12-Step program to lose the weight. This group is riddled with men who have several addiction issues. We have to deal with the addiction that will kill them first. To say the least, this is a group of men who would normally not mix.

Of the eight partnered men, four of their partners are already in Hilarie's new group and are starting to do some work. Two of the men appear to have spouses who, at this time, do not want to look at this cancer in their life at all. In all fairness, one of the guys is so new that we haven't really gotten around to his spouse yet, while the other has either been a no-show or canceled twice with Hilarie over the last five weeks. I do not perceive much willingness there, but she is only twenty-three. One of the wives did come to see Hilarie once but has decided she doesn't want what we have. At the end of the day she will probably pull her husband out of NMS. The last of the partners has seen Hilarie two or three times, and I did meet her for just a few minutes once. She appears to be very emotionally fragile, is in active bulimia, and is flailing about, overwhelmed with fear and threatening divorce at every turn.

Although we started Tuesday's group with a full complement of ten men, I am still not willing to close the group for good yet. I'll keep it open until the first of the year. My intuition tells me that we will lose two before New Year's and we could be down to six before the first blush of spring. Attrition comes with the territory. As I have said before, this program is driven by attraction, not promotion.

As each man talked, I asked incisive questions, trying to make clarifying points as I sought to get them accustomed to being transparent. I identified commonalities between the men. One of the nine men used humor to deflect feelings while another man still had a huge denial system in place. As new as these men were in recovery, many of them did see through his bull. He only has questions and doubt. For him, I'm afraid there are no answers he can comprehend.

As we proceeded, some of the men got used to the fact that they were not only allowed, but encouraged, to ask probing questions of each other. It was so odd, for them, to be in such a wide open forum. We ran overtime at about the three hour and twenty-minute mark. I am never concerned about time in group. This next week we will have one more man to process in, then we start getting down to work.

I am always excited to start a new group, to see before me the unfolding of lies and the collapse of defenses. The breadth and width of this disease is interesting to observe and I find it fascinating to witness. In the book *Twelve Steps and Twelve Traditions* from AA, on page 68 it states in the middle of Step Six that, "Only Step One, where we made the 100% admission we were powerless over alcohol, can be practiced with absolute perfection. The remaining eleven Steps state perfect ideals." My main goal for a while is to get them all to do a perfect Step One. To birth men into recovery is a difficult task to say the least, but I love and welcome the challenge.

On your mark, get set, go…I must remember it's not a sprint but rather a marathon. This group that started on November 5 will last until June three years from now. We will see who makes it and who does not. For me, at the end of the day, God's in charge.

NOVEMBER 12

REDEMPTION AND PROPHECY

This installment is directed at two different events that happened this week. The strength of each event was so profound that I just could not decide which one to write about and which one to omit, so I will report them both.

Back on April 30 I wrote a chapter entitled "Fathers and Sons." Harry had come in to see me with his father to mend some fences. It was a powerful session, but as time went on it really didn't have any lasting effect on their relationship, since only one of them (Harry) was doing any growth work. The initial bounce eventually petered out and life went back to business as usual.

This week I had a "first time" experience. I got to have a session with a man and his mom. Dean has been in NMS for over two years. When he first came into my office he was a mess. His six year live-in relationship was in turmoil and his compulsive porn use was the reported issue. I immediately put Dean into my Monday group, got him going to SLAA meetings, found him a suitable sponsor, and threw him in the deep end of the recovery pool. He read everything in sight and followed every direction. He had the good sense to know that he was drowning and he wasn't about to throw back the life preserver, whether he liked the color or not.

Within three months, Dean was on his way to connecting his head to his heart. After sitting in group with men who had sex with men, men who had hung out in strip clubs, and men who committed voyeuristic crimes, he finally felt safe enough to get honest about his own sexual behavior. Dean also had a history with prostitutes, both in this country and overseas. As he started to get honest he also came to see that the story he made up about his live-in partner was just that, a story.

Dean was an under-forty, high-ranking employee at a large Seattle corporation. He was enrolled in an MBA program. He was a father of a young son who he co-parented well with his ex-wife. From the outside, Dean presented as a man of high integrity. On the inside, his life was a secret shrouded in shame. The more honest Dean was, the healthier he became. As his life story unfolded, he realized that it was in his best interest to go into a "no-contact" period with both his live-in partner and also his nuclear family. Dean's commitment to his own personal recovery was noteworthy and was held in high regard within the NMS community.

Over the course of the last year, Dean has delivered his disclosure letter to his partner and they have begun to reconcile. He also had to get honest about the truth of this relationship. He was married at the time they partnered. Dean had to get comfortable with the truth that he in fact had an affair. His spin always kept him from touching that word. Today he can claim it with the sadness it deserves.

In the past nine months, Dean has also re-engaged with his mom and step-dad, but certainly at arm's length. By doing his recovery work he has come to see the narcissistic tendencies in his mom. I referred him to the book, *The Object of My Affection Is In My Reflection*, written in 2008 by my friend, Rokelle Lerner, to help him get some knowledge and language about what growing up with that kind of a parent does to a child. Rokelle explains in her book what drives a narcissist when she writes: "They need you and crave what you can give them. They're spoiled and wounded children desperately in need of someone to be in awe of them." When Dean read this he gained some clarity about how he was raised. He also understood his need for some strong personal boundaries when it came to interacting with his mom.

His mom had sought some counseling for herself, and Dean did attend a joint session with his mom and her therapist several months ago. Now it was time for her to return the favor. Dean's intention was to read his mom his Ninth Step amends letter in my office. He felt he needed a safe place to be so vulnerable.

This past Monday it happened. On page 76 of the AA Big Book it reads, "We subjected ourselves to a drastic self-appraisal. Now we go out to our fellows and repair the damage done in the past." After some brief cordial conversation, Dean began to read his letter. It was thorough and fearless. He pointed to his history of lying, dating back as far as he could remember. He took ownership for breaking up his marriage with an affair and how indirectly that stole from his mom's relationship with his now ex-wife, whom she thought of as the daughter she'd never had. He also acknowledged the damage he did to his mom by keeping his child from her during the "no-contact." Dean's letter was very real.

As he read his letter he wept. He was very in touch with his emotions and I was very proud of him. During the past two years, Dean has been able to access his heart. Throughout his reading she sat stoically without any external affect. When I asked her for feedback, she said, "So I still don't understand why you stopped talking to me!" Her lenses only went toward herself. It was all about her reflection. When Dean and I de-briefed he saw clearly her limitations. He also found some measure of redemption for doing this part of the work, proving once again that the process does work, and his mom is still his mom.

The second event happened on Tuesday, both in session and in my new group. About a month ago during an initial session with a new man, Nash, it was clear to me that he had an unhealthy relationship with alcohol. I tend to shy away from focusing on that issue, only because many of the men can't imagine stopping everything at once, and the typical initial focus is to stop the sexual acting-out.

When dealing with alcohol, I always ask new men to stop drinking for thirty days. I do that for two reasons; first, I want to see how much they protest, and second, I tell them that alcohol as a class of drug is a depressant and the last thing they need to be now is more depressed. Then I add that alcohol by definition is a dis-inhibitor and they really don't need to be more disinhibited either. My suggestion usually finds no push-back. But Nash wanted to haggle.

He had only been in Washington State for a few months. He came here for his fiancé while still working out of state. Nash's living/work/relationship situation is horrific and toxic to say the least. His denial about how he sees life is off the chart. I took time during that initial visit to go into great detail about the existing DUI laws in Washington State. The last place I went in my little FYI speech was to money. A DUI in this state, when it is all said and done, will cost in excess of $15,000. That's a very expensive six pack.

This past Tuesday, Nash came to see me for his one-to-one. His latest story started to unfold as our time was winding down. It appeared that just two days before, on Sunday, he had driven to a bar to watch a football game, drank too much and within two blocks of the bar got pulled over, blew a 0.14 Blood-Alcohol Content (BAC) and got hauled off to jail. He called his mom to come get him. Nash's abstinence lasted fourteen days.

As he described the events, he couldn't get off the fact that the police were waiting for people to come out of the bar and that his improper lane change was something that everyone does. He was quite the victim, if you can be a victim with a 0.14. We talked legal aspects for a while, and Nash said that he already had an attorney and he wasn't very concerned with it all. How numb can someone be?

I told Nash that this story needed to be shared in group. He really didn't see how it was anyone's business. After I pushed really hard, he asked me if I could let him tell the group later that night. I was fine with that.

In group, Nash went last. During his check-in he told the story. The men were amazed that he would put himself at risk by being in a bar with his history of picking up women in bars for opportunistic sex. As he started to push back, he revealed there was more to his story then I knew. As it turned out, he had a very toxic interaction with a woman at the bar. He got leaky and told her about being in SLAA and having just cancelled his wedding because of his cheating. The men were floored by it all. Using honesty as a ploy to get laid! And after all the disclosure, she still invited him over to her place! How sick is that!?

Nash comes to this barfly with his resume, she reads the white and not the black and then she wants to hire him! And nowhere to be found in his consciousness was his fiancé, their "no-contact," her pain, or his recovery. When I confronted Nash in group as to why he didn't disclose the part about the woman in the bar in my office earlier in the day, he was flippant and said he didn't have time.

The end of the story was that Nash was very proud of himself for saying no to sex in the bar. He just couldn't understand why everyone was pushing on him so hard about his toxic decisions. Denial is a bitch. He went as far as to say that if he had gone home with his barfly, he never would have gotten the DUI! How about that for distorted logic!

Nash is in his early thirties and still has a bucket of piss and vinegar left in him. I believe that without KeyStone he will not "Get It." He might understand in the future after he gets hurt some more. In my heart, I believe Nash will be gone from NMS and this "Recovery Thing" long before New Year's. I didn't want to be right when I told him about the DUI laws and to stop drinking. I never want to be right. When I'm right, someone is bleeding, whether they know it or not. All I know is that "Hurt People Hurt People." Nash's distorted thinking will end up creating his own self-fulfilling prophecy. But, as I always say, misery is optional.

NOVEMBER 26

NEITHER SNOW NOR RAIN...

Last week I was sitting on the beach in Galveston, Texas getting some much deserved R & R. My wife and I took a long bike ride on the Galveston Seawall overlooking the Gulf of Mexico, strolled the sidewalks in the historic Strand District, and saw a pro basketball game in Houston before heading back to the land of the winter gray. Gray I can handle, but this week was an anomaly weather-wise for sure. On Monday a severe cold front came through, leaving Seattle with uncommon single digit temperatures and four-plus inches of snow. Whenever the weather gets that nasty the city shuts down, but I am a New Yorker and it's just another day on the job in my head, so off I go.

To my amazement all of my appointments showed up. I even started my workday by meeting a new man. As our bright winter sunlight started to turn into the ominous chill of night, five of my new men said they were willing to come to group. I was impressed.

With Galen bailing out after two groups to follow his wife in another direction and two others, Jerry and Kyle, across the country in KeyStone for a thirty-day stay, we were now down to seven. With a commitment from five to show up, I was thrilled.

Addicts make excuses all the time about why they can't make it. I have heard every excuse in the book, from "I had to work late" to "My kid's homework assignment needed to be completed." I always push back. My usual push-back usually sounds like this: "If you had kidney disease and needed kidney dialysis once a week and it was only offered to you on Tuesday nights for three hours, I can guarantee nothing in your life would stop you from coming." How about that for a reality check on what is or is not important?

Yet oftentimes people do not take this disease as seriously as other life threatening illnesses. It is easy to see how recovery can, without all that much thought, go to second place on the to-do list of our lives. On this night five committed and four showed up. They got their weekly dialysis treatment. The bad blood got sucked from their bodies at least for a while.

Kasey, Najeed, Blake and Ernie proved to be the hearty souls who braved the inclement weather to sit in a group of men trying to heal. This was only the third group for these men, so the process is still real new. Our first order of business was to try and process Galen's quick departure from NMS. Their feathers were unruffled. Mainly they expressed fear and sadness, but there wasn't a whole lot of energy about it in the end. I shared with them that I supported Galen three weeks ago, as his wife's resistance to this process was becoming more evident, and agreed that he might be better off following her elsewhere. My Wednesday group had just gotten over this with regard to Owen and that was nine months in. Owen's departure was hard for everyone. This was pretty painless.

Then I gave everyone an update on Jerry and Kyle. They had in fact both made it to KeyStone. I had spoken to both of their primary counselors, giving them my insight as to some of their issues. I filled both of them in on their marriages as I understood them to be. Now all we can do is wait for the KeyStone ten-day communication black-out in order to see where they are when they finally come up for air. I did find out that Jerry arrived at KeyStone hung over from a night of drinking. What a web we weave.

Last week while I was away, I set up for my newest group to do their bye-night with my next newest group in a social setting. Masu of the Wednesday group was nice enough to offer up his home. Altogether there were fifteen men at his house for food and fun. For my Wednesday guys, this mix of groups wasn't new since early in their NMS experience I had set up the same scenario with my older Monday Group. It's the newest guys who always feel like a bunch of social misfits.

Each of the four men reported having a good time and two of the four were able to get honest about how awkward they felt, while the other two had no idea what was going on internally for their recovery brothers. Blake talked about feeling insecure around Masu's nice house. The affluence tweaked him! Najeed talked about the head games he was playing about who would and who would not come up to talk to him. He was creating his own litmus test, except it was all in his head. The Intimacy Disorder was running amuck in my new men. In time, that will pass.

We talked about the upcoming Holiday Party on December 9 and how they needed to push through any discomfort and try to have a good time. Ernie is planning to come with or without his wife. Kasey and his wife are coming, but they are planning to come separately. That is not a unique idea for our crowd.

The final hour was set aside so I could present my "Cycle of Addiction" workshop lecture. Once again, as these new men start to examine their own life history, they start to realize that there is a reason they are here and this is not an accident or a clerical error. At the end, as always, I introduce them to the Meadows and the invitation to attend their own Survivors week. For me it's just planting seeds. Blake is committed to go by April. Najeed has a bed date for KeyStone on December 13. He and my other two will overlap by a week or so. That will mean that three of KeyStone's fifteen beds would be occupied by NMS men. That's a good thing. They will bring their inpatient treatment experience back to group with them and our group will become stronger for it.

As we huddled up to say the Serenity Prayer, I thanked them all for coming in on a night it would have been easy to take a pass. "Neither snow nor rain nor gloom of night stop these couriers from the swift completion of their appointed rounds." That motto is inscribed on the General Post Office building at 8th Avenue and 33rd Street in New York City. I have read it many times in my life. As Keanu Reeves says in a great line from his not very famous movie *Hardball*, "The hardest part of life is showing up." These four men made it to their appointed rounds. They showed up.

~

November's word is illumination. Just having the chance to throw light on the eternal question of "Why" gives a sense of clarity where there was none. Moving towards knowledge, revelation and insight brings a sense of clearing to any man who has been lost for decades. The process of illumination, the movement towards becoming lucid or attaining some wisdom where there was none, lifts one's soul. Standing in the light starts to bring peace.

December

~

Service

DECEMBER 3

TUESDAY

I thought it might be interesting to just re-tell a day, just an ordinary day in the life of NMS. As usual, I am out the door at 9am. Seattle traffic is like flipping a coin in a wind storm, you just never know. I have about five different ways to get to work, and even with the help of the Internet it's still a crapshoot. With my Bluetooth snug in my ear, off I go weaving my way through myriad driving obstacles. My drive time is my time to make and receive phone calls. I'm a captive audience and I do get a lot done that helps me keep up with my life.

Tuesday's first call is usually to Gavin to catch up on what went on in his group on Monday night. For the past three years he has been diligent and more than proficient at running an NMS group for me. He has no formal training other than his own participation in NMS and a wide library of ingested recovery books. I am a firm believer in the gift of peer counseling. To have walked in those shoes is priceless.

Gavin's own recovery has been stellar and he has served as a beacon in our community. He repaired a very broken marriage, and two years ago became a dad for the first time after years of marriage built with many secret compartments. Gavin today says what he means and he means what he says, and he does it all with almost no discernible ego. He is so bright and perceptive that very little gets by him. He is a great fit for my non-micromanaging style.

One of the pieces that really made this work is that six of his seven men had gone to KeyStone. That is the highest number of men in one group in our history, and the seventh man did a week at the Meadows. With that much "treatment" in the room the group can almost run itself. They know how to hold each other accountable and that makes Gavin's job so much easier.

The latest ongoing issue belongs to Kelly. He's great, I love him, but his fear of real life is getting in his way. We have walked hand-in-hand with him through a very messy divorce. His ex was living with another guy before the marital bed was cold and, in the middle of it all, was his little son. It was ugly. In his honesty, Kelly disclosed that ten years ago while they were both drunk and she was wailing on him—he's six-feet, seven-inches and 250 pounds—he pushed his wife down. After the lawyers got through with him he was being forced, via blackmail, not via the courts, to seek domestic violence treatment in order to increase his parenting time with his son. Like I said, it was ugly.

With all his recovery work and domestic violence work, Kelly just doesn't trust women much these days and I can't really blame him. Now, one year after the legal mess is over, he has a distorted view of dating. He equates "dating" with marriage, divorce, losing half his money, child support, and the court system. Kasey's divorce left a bad taste in his mouth, but the thought of living a monastic life is not very appealing to him either.

The present day conundrum is around women. Kelly hasn't acted out in any of his bottom-lines in years. He's a good man with a bad past. He's too moral for a string of one night stands, yet he's afraid to date to mate. He thought his answer was to try to find a "Friend with Benefits" which he has supposedly found, but as with most women, she is really looking for more. Kasey gets hung up in word games. They have been together for over four months, but Kelly will not say he is dating nor that he has a girlfriend. He only sees her and is not open to seeing other women. Kelly believes she's not the one, and he is being honest with her about his intentions, and yet I am sure that she is just marking time trying to wear him down. It's a mess. That call to Gavin lasted from 9:07am until 9:42am.

By then I was getting close to my office. It'd been a bad traffic day but I was good. Then I get a call from my ten o'clock telling me he'll be a little late. I'm good with that; I'll have time to read a sports section, drink my coffee and sit for a minute.

Tyler shows up with his boyish good looks and a bag full of stories about his crazy wife. He's new at this. I've known him for three months and he's been in my new group twice. Tyler's wife is now seeing Hilarie and attending the new women's group but is so hurt and in so much pain that her behavior is toxic. We have seen it before.

They are both under thirty and they have two children, each under two. She caught him in multiple affairs and she wants to be his mom, cop, counselor, sponsor, and executioner. Tyler's trying, but this fire is not about to go out any time soon. He has little or no ability to create a boundary with her of any kind. Her illness has taken her in a downward spiral driving her to locate one of his tryst partners and confront "The Slut" face-to-face. She just can't seem to stop.

When they met, Tyler told her that he had had sex with over 150 women and had cheated on every girlfriend he had ever had. She read the white and not the black of the resume he handed her. Now she wonders why Prince Charming can't be faithful. We have seen this all before. A "no-contact" would be in order just to get them out of each other's face and space for a while, but with those two little ones it's a hard call. In a perfect world he'd be in KeyStone.

I got Tyler hooked up with Sam as a sponsor and that seems to be working out well. Tyler and his wife had both gone to their first speaker's meeting this past Saturday night as Toby shared his recovery with almost 100 people. He thanked his wife for doing her own recovery and helping them get a new language. Tyler's wife didn't seem to catch that fact in the two hour discussion that she demanded following Toby's presentation.

Tyler is crawling on eggshells with his wife, not walking. I have to try to get her to back up. I tried to help him with some new language to "Back her up" and suggested to him to have her call me. We had a good session. He has willingness but he's in a pressure cooker to say the least. I gave Tyler a reading/writing assignment with some exact instructions as to what to share and what not to share with his wife. We'll see if he can keep it. I told him to make some calls and I would see him again tonight in group.

I literally had three minutes before the next session, just enough time to scarf down a hardboiled egg and slice a persimmon, all the while checking my voice messages, just trying to catch my breath and clean house all at the same time. This is just an average day.

Tuesday noon to 2pm session. This appointment has been in the book a long time, and is one I am not looking forward to at all. This is our bi-monthly couple's coaching session with Will and his wife Vanna. The process is getting down to crunch time and I've used up all the tricks and tools I have at my disposal to keep both of them in the game. We are definitively in the fourth quarter of this contest.

Will came to see me in May of last year. He had already moved out and his wife had given him a "Honey Do" list of how to make things right with the marriage. On the list was for him to go to the Meadows. She loves to do research on the Internet. She thought it would help. When I met Will and he showed me her list, I told him that the Meadows is a good thing, but I get to tell him when it's the right time, not his wife. I was clear that she was not going to write his treatment plan for him, so the Meadows went away at least for the time being. I didn't get to meet her until the first of this year. There is some contention as to whether Will really did try to invite her into recovery. Last year she and I did have two short phone conversations and I know she also called Hilarie twice. It appeared she didn't want any part of NMS but the truth is probably somewhere in between.

Will's method for relationship is to use logic and minutia to wear his wife down in hopes of controlling the situation. In the ten years of marriage this strategy has crippled her spirit. As it appeared last fall that her marriage was spiraling out of control, she met a man who took her mind off the chaos and paid some attention to her. What started out as intrigue ended up in an affair, and she didn't really even like him. It had all the elements of revenge.

Will was able to follow her every move through snooping via phone records, text messages and emails. He is very tech savvy. As the evidence mounted, he was on his way out the marriage door. She was seeing a therapist about her childhood trauma, but continued to act out in this tryst. Will managed to go with Vanna once to see her counselor where he confronted her there with all the evidence minus the "Kodak Moment." She told him she was done with that man, but the very next weekend went back into his arms. Both their worlds were spinning out of control and all this at the expense of Vanna's oldest teen daughter from a prior relationship and their pre-school girl.

As the year ended, I was finally ready to send Will to the Meadows. He came back with some clarity but still not a lot of effect. Divorce was looming large and he was at an emotional dead-end. It was at that point that Vanna called me and came in this past January.

Vanna was clear from the beginning that she was not seeing me to save her marriage. She was very outspoken that she was doing this to save her life. She had become suicidal and she believed she needed a full course of five weeks at the Meadows. Even though I was clear she was suffering from severe PTSD, I wanted her to go to Cottonwood. I would leave it to Rokelle to make the next treatment call. Vanna jumped into the deep end of the recovery pool in a blink. I hooked her up with Beth as a sponsor and she became willing to go to any lengths to get well. She saw me every week and we started to examine the layers of her life's onion. All the while my goal was to get Will to stay still.

It has been an amazing eleven month ride with them. They both did their own disclosure letters, their own cost letters and their own empathy letters. She is a wonderful writer and can really emote with passion. After Vanna read Will her disclosure letter about her affair, she was writhing in self-loathing and pain. I looked at her and told her that she was never going to have to hike her skirt up again to get someone to love her. She can speak from her heart. She heard my words.

Will, on the other hand, tries but has yet to make the journey from his head to his heart. Vanna has gone deep into step-work and is healing every day. Will had been stagnant in his step-work, still on Step Four at the one-year mark. As she started to heal, she started to want more of him. They were in a "no-contact" for a very long time and haven't lived together for a year and a half. About three months ago I pushed them out of the "no-contact" and asked them to date each other.

Back in August, Will made a commitment to go back to the Meadows for Survivors II in December and to complete his Fourth Step by year-end. Vanna goes to five to seven meetings a week and believes in the power of the Steps. In short order she had passed him by. Now her recovery health makes her demand more from a husband. She believes that the kindness she needs is not in Will for him to give. She is unwavering. Last week she laid down a "Deal-Breaker": if he was not willing to go to some kind of month-long inpatient treatment to deal with his contempt for her that pre-dates her affair, his constant state of righteous indignation and his internal and external rage, she will divorce him. Today's meeting was for him to give her an answer.

I have been ambivalent concerning this point in the process. I usually recommend people for inpatient treatment to stop acting-out behavior, not to make a man a better husband. I believe that all of the men could benefit from that kind of intensive work but I'm not even sure where I would send him. Will hasn't acted out on his bottom-line behavior in over a year, but he just doesn't have a high emotional IQ and now she loves herself enough to finally select who she is married to instead of just settling.

The couple showed up in the session with maturity and discipline. They both showed up with their highest and best selves. In the end Will said that he was going to follow the recovery plan that has been in place since August and that if the Meadows suggests more work he will be open to it. He is leaving this weekend for Arizona. Vanna was sad that he wasn't willing to just give her four weeks of his life. She stated that she is going to see a divorce attorney this week, but again reiterated that she will move heaven and earth to make it work—money and child care-wise if Will decides to stay and get more help. In the end everyone could breathe again as we all bought a little reprieve.

If in the end their marriage does not make it, I will be sad. I like them and they are both trying so hard to repair what had been destroyed so many years before. By the end of the session I was spent emotionally. Two sessions down and two to go; my day was only half done, so to speak.

My lunch was scarfed down standing up. I did manage to check my phone before calling Damon into my room. He's been coming for three months and I really like this young man. The deck is so stacked against him, but he can be honest and vulnerable and I love him for that. At 300+ pounds, he certainly has a physical presence, but internally he is very small and very fragile.

The first thing we talked about is the fact that his wife, Norma, finally made it to see Hilarie. After she signed a release of information form, Hilarie told me that twenty minutes into her session she recommended inpatient treatment. Damon's wife is bipolar and suffering from PTSD. The two of them together are a mess but she showed up and wants to continue. Hilarie referred Norma to a colleague of ours who is down the hall in our building, Elaine Duncan, who has been trained in EMDR, a technique used to help trauma clients. Even though I know she needs it, I thought that the referral was a bit premature. Norma needs a women's support group just like the one Damon has with the men. In that way she can start getting into her own recovery to deal with her extreme love addiction. Simply stated, Damon is Norma's entire universe and that puts pressure on Damon to not go to meetings, to not go to fellowship and to not make phone calls. She has to stop making Damon her "IT" for either one of them to heal.

Hilarie agreed and is going to continue seeing Norma, putting a hold on the EMDR work. Hopefully she will be open to reaching out to women for support. She has agreed to accompany Damon to our annual Holiday party next week.

Damon is able to be empathetic and a little challenging with the men in his group. I pushed him a little about Blake, a group member who over the last almost three years has lost over 200 pounds working a 12-Step program for his eating disorder. Blake has reached out to Damon about the food issue but he has not responded. I did get Damon to agree to go with Blake to one of his Food Addiction (FA) meetings. That kind of willingness is at least a start, a first step for change.

The two hours flew by. He is a very affable young man. The prognosis is highly guarded to say the least. He still sees life through the lenses of his wife's pain. A huge piece of him just wants to fix her first. I'm glad he keeps showing up.

My 4:00pm-5:30pm slot was for a first-time guy. We talked on the phone a few days ago. I'm never really sure if any new guy will show. This is a very scary topic to broach with anyone. As I opened my door I saw him sitting there waiting nervously. As I went out into the lobby to shake his hand and introduce myself he stood up, and indeed he did, all six-foot five-inches of him.

After he found a seat in my office I said "I'm guessing six-five?" and he said I was right. I went on to tell him that I used to guess heights for a living. He looked at me oddly when I said that. After a brief explanation I asked him if he ever played basketball and he said no. I make up that he must hear that question a lot. He told me that he was only five-foot eight-inches in high school, and played a little baseball but never basketball. We quickly moved on. His name is Conrad and he is in his early thirties. He told me that his wife of one year was serving him with divorce papers the next day. I could see through the shell-shocked response of numb that he was hurting.

I did manage to make Conrad laugh a little but it was hard. His wife's extreme response to his behavior that appears to be marginal acting-out in my world leaves me with more questions than answers. He moved here from California to go to a local university fifteen years ago and never left, yet he doesn't have any friends. Conrad is now trying to find himself professionally by attending a post-graduate program.

Conrad is truly lost inside his own head. I briefly explained NMS to him and invited him to come back in ninety minutes for his first group session. I really think he just didn't know where else to go. He has been living in a hotel for two weeks. With an internal neon sign on that screams in huge letters "broken" he agreed to come back. As I shook his hand I said to him, "you're going to have to start to trust someone at some time, it might as well be me and it might as well be now!" I was hoping he'd come back as I took my dinner break.

Tuesday night group 6:30pm to 9:30pm. With two group members in KeyStone, we were down to eight counting the new guy, Conrad. As each of the other men filtered in, I introduced them one by one to Conrad. By 6:45pm, we were ready to start. I changed protocol and had each man tell a little story of who they are and how they got there. I wanted Conrad to know that I had put him in the right room, and indeed I had, and I think he knew it. He told a little of his story mostly in vague broad strokes but it was enough for him to find commonality with everyone, and everyone with him.

I started by getting feedback on what they all got out of Toby's talk from the speakers meeting last Saturday. For a couple of them it was their first speaker's meeting and the first time that they saw the SLAA community in such large numbers. Tyler talked about the grilling he got on the ride home. They left immediately after Toby was finished instead of hanging around and going to fellowship. His wife didn't want any part of it even though there were women from her group there.

We spent a lot of time on Nash again. He shared how he had broken the "no-contact" with his fiancé Nora and invited her over for Thanksgiving dinner. I already knew that, and I knew that she had spent the night in his bed, supposedly nonsexual. Then they put it out for the entire community by showing up to the speaker's meeting together. He was just adamant that it was his decision alone and he didn't need to follow any of these imposed rules. I asked him whether he told her about the DUI or the girl in the bar, during all that time they spent together, and his answer was no, it didn't come up. That's Nash.

The other guys didn't have enough recovery mettle to hold Nash's feet to the proverbial fire. I didn't push very hard, I didn't want to run him off. All the men did a check-in and in the final hour I did another workshop lecture. This week's workshop was on the "Iceberg of Addiction." Many of them really could see how the diagram matched their life.

We finished the group session by again welcoming Conrad to the group.

I encouraged all the men to call him this week and then we circled up for our version of the Serenity Prayer. Instead of holding hands we put our arms around each other's shoulders. Then we each placed our right foot into the circle (because we don't want to be left behind!) and said the prayer, "God, grant me the Serenity to accept the things I cannot change, the courage to change the things I can and the wisdom to know the difference."

Afterwards, Nash wanted a minute of my time before leaving. Standing in my lobby as I was preparing to leave, he wanted to know why I had not set him up with a sponsor the way I had some of the other men. I started by defining what that relationship would look like, and then asking him why I would want to set him up to fail, since he is driven by self-will; and I asked him why I would do that to one of my alumni, knowing that whomever I pick will be trying harder than Nash would. I didn't believe Nash would do any work and at best, he was just going orbit us. He wanted me to validate that he was doing good recovery, but I wouldn't do it. What a dope-fiend move, a classic bait-and-switch. I didn't blink. I told him his recovery wasn't about me at all and that it was all about him. We left the dialogue there. It was 10:00pm when I walked out the door. I felt good about group and very tired.

On the ride home my phone rang. It was Nash's fiancé Nora. She is struggling with knowing what to do. She changed her entire life for this man, moving to Seattle from LA to marry him and start a new life and it is starting to sink in that's it's all a lie. Not too bad for a twenty-five year-old. She announced that she is giving Nash back his ring and that's she done. I commended her for her strength. I also cautioned her that just because she says it's over doesn't necessarily mean that Nash will go quietly into the night. My vote is no. His false pride and huge ego will probably drive him to try to get her back. I told her that if he does make a run at her she should use the KeyStone card; it's Nash's only chance. She is a brave young woman dazed and confused. I told her to keep me in the loop. I pulled into my drive way at 10:45pm

Kissing my wife hello I was back in my world—a great marriage, great family and great blessings. Within forty-five minutes it was lights out trying to shut down all the chatter in my head. Tuesday is done, tomorrow the fight continues.

P.S. Nash didn't call a single man the rest of the week to tell them he had been fired as a partner. No man is an island.

DECEMBER 10

'TIS THE SEASON

I can bet the farm on it. On the second Thursday in December it will rain and the traffic will be horrible. It's a given, but also what is a given is that members of our NMS community will dress up and fight the elements to show up at our annual Holiday Party. This year was no exception.

The weather wasn't nearly as bad this year as it was for the party of 2007. That day here in Seattle, we experienced what has become known as the "Hanukah Windstorm." People died, power was lost for many in the area, and there were terrible traffic jams coupled with a surge of flooding that turned a thirty-minute commute into a four hour ordeal. It was a mess. Yet through it all, sixty-six brave hearts made it for a night of community and fun, not to mention heat and electricity. Now that was a night to remember!

The party in 2006 had a different name. I have said throughout this book that my men suffer from an Intimacy Disorder which translates into a ton of fear about being in a social setting, especially without alcohol. Since I chose the date for the party a year in advance, I try my best to make it very difficult for any man to come up with an excuse as to why he can't come. Yet some will always try. My job is to try to take away their run card.

Back in 2006 we had a member named Luther who had blown up a marriage seventeen years earlier and continued to blow up his life by sexually acting-out. He had an elaborate denial system wrapped around his distorted world view of Christianity. To make a long story short, Luther told me he would not come to a holiday party because he did not want to participate in any event that would be "Taking the 'Christ' out of Christmas." He was headstrong even in the face of our Jewish and non-believing members. It sounded strong with conviction but it was far afield from the morals he demonstrated in his life on a daily basis. I believed it was a smoke screen for his Intimacy Disorder.

I decided to take another approach. I asked Luther if he would attend a Fourth of July party if we had one and he answered with a resounding yes. Then I asked him the same question about Labor Day, Memorial Day and Thanksgiving and again he affirmed he would attend. Then I asked him about a New Year's Eve Party and again he said he would come, so I made an executive decision and re-named our party the "Pre 2007 New Year's Eve Party"! I took his "out" away. He did come and he actually had a good time in spite of himself.

With each party comes its own set of drama and trauma. It's hard for people to set aside their crap for just one night to have fun. At last year's party, Keith and his wife Elaine had a fight on the car ride to the party and it escalated in the parking lot. When Elaine walked in she was crying and a mess. That was last year; this year they were happy as a clam and grateful to be there.

Last year one of my newest guys at the time, Will, put on an amazing juggling act during our open-mic segment. He was awesome. This year he was not at the party, but was at the Meadows going through the Survivors II retreat. Last year Will attended our party alone. He was in the middle of a "no-contact" with a wife I had not met since Will arrived in mid-May. Now Vanna was here and in a leadership role for women working their own SLAA Program. How things have changed for them in just a year!

Our crowd was once again late arriving; traffic as usual was a mess. It took Troy two hours to get there from the Eastside, but he came. It also took Hilarie over two hours. By 7pm our count was up to forty, so I told the caterers to start dinner. By 7:15pm we were up to sixty-five.

At 7:30pm I started my annual speech which I jokingly call the "State of the Union" address. The speech is a time for us to reflect on some of the high and low points of the past year. I always start by saying that I am sure that ten of you will not be here next year and that another ten to fifteen will be, even though I haven't met them yet. Attrition is a scary aspect of this program. I continue on by saying that this year we lost nine men. Of the nine, one man, Matt, had been here over four years and another, Kirby, was with us almost two. Last year Kirby cracked us all up with a ten minute comedy routine. I guess he got cured.

All of the other seven men who quit NMS were with us less than nine months, and one was with us for less than a month. I read their names out loud and we take a moment to pray for them and remember why we are still here. That's an AA tradition.

We also grew in number by thirteen as I shared about starting a new group that is already at ten. Then I had them stand so we could acknowledge them. Other than the three current members in treatment, we only had two men not attend. Kelly had his son that night and then there was Nash. He claimed he had to stay in LA for work but my guess is that his Intimacy Disorder got to him, not to mention the DUI legal mess he had here. Besides his now ex, Nora, was at the party.

From there I talked about our newest alumni group that graduated in June. I had them stand for some recognition. I combined that with the fact that we had sixteen of the twenty active alumni there. Chuck and Danny are both recently home from the hospital where they both had major surgery. This was the first missed party for both of them. Neil had told me he had a conflict a while back and Edward had to attend his own work holiday party. I am so proud that sixteen of twenty men chose to come back. Hugo and Craig also once again lent their musical talent to our house band, which they started six years ago.

I then talked about my women's group and how much it meant to me to have six women trust me with their secrets. Sophie just couldn't bear to bring herself back to the party where she had been four other times with her soon to be ex-husband. She did say that she would come back next year. Teresa was going to come until child care fell through at the last minute. Her husband Kevin did come.

I talked about our collective blessings. Craig and his wife became parents of a baby boy and Darryl and his wife became parents of a baby girl. Sam is back home now living with his wife, Zoe, and the same is true for Dante now living with his partner, Tonia. We have four men who have re-partnered this year with new women; Ellis was there with a date, and Eddie was here with his first-time girlfriend. Caleb's and Trent's partners couldn't make it.

I gave a shout out to Hilarie who this year spoke in China and Spain on Internet addiction. The "Atta boys!" continued for Quinn who is giving Jerry—who is currently in KeyStone—a safe place to live. A collective ongoing thanks to Keenan and Stan from Monday night for driving our "old man" Shane to group every week. Shane will turn ninety-three next month.

I talked about the five couples who are trying to repair their partnerships: Dean and Jessica, Larry and his wife Nan, Masu and Dolores, Will and Vanna, and Keith and Elaine.

I told a cute and funny story about Kevin throwing a surprise fiftieth birthday party for his wife Teresa. What makes it funny is that Kevin had to lie, deceive and manipulate to make it work. A day before the party, Teresa called me up at a DEFCON 1 level of fear, telling me that she was sure that Kevin was cheating on her again because he was being secretive. I had to talk her off the divorce ledge without blowing his cover for the surprise. Fortunately they had a couples session with me planned in a few days. All I told Teresa was that if divorcing Kevin is a good idea today it will be a good idea on Tuesday. I told her to find her "pause button" and wait. The next night with fifty people in attendance, including her parents who flew in from another state, it all made sense to her and she had nothing but appreciation and gratitude for her husband.

The last announcement was huge. After dating for three years, Carl and Margo are going to get married in July. Another NMS wedding! This is the first marriage for Carl, who is over fifty. He got up and said a few kind words about his journey out of shame to a life of grace. His fiancé then got up to the mic and said how grateful she was for NMS giving her a healthy and caring man. It was very touching. Looks like I'm going to get a chance to dance at another NMS wedding.

For me the highlight of my annual talk is when I give out our efficacy stats. Over the past decade we have had nearly 200 men in NMS. Of these, we graduated forty-four, of which thirty-five are still active. One man moved to Mexico. Another, Patrick, has made church his recovery home. Keenan and Alex stay solely in the MKP world, and Ivan died unexpectedly on September 11, 2008 at the young age of sixty-five.

We have thirty current members of NMS in four working groups. Four members left the program when they moved out of state for work. If you crunch the numbers, over forty percent of all the men ever in NMS are still connected to our program. If you compare that to the national rates of success for an inpatient alcohol and drug treatment center, which is at about fifteen percent, we are doing really well. NMS really is making a difference in people's lives.

Every year I bring a huge poster of Ivan and hang it up for all to see. I share about him and how much I miss him. Every year at our party Ivan, with his booming baritone voice, would sing the Louie Armstrong classic, "What a Wonderful World" and stop the show. At this point, the band plays it and we all well up, remembering our late, great recovery brother.

I ended my speech by thanking my wife for all her support and her willingness to tolerate my long work days. I am clear I could never do this without her. Then I go on to thank Hilarie and Ida for the work they do with the women in the program. Lastly, I take time to acknowledge the work that Gavin does every Monday night with his men's group. His clarity about this illness, his ability to bring God into the room, and his gift of compassion, make him a wonderful peer facilitator. I am blessed to have someone I can trust with this calling.

After I finished talking, I turned the room over to Troy who was about to create our annual group photo, this time with seventy-seven people, no small task. It's great watching Troy take charge, telling people what tables to move and what chairs need to go where. After about twenty minutes of arranging and rearranging we somehow miraculously found our way into this moment of simultaneous joy now captured for posterity. It should be up on my wall with all of the other years' holiday party group pictures before the year is out, and everyone sitting in this picture knows exactly where this picture is going! In full view for anyone to see who comes into my office. No More Secrets!

Now it was time for the entertainment. Over the years our house band has been comprised of a wide range of present and former NMS members. Back in '05 and '06 we had a sax player, Cameron, who was a graduate of Julliard and toured the world professionally. To me he always sounded like Jason Sanborn. From '05 to '07 we had a drummer who had played in bands since he was fourteen and wrote a great song about NMS; sorry to say that when he left NMS he took his song with him.

This was the first year we didn't have any horns and last year was the first year we didn't have a drummer, but the sound was still outstanding. This year one of Ida's women, Daniela, stepped up to play a great conga and add some back-up vocals. I was amazed by her talent.

Craig, along with Eddie, stepped out of the band to do an open-mic classical piece. Craig is such a gifted violinist that his melodic play fills a very silent room. Minister Luke played a guitar solo and sang. He played a "non-churchie" song about spirit and light. Gavin surprised everyone with his soft guitar and vocal adaptation of The Beatles classic, "Black Bird."

For me, of the eleven performers, the one that surprised me the most was Stan's show, and boy what a show it was. Stan is a gruff, kindhearted Bostonian with an edge. He has never performed at any of the other three parties. I wasn't even aware he wanted to give it a go at all, so when he stepped up he got everyone's attention. He started by weaving his journey into NMS and recovery with taking risks and doing things he said he would never do. As he continued on in his story he shared with us that over thirty-five years ago as a high school senior he was the only boy who had a beard in his school, so the drama people came and asked him if he would play Tevye the Milkman in their production of *Fiddler on the Roof*. Stan said it was the best experience he had in high school—and that includes being a star football player. It was at that point that he announced he would sing, "If I Were a Rich Man" with tambourine in hand all by himself. He was transformed back in time, accent and all. He even threw in a little hip-wiggle during the chorus. As the song hit its crescendo, his booming voice made every jaw in the house drop, woo…what an experience.

Evan wrote and read a poem based on his Fourth Step about his relationship to time. Elaine and her group mate Dianne played a game of "Character Defect Charades" with the audience; it was a hoot. Keith brought in a kids' book that he had designed as a learning guide for the Grand Canyon. Cam did a whistle and soft *a capella* song combo. The final hit performance of the night was Ida leading a sing-along with some of contemporary music's best sex and love addicts songs. It was so funny and telling. She did end by saying that her last song was my favorite: "Bend me, shape me, anyway you want me, as long as you love me it's alright!"

This venue gives so many of us a chance to show a side of us that we would never see sitting in my men's group or a SLAA meeting. It is always amazing to me just how talented we are collectively as a group of people when we are not in our active addiction or sitting in a barrel full of shame.

With about forty-five minutes left in the night I looked up and saw that one of our missing alumni, Edward, had just walked in with his wife from his company party. It was such a nice surprise to see him. Many of the people in the room did not know Edward since he spends most of his recovery work in MKP these days. I shared about how we met. Edward had, at the time, the unique distinction in NMS history of being the only member who I welcomed into NMS sight unseen.

It's been nearly a decade since I got a call from KeyStone asking me if I would talk to this guy about coming into my program. Edward was under thirty at the time and was from northern California. It was clear to KeyStone that he could not go back home. He really didn't have anywhere else to go and I had a client in KeyStone with him at the time. After talking to Edward on the phone, I told him to come here and we would get him a place to stay and that he would be safe. Now years later, he is stable, married, employed and a stepdad. He never did leave Seattle. His smile says it all. What a gift for me to witness. Over eighty-five percent of our alumni were in attendance that night. At the end of the day, wow!

By 11pm only a handful of people were left. The band was packing up and we all just couldn't figure out a way to not have this night end. I'm sure as I process everyone's experience at the party over the course of the next week I'll get to hear about all the subterranean bullshit that was not visible to the naked eye. When you put a group of seventy-seven hyper-sensitive people in one place, feelings come up and people get challenged. It comes with the territory. Picasso said that, "Art never is chaste." Neither is recovery.

Home, hearth, holiday and a Hallmark card, *It's a Wonderful Life* and "Tis the season" all wrapped up in five hours. Not pure by any means, but in the end we did a hell of a job and had one great growth opportunity. NMS, we rock!

DECEMBER 17

WIVES AND LOVERS

We have four men currently in inpatient treatment, three at KeyStone and one at the Meadows doing their full treatment program. Three of the four men have wives. Two of the four men are dads. When a man leaves the family for a month, the family is forced to reconfigure in order to survive. Some do it better than others. This installment is about the women connected to the men. Recovery does not happen in a vacuum or a cocoon. As their stories unfold, the future history of their family unfolds with it. Sometimes the multi-generational influence of this exact moment in time is very hard to see, especially in the middle of a very large and scary trauma. Some see it better than others.

Will and Vanna were at a crossroads. His recovery had plateaued even though he had long term sexual sobriety from his very limited bottom-line list. Will's manifestation of this illness is so hard to see. Once the porn and masturbation went away, we addressed his incessant snooping. He settled into a new language of recovery but not with a lot of internal change. The more work Vanna did, the more she wanted a kinder, nicer, more thoughtful husband, to the point that she was willing to end the marriage if he did not go to an inpatient treatment center. I warned her that I did not know of a treatment center designed to make a man a better husband. Will was committed to go to the Survivors II five-day retreat at the Meadows for more introspection. As he left for his week, Vanna went to see a divorce lawyer. The situation was reaching an ugly crescendo as he left for treatment.

I could understand what Vanna was feeling and I could see Will's reluctance to just capitulate to her demands. My stance was that he should go to the five day retreat and let the treatment team at the Meadows determine the next phase of Will's treatment. The Meadows is a top of the line facility and I could stand by their recommendation. By the fourth day of his projected five day stay, they suggested to Will that he stay for their full treatment program for love addiction. Will did his usual and excruciating examination and cost-benefit process and finally decided to "Just Do It." He is such a micro-manager of life, his own and Vanna's, that it is very difficult for him to just let go of control. This was a huge step for Will.

Two weeks prior, Vanna was pleading to Will in my office that he should go to an inpatient treatment center in order to get well and save the marriage. She proclaimed that she would move heaven and earth to help make it happen, both around money and childcare. As Will now informed me of his decision and his doubts, I assured him that Vanna would live up to her word; this was a clear case of be careful of what you wish for, you may get it!

I can't count the number of text messages I got from Will and the calls from Vanna, all concerning the minutia of his decision. Because Will had completed Survivors II, his stay was going to be four more weeks including a family week. Left inside his own head, Will made all sorts of plans as I just listened and watched him spin. At one point he wanted to have his parents come with Vanna for the family component. After seeking some guidance, he finally settled on just Vanna coming out. His parents are not going to divorce him even if he doesn't get well. The focus has to be on the marriage.

Vanna called me yesterday upset by the tenor of the email invite she received from Will. It sounded cold, as if he was just being a good soldier, not personal enough for her to want to uproot her kindergartener during Christmas. Now I needed to talk her down off of her ledge. In the end, Vanna has decided to attend family week and to even bring their child on visiting day.

Will now has some hope, and Vanna now has some resolve to continue on. I keep telling them both that they have to play the entire hand out, they have to put all their cards on the table, and nobody folds. They both need to do this. It says it all in the SLAA Basic Text on page 38, "The only standard for 'success', considering my past history, would be that I was now really *present* [italics in original] in the relationship, minus addictive distractions. If we were to get back together, I could now discover what was, and was not, there. If we were incompatible, I knew that I would be able to leave the relationship without regret, and without the agony of irresolution and guilt over 'how things might have been different if only I had tried harder'." I am hoping they make it, as I am very fond of the both of them. But the one thing I am sure of is that they are both going to show up for the dance.

One of the two men at KeyStone with a wife is Jerry. He is thirty-seven and Sally is thirty. They have been together for six years and they do not have any children. His behavior blew up their relationship and landed him in KeyStone. I always am amazed when a woman stays to try to do this work when she does not have any children to factor into her decision-making process. Kids tend to make a woman stay. It would seem to make sense that a wife would just "Cut and Run," but Sally is committed to roll the recovery dice. On Tuesday she went out to KeyStone to receive a disclosure letter from her husband that would have devastated most women. She did have a lot of information before disclosure after finding his Internet account showing porn and the type of sex workers he likes to hire.

She sought a ton of help on her trip out. She called me from Philadelphia after both sessions. It was suggested to her that she not go out to eat with him when they give her that option after disclosure, and she didn't. She held the boundary and her hurt into the next day when he asked for a hug and she declined, not in anger but in the clarity of honoring her own feelings. Sally's three months of living alone plus, going to Hilarie's group while attending SLAA, has taught her how she wants to be treated, where she starts, and where she stops. I told her Thursday night that I am watching her go from a girl to a woman.

Jerry will be home on Wednesday and go back to living with Quinn. He sounded great on the phone today with a ton of acceptance and surrender. I have hope for them both. The Clinical Director told me how solid and well prepared Sally was for her two days there. It seems that not all of the women come out with such a clear vision.

The other man in KeyStone is Kyle who is over forty, married, and has two sons, ages ten and four. His wife Lindy has been resistant to this process and has been in Hilarie's group only a few times with little or no openness. I have had collectively about three hours of phone conversation with her, and the best way to describe her is that she is "Consistently Inconsistent." She's a "Herding Cats" woman I have described before. She has very little ego strength and her own pathology really prohibits her from fully participating in any kind of meaningful or difficult dialogue. I am totally exhausted by our talks. Throughout his entire time in KeyStone and from before Kyle went, Lindy has refused to go out to get disclosure, even though Sally from her very own group was going and she wouldn't have to go alone. The prognosis for any real substantive change is highly guarded.

Kyle has seemingly made some progress there, but when it comes to his wife, he is still a co-conspirator in the dysfunction of their marriage. Both he and Jerry come home on Wednesday. Even at this late date, I have no idea how life for Kyle and his wife will look. Both KeyStone and NMS are on board with them doing a hard "no-contact." Quinn has agreed to let Kyle stay there along with Jerry, but I believe that either Lindy or Kyle or both of them will sabotage any real "no-contact," any real change in the way they do business, at least initially. I pray I am wrong, but I have seen this dynamic before in very sick couples.

After examining three different couples, three different women and three very different points on the spectrum, all I can think of is a quote from Plato: "The God of Love lives in a state of Need." Romantic love is one of the most addictive substances on earth. Faulkner profoundly said, "The past is not dead, it's not even the past!"

A little FYI. Since a conversation I had before the Holiday party with Nash about how his work was going to interfere with his attendance at our party, neither I nor any of his group members have heard from him. His jilted fiancé, Nora, after many late night calls to me, finally came to see me this week. I can clearly see how denial works in the frontal lobe of a twenty-five year-old. She is at day fifteen of a self-imposed "no-contact" with Nash, attempting to get over being stood up five days before her wedding. Her answer to her emotional rawness was to tell me that she has a date for Saturday night with a "Hot Guy" and she is dropping out of group. She just wants to move on! She believes that a "transitional object" might just be the answer to her pain. I hope she doesn't have to experience a transitional baby or transitional STD. They last a lifetime. Nora's need to be loved, adored and admired is driving her to capricious decision making, but after all she is just twenty-five!

Sometime in the next fifteen years, before she hits forty and her looks start to fade, her life will most likely blow up again, but this time with two kids and a much larger mess. I hope I am wrong; again, whenever I am right someone is bleeding. But for now she is sure she knows best about what she is doing. She should take a hint from Emily Dickenson when she said "Parting is all we need to know of Hell." I will pray for Nora.

DECEMBER 24

LAST GROUP OF THE YEAR

As we all retreat into the throes of the holidays, I want to share about the only group I ran this week. I gave three of the four groups the next two weeks off. I did, however, have my newest group meet on Tuesday. It's just not wise for them to go three weeks without meeting.

We had six men in attendance. Three of our group members, Jerry, Kyle, and Najeed, are in KeyStone. Nash has gone away quietly into the night, so that left us with six. We have two new men who will join us in January, capping the group at ten. Ralph attended the Holiday party and has started to meet some men, while Edwin had only come to see me on Monday before he left town for the holidays. His first introduction to everyone will be in our first group back after the New Year on January 4.

They are all so raw, they are all so broken, and yet they are each pushing their own comfort levels to practice this thing I call intimacy. In the short time this group has been together I can see progress, and that gives me hope for the future. I know that when my three KeyStone guys return to group their openness will push the others even more.

Blake, Damon, Ernie, Kasey, Conrad and Tyler were all glad to be there. You could see the camaraderie they all felt for each other. I had arranged for Jerry and Kyle to call in from KeyStone for a phone check-in. The group loved hearing from them. Conrad had never met them, but even he chimed in. Najeed is still on black out and could not participate. After the call ended we got going in our group. I spent some time talking about relapse and the holidays. Blake, Damon and Conrad have been struggling. Darryl shared about having had a phone interview for a company based out of state that, if he got the job, he would have to relocate. That thought scares us all.

Darryl is so emotionally fragile and his wife is even worse. They would both be so over their heads, 2,000 miles from home and without support. The plan is for them to also take her toddler who she has never been a full time mom for, all while she demands that Damon meet all of her emotional needs. What a prescription for disaster, yet as broke as they are, he has to continue moving forward. Their prognosis is highly guarded. We all voiced our collective concern. Now we just have to sit back and wait for it to unfold.

Tyler, who I have dubbed "Hip, Slick and Quick" is currently out of the marital bed but he is counting on his wife's love addiction to kick back in any day. He's been the yo-yo in her "Go away I hate you, come back I can't be without you" game. It's ugly to watch but it is so predictable. We have seen it all before many times by many couples over the years.

Tyler has a commitment in place to either get a bed date to go to KeyStone by January 1 or to be out of the house. He is hedging his bets that neither will happen. He really needs to go. He uses his great looks, his humor and his wit to manage the world. Even at a young age these strategies are well honed, but with two babies still in diapers something needs to happen to give this young family any real hope of long lasting change at all. Time will tell.

Conrad is still in shock about how fast his life has come undone. Within three months he has gone from being married to being out of the house living in a hotel and his wife filing for a divorce that he does not want. He is shell shocked. Listening to him speak it becomes ever apparent that he has taken on his wife's thoughts and feelings as his own. If his wife says he is worthless than he must be worthless, if she says he is a despicable man than he must be. All of his sentences start with, "And Donna says." It is so hard to get him to see who he is, not through her lenses.

Conrad's world was her world. He had no individualized life outside of this wife's approval. Her control was so severe that he wasn't "allowed" to contact his brother-in-law directly without his wife's approval. He shared a story about how ballistic his wife went when she learned that he had sent a copy of his resume to her sister at her request so she could help him professionally. As bizarre as it sounds, even in divorce, Conrad doesn't believe that he has the right to call up people he has feelings for to even wish them a Merry Christmas or a Happy New Year! This stuff is deep and I'm sure we are just scratching the surface of his trauma. I couldn't make this stuff up even if I wanted to.

Ernie is the one group member who presents the best. His wife wants to have no knowledge of his relationship with porn or masturbation. He acts out entirely at work in his one-man office. His lost hours of productivity are taking a toll on his finances, not to mention his self-esteem. As he begins to share his struggles with his wife, she sticks her head deeper into the sand. Ernie is starting to see that everything that glitters isn't gold at home. Ernie is open and appears to have bought in. Time will tell, but my gut tells me there is still a lot of shellac left on that table.

Kasey has been with me the longest. Most of the drama and trauma has, for now, settled down. He has been out of the house since before we met and he seems to be fairing okay. He is very active in SLAA and makes and takes lots of phone calls. As strong as Kasey is, I know that under the thick skin he is hurting about not being allowed into his own home for Christmas morning with his twin girls.   His wife is signed up to go to Cottonwood the second week in January. Hopefully that will get her to do some more of her own work and help make her a little more receptive to getting out of her seeing him as the designated "Sick One" phase. Kasey is open and willing to go to Survivor's at the Meadows after the New Year. I do appreciate his leadership and his courage to speak his truth, yet he is so tied to his wife.

With just six men there, we could have finished group early, but it appeared they all had a need to stretch out the group. Several of them were making plans to spend time together during Christmas and New Year's. I told Conrad that Kelly from our Monday night group was planning a New Year's Eve party and he wouldn't have to be alone if he didn't want to be.

As we once again locked arms to say the Serenity Prayer I began the way I always begin by saying out loud: "Put your right foot in, so you don't get left behind!" I pray they survive their trials and tribulations of the holidays and return to NMS safe, sane and sober in the New Year. That is my wish for all the men I am blessed to work with.

DECEMBER 31

WHAT A LONG STRANGE TRIP IT'S BEEN!

I took the week off and went to South Florida to sit in the sun for a while. The weather wasn't what I had hoped it would be, but once again I get that reminder that the world does not run according to Jay, and I am more than fine with that. Reflecting back on the year, it all just seems to have zipped right by. Maybe it's my age. I'm not sure. I do feel good that what I had set out to do a year ago, I have done. I was true to my intention. Now I have about a month of stats and wrap-up work to write, and this baby can be put to bed. I'll be happy when it is all complete. Then I can give it to God and go back to my life. I'll leave the results up to Him. In the meantime, on Monday, I'll go back to work as the cycle starts again with the never-ending cast of No More Secrets characters.

~

AA is a school in which we are all learners and all teachers. A key aspect of AA is the concept of being of service. Passing on what has been freely given to you keeps the recovering addict humble, grateful and sober. Service provides a sense of usefulness to people who at a point felt worthless. On page 8 of the AA Big Book it reads, "No words can tell of the loneliness and despair I found in that bitter morass of self-pity." Dr. Bob Smith, one of the co-founders of AA said this about sponsorship: "It's a duty, a pleasure, a debt and insurance against a possible slip." Service is an active antidote to self-pity yet the Intimacy Disorder often prevents men from being of service to others. We here at NMS try to encourage all to be helpful to others, to be of service to others who still suffer. My hope is that this book will be of service to those who read it.

EPILOGUE

The world watched with anticipation as the events of the "Arab Spring" unfolded. In the pursuit of freedom from bondage, people without knowing it at first began pushing away the chains of a life time of oppression. We all held our collective breath looking for an outcome that was clear and understandable. We watched as the essence of their society began to shift to find its true voice. That unraveling did not take place in a vacuum. It happened in full view with the naked eye. As the inevitable end was being played out in the streets of Cairo, Anderson Cooper of CNN was trying to put words to the enormity of the internal and external struggle. He wrote a poem that he read as a backdrop to a montage of single framed pictures showing the good, the bad, and the ugly of it all and to this "Ah-ha Moment" he said, "Fear has been defeated, there is no turning back."

Addicts believe that their feelings will kill them and that their behavior will save them. That is insane upside down thinking. Only when the fear of continuing on in the addiction becomes greater than the fear of living without the addiction, do addicts truly have a chance to break the chains of their bondage.

Just like in the Middle East, this also does not happen in a vacuum. Just as the community in Egypt had to come together to overcome its collective fears, so do addicts have to go through their own individual metamorphosis in order to get to their equivalent spot of surrender; a coming to peace with the realization that fear is dead and there is no turning back. We here in NMS try to create a loving, nurturing and supportive environment that will help a sex and love addict to find the courage to set aside his or her fear of recovery just long enough to feel there is a chance at a new found freedom.

APPENDIX

LET'S TAKE A LOOK AT OUR STATS

We are proud of our successes and we are humbled by our failures. We never could have imagined over ten years ago that 18% of the men who start this program would finish as alumni four years later. Of the 140 men who have sat in our groups, two-thirds have stayed more than a year with the average being twenty-one months. That's a huge number for a 100% voluntary program. 79% of all the men were married when they entered NMS and 94% of them were still married when they left the program. Our starting age range is twenty-three to eighty-eight years of age. 28% percent of the men have been married more than once while 12% were never married before.

The initial goal of NMS is to help the men stop a behavior that will get them dead, arrested, fired or divorced. In assessing that challenge, 26% of the men have gone to inpatient treatment and another 20% have done a week retreat at the Meadows.

88% of the men participated or participate in some 12-Step program including SLAA, SAA, SA and AA. 74% of them have completed some formal step-work and 80% of them had/have a sponsor.

Helping men stay sober who are not living at home can also be problematic at best. Over 32% of our men were living at some time out of their homes. 23% percent have lived together with other NMS men in recovery, providing them with a safe harbor while they heal themselves and repair their marriages. We truly do support each other. We are blessed to have this community.

Spouses play a huge role in this dance of addiction. 20% of our NMS spouses have come to self-identify their own manifestation of sex and love addiction and 19% have gone for their own inpatient treatment experience.

43% of our current spouses are in a recovery group. Six percent of our spouses have become alumni themselves.

On the down side, 38% of the spouses refuse to do any of their own recovery work and 25% have actually become a disincentive for their partner to stay in NMS. For some, the need to have the men be and remain the designated "Sick Ones" in the marriage prevents the men from any real post-sobriety effort at leveling the playing field. 30% of our sober men remain in what they classify as unhappy marriages. I believe they are still carrying shame and guilt while lacking the courage to leave, mostly around children. It is hard to watch.

In terms of couples work, 48% have done the disclosure letter in our office, while an additional 18% did that work with their spouses when the men were in their inpatient treatment centers. 40% of the couples at one time or another had some kind of "no-contact" in place to let the flames of betrayal start to diminish.

Who joins NMS? We get a cross-section of the greater society. 63% of the men are four-year college grads. 23% of them went on to receive Masters degrees and 9% of them either received PhDs, MDs or JDs. The average age of a man when he starts NMS is forty-two.

26% of our men are in the computer tech industry, 23% are blue collar, 22% are in other professional jobs like CPA's and architects. Of all 140 men, 11% are either current or ex-military and 2% are clergy. We are people who normally would not mix, but there exists between us an uncommon bond.

Where do we come from? 47% of our men were raised in two-parent homes. Of the men raised by a single mom, 9% did not have a father figure present during their childhoods. Alcohol and drug use were present in 16% of the homes along with porn being available in 31% of the homes. 20% of NMS men were sexually abused as children, along with 22% who had at least one primary caregiver with a mental illness.

At the end of the day, when all the facts and figures have been tallied, this unique and unconventional recovery program model seems to be working. The love and caring that the NMS community generates is astounding considering the extreme level of shame, guilt and isolation with which each man enters NMS. There is something going on here that has been and continues to be divinely inspired. The credit for this goes to every man and woman who ventured into this uncharted world we call No More Secrets. "God has a plan" and "Don't leave before the miracle" are the ongoing mantras of our program.

Other Interesting Stats from the Men of No More Secrets

The statistical data on the following pages was compiled at the 140 member mark. NMS has grown substantially since.

OVERVIEW

Total number of men	140
Current members in 4 working groups	31
Alumni (17.9%)	25
Average age when starting recovery	42
Anglo	125
Non-white	11
Bi-racial	4

TIME IN PROGRAM

Current Members (31) average 18 months and counting in NMS*	
Past Members including alumni (109) average 21 months in NMS*	
Left before 3 months (11%)	15
Left before 6 months	23
Left short of one year	11
Total left before a year (35%)	49

*Out of a possible 48 months.

MARITAL STATUS when starting NMS

Never married	17	12%
Never partnered	15	11%
Married more than once	34	28%
No significant other	29	21%
End of partnership pending	10	9%
Married/partnered not living at home	25	20%
Married with children under 12	45	37%
Married with children 13-18	11	9%
Married with adult children	18	15%
Married with no children	16	13%
Unmarried-children out of wedlock	7	5%
Married men living at home but out of the bedroom	15	12%
Married-still sexual despite some program knowledge	75	61%
Marriage ends while in NMS (non-pending)	6	6%
Marriages still in place when men left NMS	55	79%

RELIGION

No God at all	26	19%
Practicing Protestant	17	12%
All branches of Judaism	14	10%
Practicing Catholic	9	6%
Practicing LDS	6	4%
Some God/non-descript concept	68	49%

EDUCATION

G.E.D.	4	5%
High School only	25	18%
Some college-no degree	21	15%
Four-year degree	88	63%
Masters	32	23%
PhD	4	3%
MD/JD	9	6%

CAREER

Technology	36	26%
Blue collar	32	23%
Other professionals	30	22%
Business	19	14%
ex-Military experience	16	11%
Education k-16	12	9%
MD/JD	9	6%
Clergy	4	2%

ACTING-OUT HISTORY

Adult porn/masturbation	131	94%
History of substance abuse	55	39%
Escorts/personals	46	33%
Opportunity sex—1 night stands	32	23%
Anonymous sex	31	22%
Long time affairs	25	18%
Legal difficulties	22	16%
Strip Clubs	21	15%
Street prostitution	21	15%
Massage parlors	17	12%
Exhibitionism/voyeurism	17	12%
Adult book stores	16	11%
Straight men having sex with men	11	8%
Under-age porn use	8	6%
Acting-out with partner + others	6	4%
Acting-out with minors	3	2%

FAMILY OF ORIGIN HISTORY

Raised by both parents	66	47%

Raised by mom, dad in the picture	19	14%
Raised by mom, dad not in the picture	12	9%
Sum raised by mom	31	23%

Raised by mom and stepdad	7	5%
Only child	16	11%
Moved often as child	14	10%
Alcohol/drugs in home	23	16%
Porn available in home	44	31%
Sexually abused as a child	28	20%
Mental illness in home	31	22%

SIGNIFICANT OTHER (S.O.) PARTICIPATION IN NMS

S.O. initially willing to participate in program	57	57%
S.O. unwilling to ever participate (men in 6+ months)	16	25%
S.O. refuses to join group	40	40%
S.O. refuses to go to NMS events	19	19%
S.O. goes to her own treatment	19	19%
S.O. recognizes need for recovery and self identifies	22	22%
S.O. of current men participating in their own group	10	43%
S.O. of current men who have never been in a group	4	17%
S.O. of current men no longer doing anything w/NMS	6	26%

CURRENT NMS MEN (31)

Current men who came into NMS without a S.O.	6	19%
Current men who are since single	2	8%
Current men's S.O. in a group	10	43%
Current men's S.O. not doing recovery	7	30%

ALUMNI (25)

Active alumni	20
Inactive alumni	5
Moved out of area	1
Died	1
Alumni who started NMS partnered	16
Alumni partner who did work	8
Alumni partnership ends	8
Alumni whose wife never participated	1
Alumni who re partnered	7
Alumni whose marriage stayed	7
Alumni currently single	6
Alumni still connected to SLAA	17
Active alumni still sexually sober	16
Alumni who became fathers	5
Alumni who joined Mankind Project	20
Alumni who continue to attend NMS	83%

NMS MEN PARTICIPATION IN 12-STEP RECOVERY

Based on men in NMS more than 3 months

Went to 30+ day inpatient treatment	32	26%
Recommended inpatient treatment on first day	31	25%
Attended the Meadows Survivors workshop	24	20%
No regular meetings	18	15%
Did 90 Meetings in 90 days	21	17%
NMS man lives with NMS man	28	23%
Prior AA experience	23	19%
Prior "S" program experience	10	8%
SLAA experience only	56	46%
SLAA + SAA experience	12	10%
SLAA + SAA + AA experience	39	32%
Has a sponsor	46	38%
Had a sponsor	51	42%
Has been or is a sponsor	21	34%
Some step-work completed	32	74%

SPOUSES OR SIGNIFICANT OTHER (S.O.)

S.O. who refused to ever come in	10%
S.O. who came in less than 5 times	27%
S.O. who refused to join a woman's group	37%
S.O. who refused to go to speakers meetings	38%
S.O. currently in a group	43%
S.O. goes to do her own inpatient treatment	19%
S.O. self-identifies as an addict	20%
S.O. does their own recovery program	12%
S.O. sponsors other woman	8%
S.O. becomes NMS Alumni	6%
S.O. who got their partner to leave NMS	25%

COUPLES

Couples who left NMS still married	94%
Couples who did disclosure in our office	48%
Couples who did disclosure at treatment center	18%
S.O. chooses to not get disclosure at treatment center	8%
Couples who did cost letter in our office	44%
Couples who did empathy letter in our office	41%
Couples who did a hard no-contact	21%
Couples who did a soft no-contact	19%
Couples who did no work at all	41%

MEN

Sober men who stay in unhappy marriages and NMS	30%
Sober men who leave NMS after marriage is over	3%
Sober alumni who came in single and are partnered now	50%

APPENDIX

ABOUT THE AUTHOR

Jay Parker is a native of New York City who ran a successful basketball talent scouting service in Texas until his own struggles with addiction took his life in another direction. He lost his business and career. Through his professional association with the former pro basketball all-star, John Lucas, Mr. Parker entered the John Lucas Treatment and Recovery Center in Houston and dealt with his addiction, turning his experience into his expertise. Mr. Parker completed counseling course work and became a Licensed Chemical Dependency Counselor (LCDC) in Texas in 1994. He began a new career in mental health as the director of education at West Oaks Hospital in Houston before moving to the private alcohol and drug treatment center, The Right Step. He moved to the Pacific Northwest to take an administrative position with Lakeside-Milam Recovery Centers in Kirkland, Washington. He met Dr. Hilarie Cash, who was at work developing observations about computer and Internet addiction. In 1999, they co-founded Internet/Computer Addiction Services (I/CAS) in Redmond, Washington. As a byproduct of his work in I/CAS, Mr. Parker started No More Secrets in 2000. He has appeared on ABC News, CNN, the BBC, and PBS, and been interviewed by publications including The Wall Street Journal, USA Today and U.S. News and World Report. He speaks at treatment centers and has addressed conferences of The Northwest Institute of Addiction Studies, the Texas Association of Addiction Professionals, and the National Council on Sexual Addiction and Compulsivity. He is an NCAA-approved speaker who addresses university and college student-athletes on the perils of alcohol and substance abuse as well as other topical mental health issues. In 2013 Mr. Parker left the field of counseling to become a recovery life coach. He is happily married with two adult children. He recently celebrated his twenty-third year of personal sobriety. His commitment to his own recovery is unwavering. Mr. Parker takes particular delight in dancing at the weddings of his clients who, like him, have turned their lives around.

Learn more about No More Secrets and Jay's approach to recovery at
www.JayParker.org.

Made in the USA
San Bernardino, CA
22 November 2014